The Gen X Series

CYBER OLYMPIAD 5

Useful for Cyber Olympiads Conducted at School, National & International Levels

Authors
Shraddha Singh
Bunny Mehra

Peer Reviewer
Manasvi Vohra

Strictly According to the Latest Syllabus of Cyber Olympiad

V&S PUBLISHERS

Published by:

V&S PUBLISHERS

F-2/16, Ansari road, Daryaganj, New Delhi-110002
☎ 23240026, 23240027 • *Fax:* 011-23240028
✉ info@vspublishers.com • ⊕ www.vspublishers.com

 **Online Brandstore: amazon.in/vspublishers**

Regional Office : Hyderabad
5-1-707/1, Brij Bhawan (Beside Central Bank of India Lane)
Bank Street, Koti, Hyderabad - 500 095
☎ 040-24737290
✉ vspublishershyd@gmail.com

Follow us on:   

BUY OUR BOOKS FROM: | AMAZON | | FLIPKART |

DISCLAIMER

While every attempt has been made to provide accurate and timely information in this book, neither the author nor the publisher assumes any responsibility for errors, unintended omissions or commissions detected therein. The author and publisher makes no representation or warranty with respect to the comprehensiveness or completeness of the contents provided.

All matters included have been simplified under professional guidance for general information only, without any warranty for applicability on an individual. Any mention of an organization or a website in the book, by way of citation or as a source of additional information, doesn't imply the endorsement of the content either by the author or the publisher. It is possible that websites cited may have changed or removed between the time of editing and publishing the book.

Results from using the expert opinion in this book will be totally dependent on individual circumstances and factors beyond the control of the author and the publisher.

It makes sense to elicit advice from well informed sources before implementing the ideas given in the book. The reader assumes full responsibility for the consequences arising out from reading this book.

For proper guidance, it is advisable to read the book under the watchful eyes of parents/guardian. The buyer of this book assumes all responsibility for the use of given materials and information.

The copyright of the entire content of this book rests with the author/publisher. Any infringement/transmission of the cover design, text or illustrations, in any form, by any means, by any entity will invite legal action and be responsible for consequences thereon.

Publisher's Note

General Trade and Mass Appeal books across various genres have helped **V&S Publishers** to gain widespread popularity. In a short span of 10 years, we have successfully published more than 1000 titles across 9 languages in our 50 subject categories. Being into the publishing business for about 40 years, we have always been a dynamic publishing house, with a massive distribution network, across India; including E-commerce platforms.

Understanding the need of inculcating knowledge and developing a spirit of healthy competition amongst students to make them ready for the world outside schools and colleges; we created Olympiad Series under the **GEN X SERIES Imprint** which, owning to its rich content and unique representation became popular amongst students, in no time. The motivation is not to improve marks in terms of numbers, but is to make sure that the students are already prepared to face competitive environment with respect to college admissions and cracking various entrance examinations, while ensuring their conceptual clarity.

Published for classes 1-10 across subjects English, Mathematics, Science, Computers, General Knowledge, the books are unlike any other in the market and are written in a guidebook pattern and exhaustively include examples and Multiple-Choice Questions.

Here, we present the latest Edition of **CYBER OLYMPIAD CLASS 5.**

Unique Features of the book are as follows:

- Authored by Subject Matter Experts' and Peer reviewed by School Principals and HOD's for the respective subjects
- Books based on principles of Applied Psychology and Bloom's Taxonomy
- Suited for Olympiad Examinations held at School level, National level & International Level irrespective of organizing body.
- The only Olympiad Book in India written in Guidebook Pattern with Concise Theory, images and illustrations.
- Exhaustively include Examples, MCQs, Subjective Questions, and HOTS with Answer Keys & Solutions.
- Multiple Model Papers for thorough practice also given inside the book with solutions.
- OMR sheets appended at the end of the book for simulating exam environment.

Besides, we are also planning to launch an App very soon for the Olympiad preparation which further testifies our constant endeavor to keep up with student demands. We have made sure to closely follow syllabus patterns of not only Olympiad conducting bodies but also education boards & organizations like CBSE and NCERT, to make sure that our books prove useful to students; helping them to boost their academic performance in schools as well.

P.S. While every care has been taken to ensure the correctness of the content, if you come across any error, howsoever minor, do not hesitate to discuss with teachers while pointing that out to us in no uncertain terms.

We wish you All the Best!

01 LEARNING OBJECTIVES

They list the whole chapter as subtopics, helping the teachers to guide children in a step-by-step manner.

02 DID YOU KNOW

Enhance your knowledge by getting acquainted with some amazing facts across various subjects like science, Mathematics and English.

03 MULTIPLE CHOICE QUESTIONS

MCQs act as an excellent learning aid, helping you to understand and work on your mistakes.

04 THINGS TO REMEMBER

A quick recap of the chapter in a summarized format helps in faster revision along with conceptual clarity.

05 HOTS

The High Order Thinking Questions aim to help the student to solve Application-based questions and gain practical understanding of the subject.

FEATURES

SUBJECTIVE QUESTIONS
Help to place the knowledge gained in orderly fashion by using **"WH"** questions, mostly in the form of bullet points.

06

ACHIEVER'S SECTION
Offers a quick revision of the book along with some new facts for the students to discover.

07

A SET OF OMR SHEETS
To allow the student to practice question in an exam-like format which would help them to get the "feel" of how Olympiad exams take place.

08

MODEL TEST PAPERS
Two model test papers are provided at the end of each book, which help the student to test the knowledge which they have gained after thorough reading of all chapters.

09

ANSWER KEY & SOLUTION
Detailed Answer Key along with explanations aid the pupil to indentify, understand the mistakes they make during the course of Olympiad preparation.

10

COMPLEMENT SCHOOL SYLLABI
The syllabi across all Olympiad examination closely follow the pattern of academic books. Hence, they not only provide a competitive examination experience, but also help to revise topics for school examinations as well, while strengthening conceptual precision.

ENHANCEMENT OF ANALYTICAL & LOGICAL REASONING
Practicing analytical ability questions, not only helps in developing intellectual ability but also plays a vital role in building critical thinking ability which helps an individual to think about a question or a crisis like situation in day to day life; from all aspects and directions.

Note to Parents

Dear Parents,

Olympiad examinations come with a plethora of advantages. First and foremost among such advantages is the application of knowledge studied, in the form of multiple-choice questions. It helps the child not only to step away from rote learning, but also helps them to exhibit their competencies across various subjects.

In addition to this, Olympiads help the student to understand the importance of revision and practice, and to imbibe upon these practices; which also prove useful in academic performance of the child.

The Olympiads are conducted across multiple subjects, and help the child to recognize their field of interest, thereby encouraging the students to make a career in the field where they can excel the most.

However, cognitive development of a child is not just limited to the four walls of classroom. Following steps can be encouraged by you, to ensure their ward is able to grasp various concepts with ease or lesser difficulty:

☞ **Eat a balanced diet:** Ensure intake of vitamins and minerals to keep you active. Include fruits and super foods like millet in your diet to ensure healthy functioning of organs. Huge intake of junk food should be avoided.

☞ **Indulge in outdoor activities:** Outdoor games break the monotony of life. Play your heart out in greenery to keep yourself alert, active and fit.

☞ **Sleep well:** A sound sleep of 7-8 hours refreshes the brain and makes it ready to understand new topics with more clarity. A sleep derived person faces difficulty in doing even the simplest tasks of day to day life.

☞ **Reduce your Screen time:** More screen time leads to not only weakening of eyesight but decreases concentration span. Regulated Screen time should be encouraged

☞ **Do not hesitate to raise a hand:** Having a doubt in class? Do not hesitate to ask your parents or teachers. This ensures more Conceptual Clarity and hence leads to Application based understanding of various subjects and topics.

☞ **Teach and Learn:** No need to do rote-learning. Once you understand a topic teach or explain it to your friends, siblings and parents. It brings clarity and ensures the child does his revision this way.

☞ **Keep smiling:** A positive attitude promotes a growth mindset and encourages the child to be more inquisitive and try to learn something new, everyday!

HAPPY LEARNING!

Contents

SECTION 1
COMPUTERS AND IT

Fundamentals of Computers 1

CHAPTER SUMMARY

Computer needs two main parts to functions. They are the hardware and the software.

Hardware

Hardware is the physical part of the computer which we can touch and see. They include input and output devices or CPU components.

Input Devices

Devices that help a user to make an entry into the computer or instruct a computer to perform a task are called input devices.

Some of the input devices are keyboard, mouse, joystick, light pen, microphone and bar code reader.

Keyboard

It has a number of keys on it. These keys are pressed to type numbers, letters and symbols. The keyboard also has keys that help us perform tasks on different programs.

Using the keyboard: The keys on your keyboard can be divided into several groups based on function:

A. **Typing (Alphanumeric) keys:** These keys include the same letter, number, punctuation and symbol keys found on a traditional typewriter.

B. **Control keys:** These keys are used alone or in combination with other keys to perform certain actions. The most frequently used control keys are Ctrl, Alt, the Windows key ⊞ and ESC (escape).

C. **Function keys:** The function keys are used to perform specific tasks. They are labeled as F1, F2, F3, and so on, up to F12. The functionality of these keys differs from program to program.

D. **Navigation keys:** These keys are used for moving the cursor in documents or webpages and editing text. They include the arrow keys, Home, End, Page Up, Page Down, Delete and Insert.

E. **Numeric keypad:** The numeric keypad is handy for entering numbers quickly. The keys are grouped together in a block like a conventional calculator or adding machine.

The following illustration shows how these keys are arranged on a typical keyboard. Your keyboard layout might be different.

Mouse

It is a pointing device that helps us to locate different files, folders and images on the computer screen. It has two or three buttons which help us to open, save, create and perform varied functions by clicking on them. The scroll wheel between the mouse buttons help us to move up and down on a page.

Doug Engelbart designed the first computer mouse in 1964, which consisted of a wooden casing with two rollers and a button on top.

Joystick

This input device has a stick fixed on a base. It can be moved to control the actions done on the screen. It is also used to play computer games.

Microphone

With the help of this device, the user can record sounds or his own voice. The sound then gets stored in the computer which can be used like any other audio file.

Bar Code Reader

It is a device used to read bar codes printed on any commercial product. It is commonly used in shopping malls and at billing counters.

Touch Screen

It is a touch sensitive device which helps you to input data into the computer. One common place where a touch screen is used is the ATM. Most ATMs have a touch screen. You touch the screen at certain places to key in your task preference - PIN number, amount, etc.

Output Devices

Devices that are used to view the result of an operation are called output devices. Some of the output devices are the monitor, printer, speakers and headphones.

Monitor

It is also called the Visual Display Unit or VDU. It looks very similar to a television screen. This screen is where we watch movies, play games, write letters or create drawings.

Printer

It is used to print hard copies of the digital file present in the computer. The hard copy gets printed on the paper.

Speaker

It emits sounds from the computer. You can listen to songs on the speakers.

Headphone

It is used to listen the sounds without disturbing others. The sound can be heard only by the person wearing the headphones.

CPU Components

The CPU is the brain of the computer. It controls and manages all the tasks performed by the computer system. The CPU is divided into two. They are the Control Unit and the Arithmetic Logic Unit (ALU).

The Control Unit controls the fetching of instructions from the main memory and the subsequent execution of these instructions.

The ALU carries out arithmetic operations on integer and real operands.

The devices fitted or placed inside the cabinet are the components of the CPU.

Software

It is a set of instructions given to the computer as input or a programmed language which helps to run the hardware components of the computer.

Software can be of two types: Application Software and System Software.

System Software

It provides a platform for running various computer programs. It is designed to control the running of the hardware components. The operating system or the OS is the best example of a system software.

The other system software are:

- The BIOS (Basic Input/Output System) which gets the computer started after you switch it on and make ready the other hardware components to receive instructions.

- The boot program loads the operating system into the computer's RAM.
- An assembler takes instructions and converts them into bits that the processor can use to perform its basic operations.
- A device driver controls a particular type of device that is attached to your computer, such as a keyboard or a mouse.
- System software also includes system utilities, such as the Disk Defragmenter and System Restore.

➡ Devices that help a user to make an entry into the computer or instruct a computer to perform a task are called input devices.

➡ Devices that are used to view the result of an operation are called output devices.

➡ The Control Unit controls the fetching of instructions from the main memory and the subsequent execution of these instructions.

➡ The ALU carries out arithmetic operations on integer and real operands.

1. A mouse with a sphere that is moved for navigation instead of moving the whole mouse.
   (a) Zip Disk
   (b) Trackball
   (c) Optical Mouse
   (d) Keyboard

2. A device that emits computer audio audible to everyone
   (a) Speakers
   (b) Trackball
   (c) Printer
   (d) Magnetic Tape

3. A magnetic device using which the cursor is moved by touching with the fingers.
   (a) Light pen
   (b) Trackpad
   (c) Trackball
   (d) Touchpad

4. A device that converts soft copy to hard copy
   (a) Printer
   (b) Mouse
   (c) Magnetic Disk
   (d) Scanner

5. What is the common name for a video camera that streams video over the Internet?
   (a) iCaming
   (b) Netcam
   (c) Intercam
   (d) Webcam

6. Which of the following is NOT a type of flat-screen display?
   (a) LCD
   (b) LED
   (c) CRT
   (d) Plasma

7. Which of the following is NOT an impact printer?
   (a) Daisy Wheel
   (b) Drum
   (c) Chain
   (d) Thermal

8. What unit of measurement is used to measure digital camera image resolution?
   (a) Megabytes
   (b) Magahertz
   (c) Megatons
   (d) Megapix

9. Caps Lock, Num Lock and Scroll Lock are called ______.
   (a) Keyboard Shortcuts
   (b) Toggle Keys
   (c) Number Keys
   (d) Modifier Keys

10. A Dot matrix printer is an example of what type of printer?
    (a) Inkjet Printer
    (b) Laser Printer
    (c) Impact Printer
    (d) 3D Printer

11. What is dot pitch used to measure?
    (a) The sharpness of a monitor's display
    (b) The resolution of a printed document
    (c) The megapixel count of a digital camera
    (d) The shape of individual pixels on a screen

12. Which part instructs the ALU?
    (a) Memory
    (b) Control Unit
    (c) Keyboard
    (d) Monitor

13. A ________ is a peripheral device that allows a computer to connect and communicate with other computers.
    (a) ISP
    (b) Web browser
    (c) Telephone Lines
    (d) Modulator-demodulator

14. Motherboards, memory modules, and network interface cards are all types of
    (a) PCBs
    (b) CCDs
    (c) CPUs
    (d) VLBs

15. What is the purpose of UPS?
    (a) It ensures to connect power to the devices when the electricity goes out.
    (b) It balances the bandwidth of multiple network connections.
    (c) It allows single computer to work with multiple monitors.
    (d) It prevents unauthorized devices from accessing a wireless network.

16. "Power strip" is another name for which device?
    (a) Power Adaptor
    (b) Power Supply
    (c) Power Board
    (d) Fuse Box

17. What is the standard resolution of VGA display?
    (a) 1860 × 234 pixels
    (b) 640 × 480 pixels
    (c) 1024 × 768 pixels
    (d) 1920 × 1080 pixels

18. Which of the following is an example of an optical disc drive?
    (a) Tape Drive
    (b) DVD Drive
    (c) Internal SSD
    (d) External Hard Drive

19. What is the purpose of a CPU heat sink?
    (a) It blows cool air onto the processor.
    (b) It stores energy create by the processor to power the computer.
    (c) It dissipates heat from the processor.
    (d) It keeps the processor warm enough to function correctly.

20. Which of the following is the most recent type of hardware interface?
    (a) USB   (b) Fire Wire
    (c) Thunderbolt   (d) eSATA

21. What type of component may come in a dual-core version?
    (a) RAM   (b) CPU
    (c) SSD   (d) PCI Card

22. A/an _________ software allows us to perform specific types of jobs.
    (a) System   (b) Compression
    (c) Backup   (d) Application

23. [image] is an example of _____.
    (a) System Software
    (b) Application Software
    (c) Utility Program
    (d) Operating System

24. What is CAD software used for?
    (a) Developing computer programs
    (b) Creating 2D and 3D models
    (c) Editing digital photos
    (d) Editing digital videos

25. .jpg, .html, and .fla are all examples of file _________.
    (a) Types   (b) Association
    (c) Names   (d) Extensions

26. What file extensions do most Windows programs have?
    (a) .zip   (b) .bas
    (c) .exe   (d) .cpp

27. Set of instructions given to the computer is called a _______.
    (a) List   (b) Note
    (c) Program   (d) Instructs

28. Which of the following is a function of an Operating System?
    (a) Memory management
    (b) Processor management
    (c) File management
    (d) All of these

29. Who first used the term software?
    (a) Winston Turkey
    (b) John W. Turkey
    (c) Dennis Ritchie
    (d) Ronald Ducking

30. Which of the following is a desktop package?
    (a) Page maker   (b) Corel Draw
    (c) Both (a) and (b)   (d) None of these

31. _____ software is used to create images like charts, logos, cartoons, etc.
    (a) Graphics
    (b) Multimedia
    (c) Presentation
    (d) Word processing

32. _______ software is used to create full motion video, animation, sound, etc.
    (a) Graphics
    (b) Multimedia
    (c) Presentation
    (d) Word processing

33. _____ software is used for the production of any sort of printable material.
   (a) Graphics
   (b) Multimedia
   (c) Utility
   (d) Word processor
34. Firefox, Chrome and Safari are all types of what software?
   (a) Utility   (b) Web Browsers
   (c) Image Editors   (d) Video Players
35. Which of the following describes installing a new software in the correct order?
   (a) Install, Download, Run
   (b) Run, Download, Install
   (c) Run, Install, Download
   (d) Download, Install, Run

HOTS

1. Identify the kind of program described below.
   - System designers use this program over wired electronic circuit to perform high-level operations.
   - Good example of it is "system boot program".
   - A computer needs this program every time it is switched ON and the computer must retain it even when it is switched OFF.
   (a) Mini Program
   (b) Demo Program
   (c) Micro Program
   (d) Major Program

2. Which of the following statements is incorrect about magnetic tapes?
   (a) It is not suitable for storage of those data that we need to access randomly.
   (b) There is no need to label magnetic tapes properly and logically to remember what data is on which tape.
   (c) It should be stored in dust free environment.
   (d) Both (a) and (b)

3. In a mainframe computer, numerous programs are loaded in a memory and its operating system runs those programs one by one and executes them simultaneously. This technique is called _________.
   (a) Multitasking
   (b) Multiprocessing
   (c) Multithreading
   (d) Multiuser

4. Main board and logic board are alternative names of which computer component?

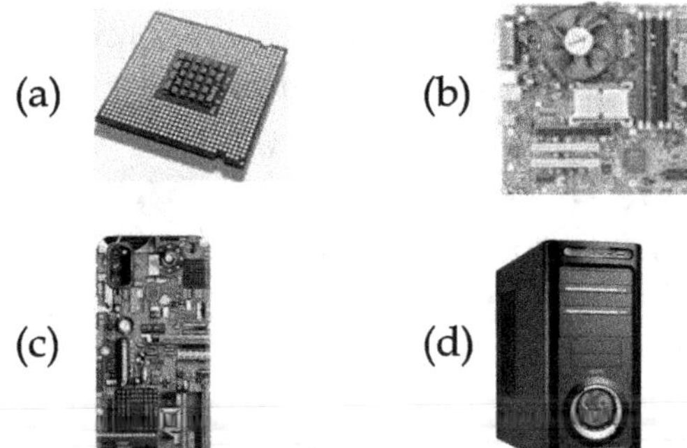

(a)   (b)

(c)   (d)

5. A CPU processes the data and instruction provided through the input devices and then passes the processed result to the output devices. Identify the device on which it is present.

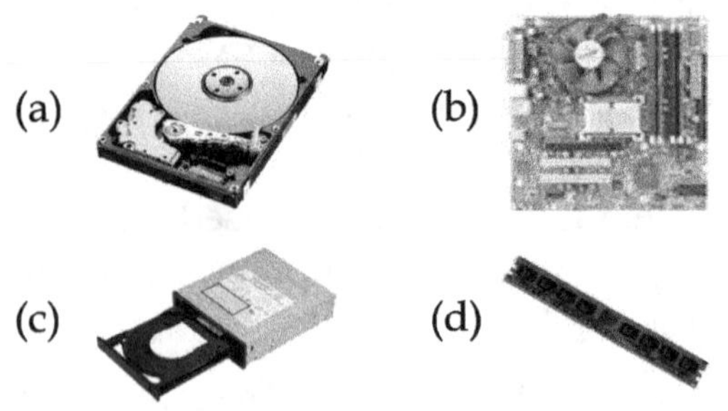

(a)   (b)

(c)   (d)

1. **What are System Programs and Application Programs?**

Ans.

There are basically two types of programs that we use: system programs and application programs. The system programs constitute what we call an operating system.

The programs that make up the operating system are:

- Control programs
- Supervisory programs
- Service programs

The control programs control and manage all the hardware and memory resources of the computer. They regulate and time the activities of the CPU and allocate memory space when it is required. They schedule the data to be received or sent through input and output devices. The service programs provide many services to the user. The most common example is the set of programs that let you save files and load them from floppies or CDs and copy, rename, delete files or folders. The Windows operating system has a few application programs associated with it. In the smaller classes, you may have used the one called Notepad for writing text. Examples of other application programs are word processor, spreadsheet and Internet Explorer.

2. **How to permanently delete files in a Computer?**

Ans.

When there are too many items in the Recycle Bin and you do not need any of them, you can permanently delete the files by performing the following steps:

- Right click on the Recycle Bin icon.
- Choose the Empty Recycle Bin option.
- When asked for confirmation, click on the Yes button. Once the Recycle Bin is emptied, the deleted files cannot be restored again.

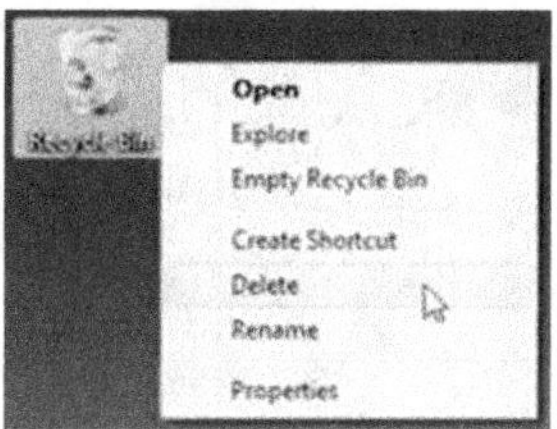

3. **List some advantages of Digital computer.**

Ans.

Advantages of Digital Computers are:

- Digital computer uses binary data strings (0 and 1) to reproduce data.
- Noise and distortions have hardly any impact on its output.
- It makes high-quality data transmission possible.
- It is very precise in its output.

4. **List some disadvantages of Analog computer.**

Ans.

Some of the disadvantages of using an analog computer are:

- Alphanumeric information cannot be processed in this system.
- It gives very little precision.
- Its memory capacity is limited.

5. **What are different types/categories of computer?**

Ans.

The computers you come across in the daily course of your day range from laptops, palmtops, mainframe computers to desktop computers. Computers are categorized based on physical structures, purpose of their use, capacity, speed and reliability. Based on the operational or working principle, the different categories of computers are:

- Digital computers
- Analog computers
- Hybrid computers

Memory and Storage Devices 2

Learning Objectives : In this chapter, students will learn about:
- ✓ Primary Memory
- ✓ Secondary Memory
- ✓ Hard Disk

CHAPTER SUMMARY

Computer memory refers to the device where data is stored temporarily or permanently. There are two main types of physical memory. They are namely primary memory and secondary memory.

Primary Memory

Primary memory is physically made up of Random Access Memory (RAM) which is otherwise known as volatile memory. It also includes cache memory. It is called volatile because this type or memory needs power supply to be accessible.

It stores data for quick and easy access. Primary or main memory is used to execute program code and store temporary data. It is also called the main memory. When the computer is switched ON, the primary memory initiates the devices and the main operating system to ready it for use.

Software which is being processed by the CPU, otherwise known as '**Executing Software**', is temporarily stored in the main memory. A typical personal computer will have between 1–4 Gigabytes of RAM outside the main CPU.

Cache Memory

Cache memory is a very high speed semiconductor memory which can speed up the CPU. It acts as a buffer between the CPU and main memory. It is used to hold the data and programs which are most frequently used by the CPU.

Advantages

The advantages of cache memory are as follows:

- Cache memory is faster than the main memory.
- It consumes less access time as compared to main memory.
- It stores data for temporary use.

Disadvantages

The disadvantages of cache memory are as follows:

- Cache memory has limited capacity.
- It is very expensive.

Secondary Memory

Secondary memory, or secondary storage, is non-volatile storage. It is called so because it retains the data even if the power supply to the computer system is cut off. Secondary memory is used to hold data and programs which are not currently being used but need to be accessed at some point. For example, the hard disk, flash memory or magnetic tapes are secondary storage devices.

A typical personal computer will have a few hundred gigabytes of secondary memory in the form of a hard disk.

Hard Disk

A hard disk is a secondary data storage device also known as hard drive or fixed drive. It is the largest storage device in a computer. It was introduced by IBM in 1956. It instantly became the predominant storage device. Hard disk is divided into tracks and sectors. Data can be accessed in a random manner from the hard disk, meaning individual sets of data can be retrieved and used/viewed in any order rather than sequentially. 1 terabyte capacity of a hard drive means it can store data amounting to 1000 gigabytes.

Magnetic Tape

Magnetic Tape consists of a thin tape with a coating of a fine magnetic material. It is used to record analog or digital data. A device that stores data on magnetic tape is a **Tape Drive**. The largest amount of data that can be stored in magnetic tape is about 5 Terabytes. Magnetic tapes transfer data a bit slower than hard drives. They are cheaper and are more durable than hard disks.

Floppy Disk

It is also called a **Diskette**. It is composed of thin and flexible magnetic storage medium sealed in a rectangular plastic carrier lined with fabric that removes dust particles. Floppy disks were a common storage device between 1980s and early 2000s. Floppy disks come in 3 sizes: 8 inches, 5.5 inches and 3.5 inches. The capacities of floppy disks vary between 1 and 250 Megabytes. These devices were slow, reading data at rates of bytes and kb/s. They are obsolete now.

Optical Disk

It was invented in 1958. It is a flat, usually circular disc with a hole at the centre. It encodes binary data in the form of pits (binary digit 0) and lands (binary value of 1) on one of its flat surfaces. Optical discs are usually between 7.6 and 30 cm in diameter. A typical disc is about 1.2 mm thick, while the track pitch is typically 1.6 micrometre. Optical discs are most commonly used for storing music, video or data and programs for personal computers.

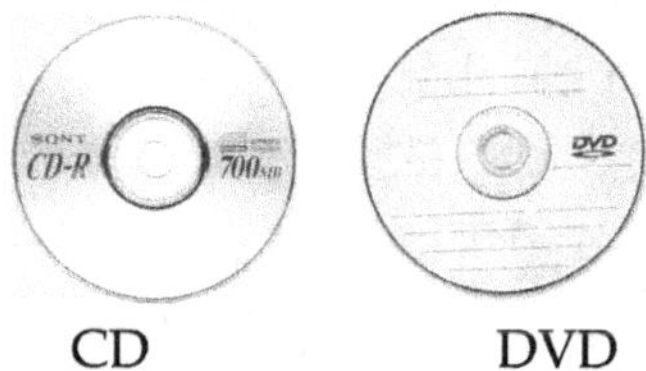

CD   DVD

Flash Drive

A flash drive is a small external storage device, the size of a thumb. It is also called a **Pen Drive**. These are removable and rewritable. They are a solid-state storage medium that are both inexpensive and durable. USB Flash drives vary in sizes from 8 Megabytes to 1024 Gigabytes. More commonly used sizes vary from 2 Gigabytes - 16 Gigabytes.

TRIVIA

When compared to a QWERTY keyboard, a DVORAK keyboard enables you to type 20 times quicker.

MUST REMEMBER

➡ Primary memory is physically made up of Random Access Memory (RAM) which is otherwise known as volatile memory.
➡ Cache memory is a very high speed semiconductor memory which can speed up the CPU.
➡ Secondary memory, or secondary storage, is non-volatile storage.
➡ Floppy disks were a common storage device between 1980s and early 2000s.

1. It is a magnetic disk storage medium sealed in a square plastic carrier lined with fabric that removes dust particles.
   (a) Floppy disk
   (b) Compact disc
   (c) Optical disc
   (d) Zip disk

2. A small plastic disc used for the storage of digital data, originally developed for audio system. What it is called?
   (a) Compact disc
   (b) Floppy disk
   (c) Optical disc
   (d) Zip disk

3. The storage capacity of a computer is called its ______.
   (a) Storage space
   (b) Stack
   (c) Pile
   (d) Memory

4. Internal memory is synonymous with which memory?
   (a) Primary
   (b) Secondary
   (c) Tertiary
   (d) None of these

5. What is the full form of ROM?
   (a) Random Only Memory
   (b) Read Only Memory
   (c) Random Order Memory
   (d) Read Order Memory

6. Which of the following is a type of internal memory?
   (a) RAM
   (b) ROM
   (c) Both (a) and (b)
   (d) None of these

7. Which is the built in memory of a computer?
   (a) RAM   (b) ROM
   (c) Hard disk   (d) Flash drive

8. Which memory is called read/write memory?
   (a) RAM   (b) ROM
   (c) Hard disk   (d) Flash drive

9. Which memory is a volatile memory?
   (a) RAM   (b) ROM
   (c) Hard disk   (d) Flash drive

10. The storage of data and instructions in ROM are ______.
    (a) Volatile   (b) Erasable
    (c) Permanent   (d) Changeable

11. What is the full form of PROM?
    (a) Processed Read Only Memory
    (b) Promoter Read Only Memory
    (c) Printable Read Only Memory
    (d) Programmable Read Only Memory

12. What is the full form of EEPROM?
    (a) Electronically Erasable Programmable Read Only Memory
    (b) Electrically Erasable Programmable Read Only Memory
    (c) Electronically Erasable Printable Read Only Memory
    (d) Electrically Erasable Printable Read Only Memory

13. Which of these is NOT a secondary memory?
    (a) Hard disk
    (b) Random Access Memory
    (c) Flash drive
    (d) CD-ROM

14. Which of the following is a dimension of floppy disk?
    (a) 3.5 inch
    (b) 5.25 inch
    (c) Both (a) and (b)
    (d) None of these

15. Hard disk is made up of a collection of disks known as ______.
    (a) Serials   (b) Platters
    (c) Tracks   (d) Bundles

16. Match the following:

Column-I	Column-II
(i) 1 Byte	(a) Secondary Memory
(ii) RAM	(b) 8 bits
(iii) PROM	(c) Ultraviolet light
(iv) EPROM	(d) Once programmer, cannot be erased
(v) Pen Drive	(e) Power Supply dependent

(a) (i) – a, (ii) – e, (iii) – d, (iv) – c, (v) – b
(b) (i) – b, (ii) – c, (iii) – e, (iv) – d, (v) – a
(c) (i) – a, (ii) – b, (iii) – d, (iv) – c, (v) – e
(d) (i) – b, (ii) – e, (iii) – d, (iv) – c, (v) – a

17. Which of the following is NOT a type of primary memory?
(a) PROM
(b) CD-ROM
(c) EPROM
(d) EEPORM

18. Which of them is another name of pen drive?
(a) Flash drive
(b) USB drive
(c) Both (a) and (b)
(d) None of these

19. It is the type of ROM, in which the recorded information can be erased by exposing it to ultraviolet light.
(a) RAM
(b) PROM
(c) EEPROM
(d) EPROM

20. 1 TB = _____.
(a) 1024 KB
(b) 1024 GB
(c) 1024 MB
(d) 1024 KB

21. Select the incorrect match.

(a) This type of storage device can be then used to transfer image to a PC.   (i) USB Flash card

(b) Storage medium in the form of circular Plate.   (ii) Disk

(c) It contains a basic set of instructions.   (iii) BIOS

(d) They tend to be slowest and noisy.   (iv) Laser Printers

22. Which of the following devices would be needed to use the storage medium shown in this figure?

(a)   (b)

(c)   (d)

23. When we visit a web page on the internet, in which memory is the page stored?
(a) RAM
(b) ROM
(c) Cache
(d) Auxiliary

24. On which of the following storage devices, can data not be written more than once?
(a) CD-RW
(b) CD-R
(c) DVD-RW
(d) Flash drive

25. Which of the following statement is incorrect?
(a) You cannot play DVDs in a CD device.
(b) Flash drive can be of 4 GB.
(c) A group of 8 bits is called nibble.
(d) Data written in CD-RW can be erased to write or record new information.

1. Sheetal wrote a computer exam where she marked her answers by darkening circles on pre-printed sheets. Which of the following devices will be used to check her answer sheet?

(a) 

(b) 

(c) 

(d) 

2. If you want to edit and save your files over and over again in the same CD, which of the following type of CDs would you need to use?
   (a) CD-WORM   (b) CD-RW
   (c) CD-ROM   (d) CD-DOD

3. Arrange the following in decreasing order of their storage capacity CD-ROM, DVD, Blu-ray
   (a) CD-ROM → DVD→ Blu-ray
   (b) CD-ROM→ Blu-ray →DVD
   (c) DVD → Blu-ray → CD-ROM
   (d) Blu-ray → DVD → CD-ROM

4. SIMMs and DIMMs are different types of which computer component?

(a) 

(b) 

(c) 

(d) 

5. Identify the device shown here and select the statement which is CORRECT about it.

   (a) It affects the number and size of programs that a system can run simultaneously.
   (b) It is the main secondary storage found inside a computer.
   (c) It is used to store and transfer data from one computer to another.
   (d) It is attached with the CPU through USB port.

1. Differentiate between Primary and Secondary Memory.

Ans.

Primary or Main memory is used to execute program code and store temporary data. Primary memory is physically made up of Random Access Memory (RAM) which is otherwise known as volatile memory.

Secondary memory, or secondary storage, is non-volatile storage for data. For example, the hard disk, flash memory or magnetic tape. Secondary memory is used to hold data and programs which are not currently being used, but need to be accessed at some point of time.

2. What is cache memory?

Cache memory is a very high speed semiconductor memory which can speed up the operations of CPU. It acts as a buffer between the CPU and main memory. It is used to hold those parts of data and program which are most frequently used by CPU.

3. What is a Barcode Reader?

Ans.

A barcode reader is a device used to read barcodes. A barcode is a pattern printed in lines of different thicknesses that can be seen on many products. A barcode reader interprets these lines to input the information of a product into the computer system. Barcodes are widely used in supermarkets for recording the sale of items quickly.

4. What is a Light Pen? What is its use?

Ans.

A light pen is an input device. It is shaped like a pen. A light pen is connected to the VDU (Visual Display Unit). It allows the user to draw or point to objects on the computer screen or the monitor.

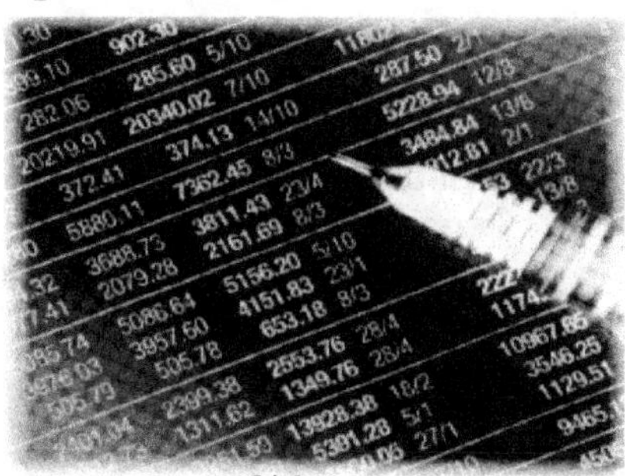

Light pen

5. Write short note on Biometric devices.

Ans.

The term biometric is derived from the Greek words 'bio' meaning life and 'metric' meaning to measure. These days many biometric devices are available that can scan and detect a person's fingerprints, face, iris, and so on. These devices are used for identification and access control. They help in enhancing the security as compared to the system of login ids and passwords.

6. Explain about RAM Briefly.

Ans.

RAM: RAM stands for Random Access Memory. RAM is placed in the form of a chip on the motherboard. RAM is a read/write memory. Information can be written onto and read from RAM. When a computer starts, it loads the operating system into RAM. While you are working on any program, you are actually working on the program loaded in the RAM. However, RAM is volatile memory. It retains the stored information as long as the power is switched ON. When the power supply is switched OFF, the information in the RAM is lost. The amount of RAM installed in a computer affects the number and size of programs that a computer can run simultaneously.

Introduction to Multimedia 3

CHAPTER SUMMARY

Multimedia is more than one presentation medium. We can also say it is the use of computers to present text, graphics, video, animation, and sound in an integrated way. Multimedia is typically used to mean the combination of text, sound or motion video. Some say that the addition of animated images produces multimedia but it typically means one of the following:

- Text and sound
- Text, sound and still or animated graphic images
- Text, sound and video images
- Video and sound
- Multiple display areas or images presented concurrently

Multimedia presentations are possible in many situations, including on the Web, CD-ROMs, and live theater. Multimedia presentations may be viewed by persons on stage and projected, transmitted or played locally with a media player. A laser show is a live multimedia performance. A broadcast may be a live or recorded multimedia presentation. Digital online multimedia may be downloaded or streamed. Streaming multimedia may be live or on-demand. For multimedia Web sites, popular multimedia players include MPEG, Quicktime and Shockwave.

The basic elements of multimedia on a computer are: Text, Images, Audio, Video and Animation.

Text

Text is the most popular of all the media types. It is distributed over the Internet in many forms including files or messages using different transfer protocols such as FTP (File Transfer Protocol) that is used to transfer binary and ASCII files over the Internet, HTTP (Hyper Text Transfer Protocol) that is used to transmit HTML pages or SMTP (Simple Mail Transfer Protocol).

Protocol

Used for exchanging e-mails. Text can be created in many applications:

- Basic text editing
- Windows notepad - an ASCII text editor
- Notepad++, a free source code editor
- Word processsors (MS-Word, Open Office) and
- Web editors (Microsoft Expression Web, Adobe Dreamweaver).

Sound/Audio

Audio media is sound/speech converted into digital form using sampling and quantization. Some Tools

- Waveform (.wav, .mp3)
- Windows Sound Recorder
- Windows Movie Maker (able to save to .wma)
- Quicktime (.mov)

Images

Graphics programs can be divided into bitmap editors and vector-drawing editors.

- **Bitmap editors**
  1. General drawing programs
  2. JASC PaintShop Pro
  3. Corel PhotoPaint
  4. Macromedia Fireworks
  5. Specialist editors
- **Vector editors**
  1. Corel Draw
  2. Macromedia Fireworks
  3. Flash - while much more than a vector drawing tool, it is capable of creating very sophisticated vector based graphics
  4. Open Office/Libre Office Draw

Animation

Animation is the process of creating motion and shape change illusion by playing static images at a rapid sequence.

This includes static media types like digital images and dynamic media types like flash presentations. Compared to text or digital audio, digital images tend to be large in size.

Video

Video is a sequence of images/frames displayed at a certain rate, e.g., 24 or 30 frames per second. Digitized video, like digitized audio, is also transmitted as a stream of discrete packets over the network.

TRIVIA

You may heat a room with Gaming PCs more effectively than a heater.

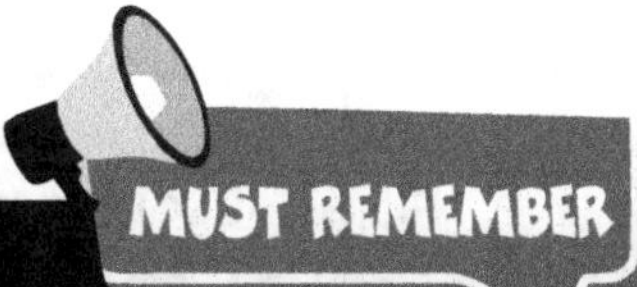

- ➡ Multimedia presentations may be viewed by persons on stage and projected, transmitted or played locally with a media player.
- ➡ Text is the most popular of all the media types.
- ➡ Animation is the process of creating motion and shape change illusion by playing static images at a rapid sequence.

1. Multimedia is _________ .
   - (a) Picture
   - (b) Sound
   - (c) Animation
   - (d) All of these

2. What is the most common way to discover a media?
   - (a) By the name
   - (b) By file location
   - (c) By file extension
   - (d) None of these

3. MP3 is an extension for _________ .
   - (a) Sound/Audio/Music file
   - (b) Video file
   - (c) Data files of pictures
   - (d) Graphic file

4. _________ is a simulation of movement created by displaying a series of pictures.
   - (a) Movie
   - (b) Picture
   - (c) Animation
   - (d) Sound

5. Picture formats can be recognized by which extensions?
   - (a) .gif
   - (b) .jpg
   - (c) Both (a) and (b)
   - (d) None of these

6. The MP3 format is synonymous with _________ .
   - (a) MPGE
   - (b) MPPP
   - (c) MPEG
   - (d) AU

7. What is the full form of MPEG?
   - (a) Motion Pictures Experts Group
   - (b) Moving Pictures Experts Group
   - (c) Motion Pictures Expanding Group
   - (d) Motion Page Expanding Group

8. Videos can be stored using the AVI format. What does AVI stand for?
   - (a) Audio Video Interface
   - (b) Audio Video Interleave
   - (c) Audio Video Interaction
   - (d) Audio Video Internet

9. What are the extensions of Windows Media files?
   - (a) .asf
   - (b) .asf
   - (c) .wmv
   - (d) All of these

10. .wmv stand for _________ .
    - (a) Windows Media Video
    - (b) Windows Motion Verdict
    - (c) Windows Media Version
    - (d) Windows Motion Video

11. What is the default buffering time for windows media player?
    - (a) 10 sec
    - (b) 2 sec
    - (c) 4 sec
    - (d) 5 sec

12. What does JPEG stand for?
    - (a) Joint Picture Expert Group
    - (b) Joint Picture Enhancing Group
    - (c) Joint Photographic Experts Group
    - (d) Joint Photo Expert Graphic

13. A play queue is a ___________ song listing that allows you to easily select and sort tracks.
    - (a) Permanent
    - (b) Stored
    - (c) Temporary
    - (d) Long

14. The _________ is a play queue.
    - (a) List
    - (b) Library
    - (c) Play list Editor
    - (d) None of these

15. An equalizer allows you to control the _________ of the songs you are playing.
    - (a) Audio volumes
    - (b) Audio frequencies
    - (c) Audio extensions
    - (d) Audio noise

16. The Quick Time format was developed by _________ .
    - (a) Intel
    - (b) Microsoft
    - (c) Apple Inc
    - (d) HP

17. The Real Video format is developed by _________ .
    - (a) Microsoft
    - (b) Real Networks
    - (c) Apple Inc
    - (d) HP

18. What is the extension of videos stored in Real Video format?
    - (a) .rm
    - (b) .wm
    - (c) Both (a) and (b)
    - (d) None of these

19. The tiny dots comprising a picture are called _________.
   (a) Images   (b) Pixels
   (c) Matter   (d) Points
20. .gif stand for _________.
   (a) Graphics Identification Format
   (b) Graphics Interchange Format
   (c) Graphic Identity File
   (d) Graphic Interface Format

HOTS

1. In the given image, face 1 and face 2 blends together in such a way that it distorts the first face to have the shape of second face and at the same time turning into another new face 3. What is this technique called?

   (a) Rendering   (b) Sampling
   (c) Morphing   (d) Retarding
2. Resolution of XGA monitor is ______.
   (a) 1024 × 768   (b) 800 × 600
   (c) 640 × 480   (d) 320 × 200

3. Mrs. Kapoor wants to gift a digital album to her friend on her birthday. All the images are static and have lots of colour shading. Which of the following format is best suited for this purpose?
   (a) AUI   (b) JPEG
   (c) GIF   (d) Bitmap
4. In _________ streaming, there is no need to store data before delivering it, here data is processed quickly by buffering.
   (a) Batch-time   (b) Patch
   (c) Real-time   (d) Static
5. When audio and video segments of a multimedia files are interleaved together to reduce the number of records to store them, it is called as __________.
   (a) Scanning   (b) Flattening
   (c) Spotting   (d) Densing

SUBJECTIVE QUESTIONS

1. Write a short note on Text.

Ans.

Text is the most popular of all the media types. It is distributed over the Internet in many forms including files or messages using different transfer protocols such as FTP (File Transfer Protocol: used to transfer binary and ASCII files over the Internet), HTTP (Hyper Text Transfer Protocol: used to transmit HTML pages) or SMTP (Simple Mail Transfer Protocol: Used for exchanging e-mails).

2. What is the use of multimedia in Entertainment industry?

Ans.

The Entertainment industry is one of the largest sectors of multimedia and growth in this industry has evolved collectively with technology in the production of film, commercials, games and many other areas of entertainment. Multimedia is heavily used in the entertainment industry, especially to develop special effects in movies and animations. Some examples are Avatar, Jurassic Park and Lion King. Multimedia games are a popular pastime and the same goes for software programs available either as CD-ROMs or online. Some video games also use multimedia features.

3. List some major E-Business list of Portals.

Ans.

Some major E-Business list of Portals are following:

- IRCTC Portal.
- Online reservation site Yatra.com.
- Life Insurance Corporation of India.
- E-Banking Sites.
- Online Shopping.
- Online Stock trading site - sharekhan. com.

4. What is the use of Multimedia in Advertising and Film making?

Ans.

You must have seen lots of impossible things happening in TV commercials and wondered how people fly in the air or jump off from high buildings without getting hurt. In advertising, promoting products require an effective medium able to catch the interest of the targeted market. Multimedia plays a vital role in advertising, creating a huge influence in the market and gaining popularity. When the animation and the graphic designs are used to sell products or services, it is known as multimedia advertising. There are various forms of multimedia advertising such as videos, online advertising and DVDs, CDs, etc. The companies can always increase their customers' base through multimedia advertising; therefore, multimedia advertising positively contributes in the marketing of the products and services.

5. How you can use sound recorder in Windows?

Ans.

You can use Sound Recorder to record a sound and save it as an audio file on your computer. You can record sound from different audio devices, such as a microphone that's plugged into the sound card on your computer. The types of audio input sources you can record from depend on the audio devices you have and the input sources on your sound card.

To record audio with Sound Recorder:

i. Make sure you have an audio input device, such as a microphone, connected to your computer.

ii. Open Sound Recorder by clicking the Start button. In the search box, type Sound Recorder, and then, in the list of results, click Sound Recorder.

iii. Click Start Recording.

iv. To stop recording audio, click Stop Recording.

v. (Optional) If you want to continue recording audio, click Cancel in the Save As dialog box, and then click Resume Recording. Continue to record sound, and then click Stop Recording.

vi. Click the File name box, type a file name for the recorded sound, and then click Save to save the recorded sound as an audio file.

MS Paint

4

Learning Objectives : In this chapter, students will learn about:

- ✓ Opening a Paint Window
- ✓ Drawing Different Shapes
- ✓ Quick Access Toolbar
- ✓ Drawing Different Lines
- ✓ Adding Colour to an Image

CHAPTER SUMMARY

Paint is a feature in Windows 7 that you can use to create drawings on a drawing area or on existing pictures. Many of the tools you use in MS Paint are found in the ribbon, which is near the top of the Paint window. The following illustration shows the ribbon and other parts of MS Paint window.

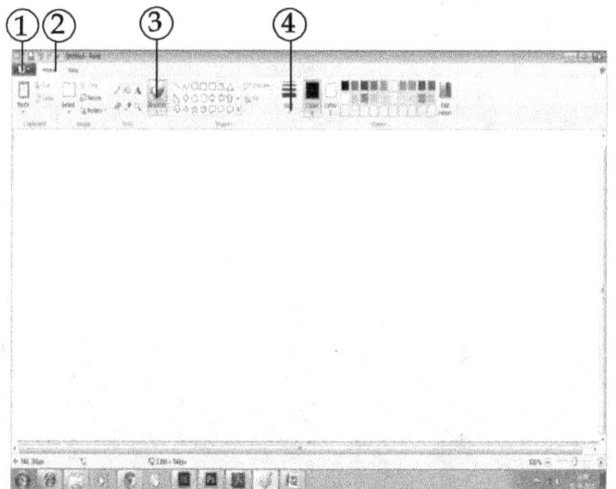

① Paint button ③ Ribbon
② Quick Access Toolbar ④ Drawing area

How to open a Paint window?

- Open Paint by clicking the Start button .
- Click on All Programs.
- Click on Accessories.
- Then, Click on Paint

You can use different tools displayed in the Paint toolbar to draw in Paint. The tool you use and the options you select determine how the drawing appears.

Drawing Different Lines

You can use Paint to draw lines of varying thickness and style. A line tool is used to draw straight lines only. A pencil tool is used to make free-hand drawing of various shapes. A curve tool can be used to draw a curved line. Dragging at a particular point on the line brings a straight line into a curve. The default size of the line is 1 pt or hairline.

Drawing Different Shapes

You can use Paint to add different shapes in a picture. The ready-made shapes range from rectangles, ellipses, triangles, and arrows — to fun and unusual shapes, such as a heart, lightning bolt, or callouts (to name a few).

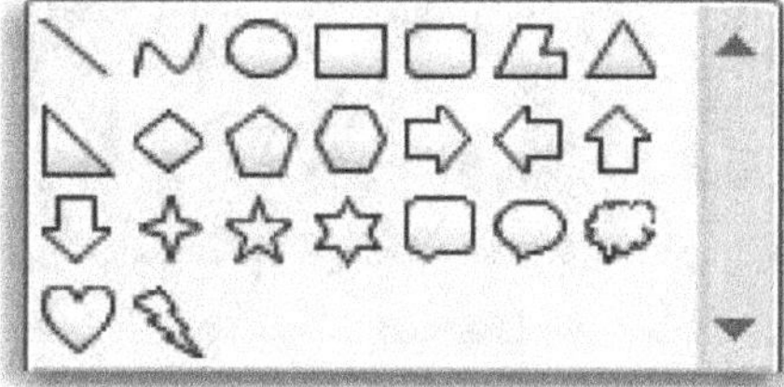

If you want to make your own custom shape, you can use to the Polygon tool ⌂ to do this.

Adding Colour

The Paint window also comes with a color palette which gives you the option of using colours for your drawing. When a tool like line tool, pencil tool or curve tool is selected to make a drawing, the desired colour can also be selected at the same time so that the drawing with the desired colour is drawn. The bucket tool also helps to fill in colour in closed shapes or figures.

You can choose colours of two types. They are fill colour and outline colour. When outline colour is selected, only the border or the outline of the figure shows the colour selected. The fill colour helps to fill in shapes with the desired colour.

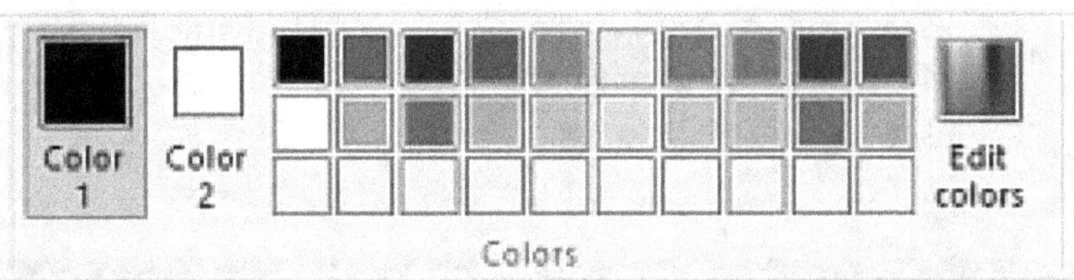

Quick Access Toolbar

The commands that you use in Paint frequently can be added to the Quick Access Toolbar so that it can be used easily.

To add a Paint command to the Quick Access Toolbar, right-click a button or command, and then click Add to Quick Access Toolbar.

Resizing a picture or part of it

Use Resize  to resize the whole image or to resize an object or part of a picture. You can also skew an object in the picture so that it appears slanted.

Saving and using your picture

When editing in Paint, you should save your work frequently so you do not accidentally lose it. After you save your picture, you can use it on your computer or share it with others in email.

TRIVIA

YouTube actually started as a dating website.

➡ Paint is a feature in Windows 7 that you can use to create drawings on a drawing area or on existing pictures.

➡ A line tool is used to draw straight lines only. A pencil tool is used to make free-hand drawing of various shapes.

➡ Use Resize to resize the whole image or to resize an object or part of a picture.

Direction (1-4): Look at the bar on MS-Paint window and answer the following questions.

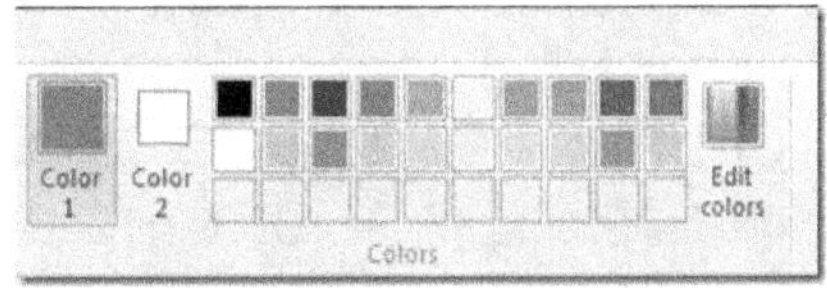

1. The image shown here is of ______.
   (a) Status Bar
   (b) Menu RIBBON
   (c) Quick Access Toolbar
   (d) Title Bar

2. What is 768 × 480 px shown in the image?
   (a) Dimension of the drawing area.
   (b) Dimension of the selected area of a drawing.
   (c) Dimension of the selection tool.
   (d) All of these

3. What is 25 × 26 shown in the image?
   (a) Dimension of the drawing area
   (b) Dimension of the selected area of a drawing.
   (c) Dimension of the selection tool.
   (d) All of these

4. In 768 × 480 px, ______ px is the length and ______ px is the breath respectively.
   (a) 768, 480   (b) 480, 768
   (c) 768, 768   (d) 480, 480

5. To change the unit to centimeter, you should go to the ______.
   (a) View tab of the Ribbon
   (b) Properties dialog in the Paint menu
   (c) Home tab of the Ribbon
   (d) Double click on the status bar

6. How do you hide the status bar?
   (a) Uncheck "Status Bar" from the view tab of the Ribbon.
   (b) Click "Hide Status Bar" in the Paint menu.
   (c) Uncheck "Status Bar" from the Home tab of the Ribbon.
   (d) Double click on the status bar.

7. Which shortcut should you use to view the drawing in full screen?
   (a) F1   (b) F2
   (c) F3   (d) F11

8. The ___ tool can be used to pick colors that you have already used in an image.
   (a) Full Colors   (b) Eraser
   (c) Color picker   (d) Brush

9. Observe the given image.

   The third row of color boxes shows:
   (a) Recently used colors
   (b) Color which you use and are not available in the default palette.
   (c) Colors that are used for background.
   (d) None of these

10. The ______ tool is used to position and enter text in your drawing.
    (a) ?   (b) **A**
    (c) \   (d) ◈

11. What is the shortcut key to undo a change in the drawing?
    (a) Ctrl + A   (b) Ctrl + X
    (c) Ctrl + U   (d) Ctrl + Z

12. The drawing you create in MS Paint can be saved as______.
    (a) JPEG, PNG   (b) GIF, TIFF
    (c) BMP   (d) All of these

13. Which keys will help you to select the whole page?
    (a) Ctrl + C   (b) Ctrl + Z
    (c) Ctrl + V   (d) Ctrl + A

14. Which of the following is NOT a valid option to rotate an image?
    (a) Rotate left 90°   (b) Rotate right 90°
    (c) Rotate 180°   (d) Rotate 270°

15. Which of the following can create an effect that can be used in making an illusion of 3D perspective?
    (a) Skew
    (b) Flip
    (c) Rotate
    (d) Stretch

16. Which of these image properties can you change using image properties dialog box?
    (a) Units
    (b) Colors
    (c) Dimension
    (d) All of these

17. The shortcut to view image Properties dialog box is______.
    (a) Ctrl + E
    (b) Ctrl + A
    (b) Ctrl + Z
    (d) Ctrl + F

18. This picture shows a grid on the circle. How is the grid created?

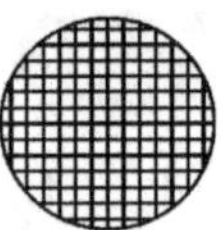

    (a) Enable Gridlines in the File of the ribbon.
    (b) Use the line tool to create the grid.
    (c) Use the rectangle tool to create the grid.
    (d) Enable Gridlines in the view tab of the ribbon.

20. How do you transform the image in Figure 1 to the one given in Figure 2?

 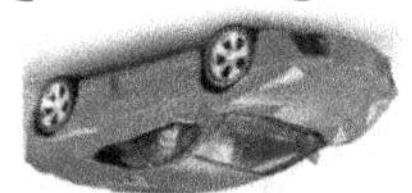

Figure 1   Figure 2

    (a) Rotate left 90°
    (b) Rotate 180°
    (c) Rotate right 90°
    (d) Flip vertical

HOTS

1. To save a drawing in one of the available formats (png, jpeg, bmp, gif and other possible file types), go to Paint button and select ____________.

(a) 
(b) 
(c) 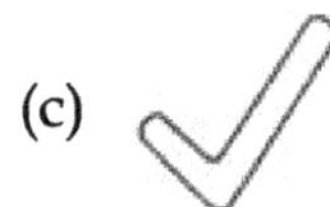
(d) 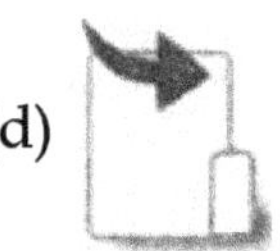

2. Which command should you use to bring a Zoomed in or a Zoomed Out image to its original size?

(a) 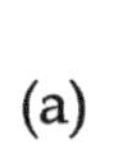 
(b) 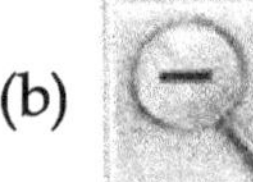
(c)  
(d) 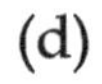 

3. What is the function of this tool in MS Paint?

    (a) Draws a thin free form line. Used to draw objects just as you would with a pencil.
    (b) Enables you to draw a text box to add typed words to an image.
    (c) Fills an area with color.
    (d) Picks up a color from one area of an image to use with a drawing tool.

4. You can set the drawing size of Paint in the computer like choosing the size of paper to use. To set the drawing size, what are the steps to follow?
    (a) Ctrl + X
    (b) Ctrl + H
    (c) Image Menu | Attributes
    (d) Image Menu | Flip/Rotate

1. List any 5 options available on toolbox. What is their use?

Ans.

The toolbox is very useful, because it contains the tools you will use in order to come up with your drawing. It contains the following tools:

Free-Form Select and Select Tool: For selecting a specific object, which then you can copy and paste in another location, or you can opt to delete that selection.

Eraser/Colour Eraser: This is for erasing your drawing or the colour you have applied.

Pick Colour: This picks a specific colour you want and makes it the active colour, meaning that whatever you do next will have that colour.

Pencil: You will use it for drawing.

Airbrush: For spraying your object with colour.

2. What is the use of Circle Tool?

Ans.

The circle tool is used to draw circles. A user can open this tool by clicking on the ellipse tool in the toolbox.

Once after selecting the circle tool, drag the mouse cursor on the drawing sheet. Click on the mouse's left button while dragging it and then release the mouse. With the help of this tool, a user can draw a full circle, semi-circle and other round images.

3. Write about Crop option.

Ans.

The top button in the Image group of Home tab is, a diamond shape with a line icon through it is called as Crop. This option is used for erasing or cropping the picture/image without disturbing the selected area/part of the picture. After cropping the large/full picture into the selected area, and after saving it, then the full picture or image before the cropping will not get saved but the image/picture after the cropping with new selected area will be saved.

4. What is Size tool?

Ans.

This tool is used only when any brush or shape is inserted into the paint program. You will be able to see the small down arrow that is appearing under the Size Tool when any of the shape or brush is selected (for selecting the line thickness). The line thickness also depends on the brushes that is been chosen.

5. Write about brushes.

Ans.

In Paint program, brushes are made used when if we want to apply the color to any picture or text with the changes in the texture width (brush nip size). Brush, Calligraphy 1, Calligraphy 2, airbrush, crayon, marker, natural pencil, water color etc are some the examples of different types of brushes.

MS Word

Learning Objectives : In this chapter, students will learn about:
- ✓ Creating a New Document
- ✓ Bold, Underline and Italic Options
- ✓ Cut and Paste Options
- ✓ Shortcut Keys

CHAPTER SUMMARY

We all know that MS Word is a software that helps us to write and create documents. The MS Word window looks similar to the one shown below.

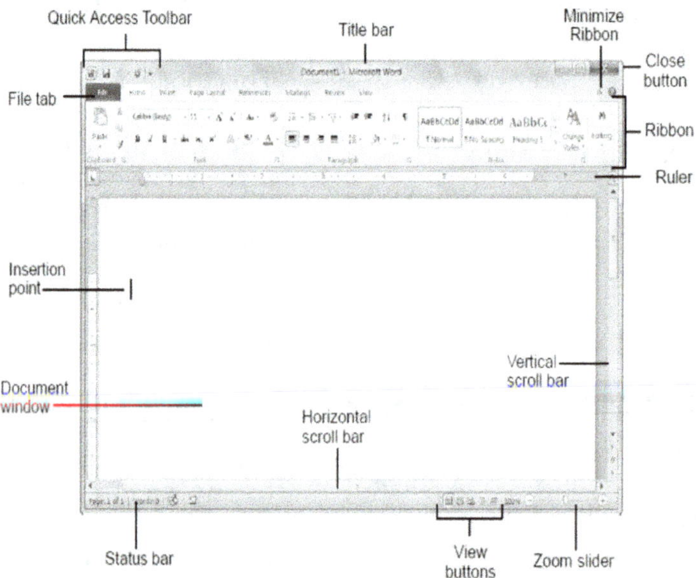

The **File** tab menu and backstage view contain commands for working with a program's files, such as Open, Save, Close, New and Print.

To Create a New Document

Click the **File** tab, click the **New** tab, and click the **Create** button. Or, press **Ctrl + N**.

To Open a File

To continue working on a file you previously saved, you must open the file. To open the file:

- ■ Click on File.
- ■ Select Open.
- ■ Find the folder you saved in the Look In field. You can also type in the name of the document in the File Name field.
- ■ Click on Open.
- ■ The file you saved will appear on the screen.
- ■ **To Save a Document:** Click the **Save** button 🖫 on the Quick Access Toolbar, or press **Ctrl + S**.
- ■ **To Print a Document:** Click the **File** tab and click the **Print** tab, or press **Ctrl + P**.

- **To Undo:** Click the ↺ **Undo** button on the Quick Access Toolbar, or press **Ctrl + Z**.
- **To Close a Document:** Click the **X** **Close** button, or press **Ctrl + W**.
- **To Get Help:** Press **F1** to open the Help window. Type your question and press **Enter**.
- **To Insert a Header or Footer:** Click the **Insert** tab on the Ribbon and click the **Header** or **Footer** button in the Header & Footer group.
- **To Insert a Manual Page Break:** Click the **Insert** tab on the Ribbon and click the **Page Break** button in the Pages group.
- **To Insert a Table:** Click the **Insert** tab on the Ribbon, click the **Table** button in the Tables group, and select **Insert Table** from the menu.

Bold, Underline and Italic

You can bold, underline, or italicize the written text on the Word file. First highlight the text you wish to format, then click the appropriate formatting button on the format toolbar.

- **B** - Bold button
- *I* - Italic button
- U - Underline button

Highlighting Text

Highlighting is useful when you want to emphasize important information. Word provides a button on the Formatting toolbar that lets you highlight text. To use this feature:

- Click the Highlight button ✎ ▾ on the Formatting toolbar.
- Yellow is the default colour. You can select a colour of your choice by clicking on the arrow on the right hand side.
- When the Highlight button is activated, continue selecting the text you want to highlight with the help of a mouse. Once done, click on the highlight button to deactivate this feature.

Cut and Paste

You can remove text from the document and also paste it elsewhere in the document. When you cut text, it is stored on the Clipboard. Information stored on the Clipboard stays there until new information is either cut or copied.

Cutting and Pasting by Using the Standard Toolbar
- Highlight the text you wish to cut or copy.
- Click on Edit, then select cut or copy.
- Bring the cursor to the position where you want to paste the text.
- Click on Edit, and then select paste.

Cutting by Using the Icon
- Highlight text you want to cut.
- Click on the Cut icon ✂ .
- The text is now on the clipboard.

Copying by Using the Icon
- Highlight the text you want to copy.
- Click on the Copy icon ▤ .

Pasting by Using the Icon
- Place the cursor where you want to paste the text.
- Click on the Paste icon ▤ .

Changing Font Color
Word also lets you change text color in a document. To use this feature:
- Select the text you want to change the color of.
- Click the Text button **A** ▾ on the Formatting toolbar.
- Select the desired color by clicking on the arrow on the right hand side.
- When completed, click once on the Text button to deactivate it.

The Paragraph Group

Many options are available directly in the **Paragraph** group on the **Home** tab of the Ribbon and in the **Paragraph** group on the **Page Layout** tab.

Paragraph group on Home Tab

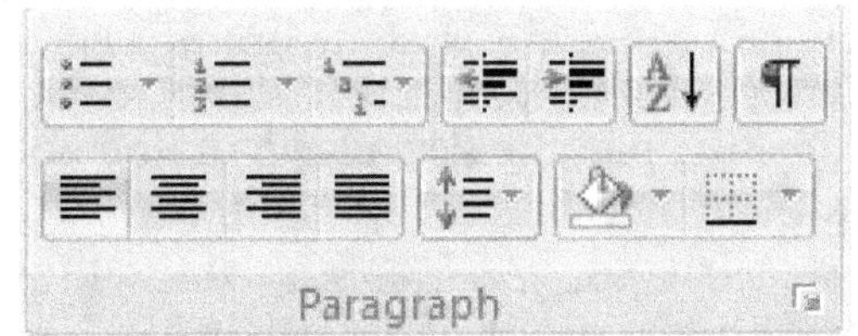

Alignment

Alignment or *justification* refers to the way in which the lines of a paragraph are aligned. There are four types of alignment, and the type of alignment of the paragraph where your cursor is located is indicated by the highlighted button in the **Paragraph** group on the **Home** tab.

- With *left alignment* (≡) (the default), the left-hand ends of all the lines in the paragraph are aligned along the left-hand margin of the text area.
- With *center alignment* (≡), the mid-points (centers) of all the lines in the paragraph are aligned along the same imaginary vertical line at the center of the text area between the margins.
- With *right alignment* (≡), the right-hand ends of all the lines in the paragraph are aligned along the right-hand margin of the text area.
- With *justified alignment* or *full justification* (≡), all the lines in the paragraph, except the last line, are extended so that the left-hand end of each line is aligned along the left-hand margin of the text area, the right-hand end of each line is aligned along the right-hand margin of the text area, and the lines are all of the same length.

Line Spacing

Line spacing refers to the vertical distance between the lines within a paragraph and determines the location of each line relative to the line above it. Line spacing can be specified by name (single, 1.5 lines, double), by a number that indicates a multiple of single spacing (for example, 2.0 is equivalent to double spacing). You can quickly view and change the line spacing to several common standard values by clicking the **Line Spacing** button (≡) in the **Paragraph** group on the **Home** tab. More line spacing options become available when you click **Line Spacing Options** to open the **Paragraph** dialog box.

Indents

The *indent before text* refers to the width of the additional empty space that is inserted between the margin and the text on the left-hand side of a paragraph of left-to-right text, and the *indent after text* refers to the width of the additional empty space that is inserted between the text and the margin on the right-hand side of a paragraph of left-to-right text. You can quickly increase the indent before text to the next tab stop by clicking the **Increase Indent** button (≡) in the **Paragraph** group on the **Home** tab, and you can quickly decrease the indent before text to the preceding tab stop by clicking the **Decrease Indent** button (≡) in the **Paragraph** group on the **Home** tab.

You can set the indent before text (the left indent for left-to-right text) to values that do not correspond to tab stops, and you can also set the indent after text (the right indent for left-to-right text) in the **Paragraph** group on the **Page Layout** tab.

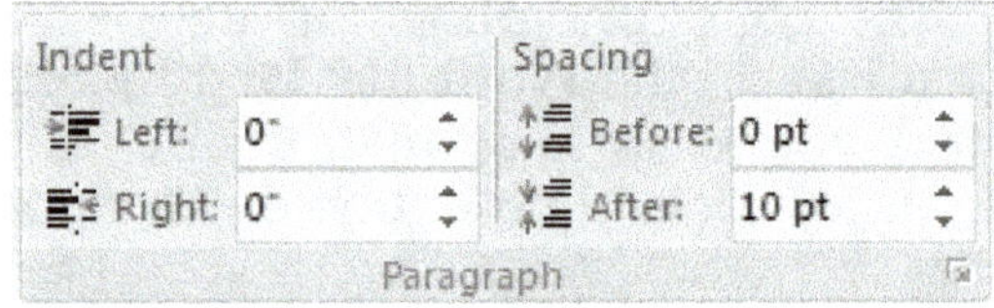

Paragraph Spacing

The spacing between your paragraphs is determined by the *spacing before it* and the *spacing after it* that are set for each paragraph. You can modify the spacing before a paragraph and the spacing after it by changing the values in the applicable boxes in the **Paragraph** group on the **Page Layout** tab.

Borders

If you want to add borders around the paragraph where your cursor is located, click the **Borders** button (≡) to add the current default borders. If you want to select a border style that differs from the current default border style, click the small arrow on the **Borders** button, and select one of the border styles displayed.

Shading (Colored Background)

If you want to add shading with the current default background color to the entire text area of the paragraph where your cursor is located, click the **Shading** button ( ) in the **Paragraph** group on the **Home** tab.

Using Drop Cap

A *drop cap* (*dropped capital*) is a large *capital* letter used as a decorative element at the beginning of a paragraph or section.

Open a document in Word 2010 and select the letter you want to insert as drop cap. Click on the **"Insert"** tab,

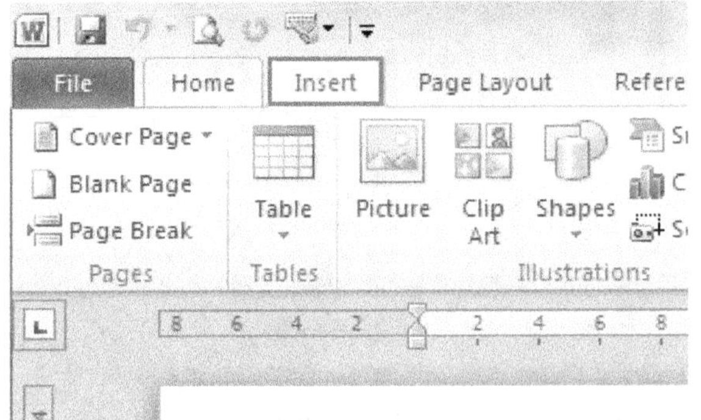

and in the **"Text"** group you can find **"Drop Cap"** button. Click it, and hold the mouse pointer over your choice to see a preview in your document.

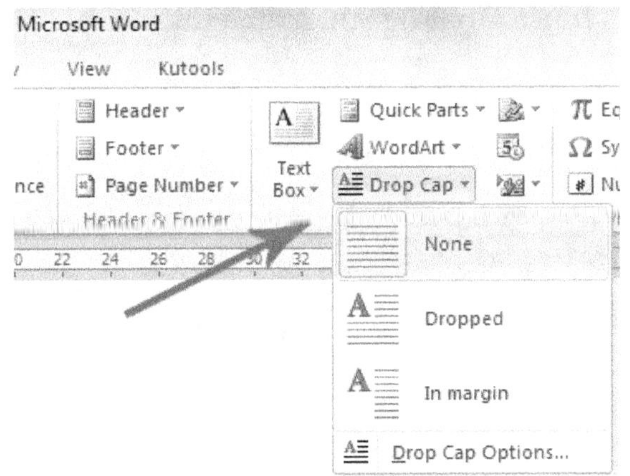

Working in Different Views

Depending on what you currently want to do with a document, you can work in any of Word's *views*: Print Layout, Full Screen Reading, Web Layout, Outline, and Draft. Each view serves a particular purpose, as described below.

The Document Views group contains the same five view icons as the ones in the status bar.

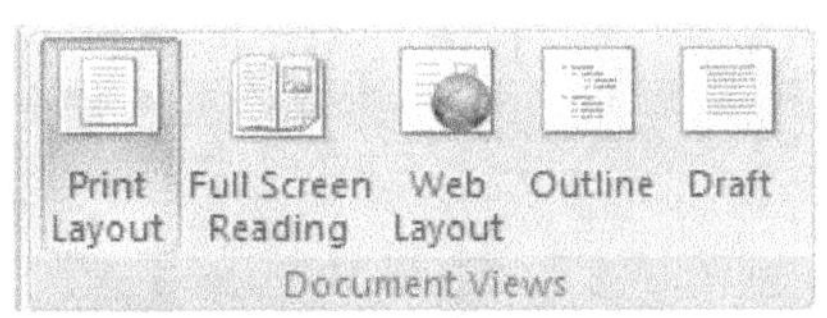

Print Layout view

Standard documents, such as letters, memos, and reports, are often written and edited in Print Layout view. One advantage of working in this view is its adherence to *WYSIWYG* (what you see is what you get). The margins, headers, and footers correspond to the printed output. Pages are shown as equivalent pieces of paper with physical breaks between pages.

Full Screen Reading view

If want to read or review a document, Full Screen Reading view can help simplify the task where you can see the document spread over full screen.

Web Layout view

Use Web Layout view to create, view, and edit pages as they'll appear online when opened in a browser.

Outline view

Use Outline view to create, view, and edit outlines.

Draft view

Work in Draft view when speed is of primary importance. In Print Layout view, physical pages and breaks are drawn. Draft view displays a document as a continuous text scroll; page breaks are denoted by dashed lines. Because repagination occurs almost instantly as you compose, this is an ideal view if you have an older, slower computer.

Inserting Graphics-Pictures and Shapes, Clip Arts, SmartArt and Text Box

You can do all kinds of things with graphics in Word 2010. Look for all the different types of graphics on the Insert tab, in the Illustrations group.

Adding a picture in a Word document:

1. From the Insert tab's Illustrations group, click the Picture button. The Insert Picture dialog box appears.

2. Use the dialog box controls to browse for the image you want.

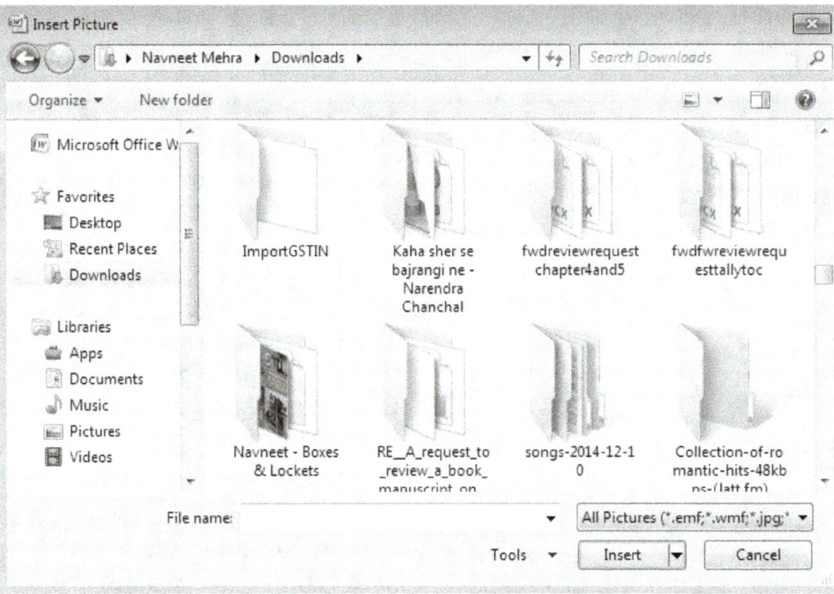

3. Click to select the image.
4. Click the Insert button.

The image will be added into your document. After you insert a picture, the Picture Tools Format tab appears on the Ribbon.

Inserting clip art in Word

Clip art is a collection of images, both line art and pictures, that you're free to use in your documents:

1. On the Insert tab, in the Illustrations group, click the Clip Art button. The Clip Art task pane appears.
2. In the Search For box, type a description of what you want. For example, a picture of a computer may go well with your report on computer education. Type **computer** in the box.
3. Click the Go button. The results are displayed in the task pane. Check the results and note that you may have to scroll a bit to see all of them. If you don't find what you want, go back to Step 2 and refine your search.
4. Click the image you want. The image will be added to your document.
5. Close the Clip Art task pane by clicking the X in its upper-right corner.

Adding a shape in Word content

Word comes with a library of common shapes ready to insert into your document:

1. Choose a predefined shape from the Shapes button menu, found in the Illustrations group on the Insert tab.

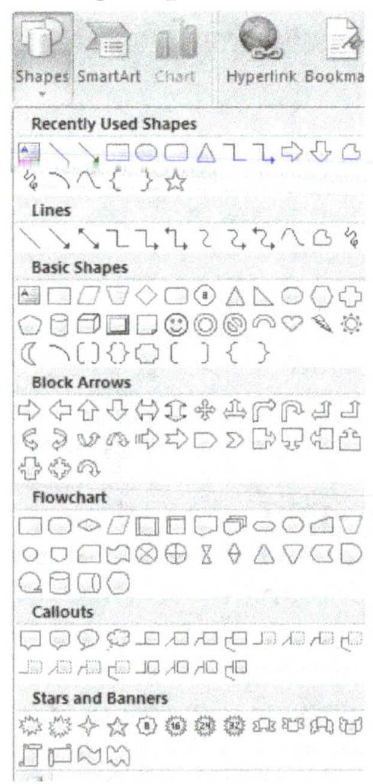

The mouse pointer changes to a plus sign.

2. Drag the mouse in the document where you want the shape to appear. Drag down, from the upper-left corner of the shape to the lower-right corner. The shape appears at the location where you draw it, as a size determined by how you drag the mouse.

SmartArt

Clicking the SmartArt button in the Illustrations group on the Insert tab summons the Choose a SmartArt Graphic dialog box. You can use that dialog box to quickly arrange a layout of graphics in your document.

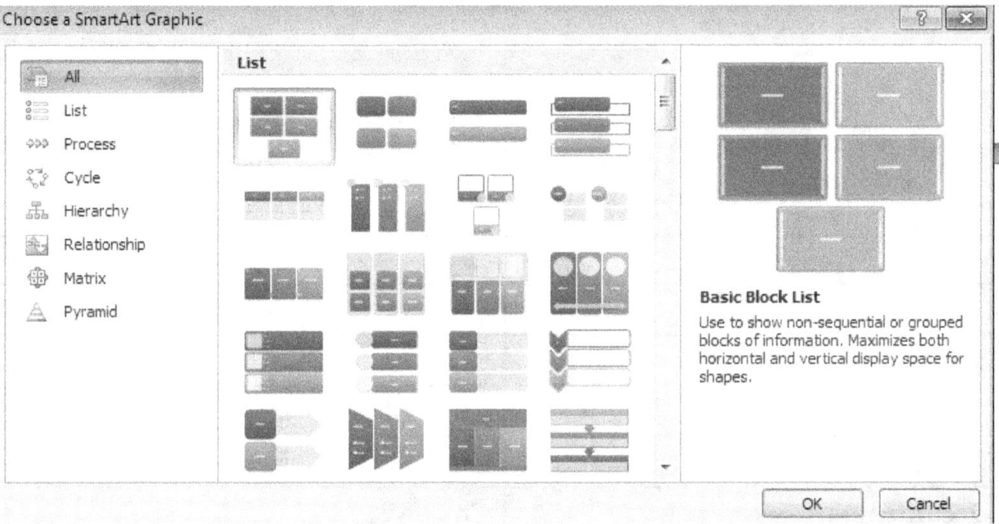

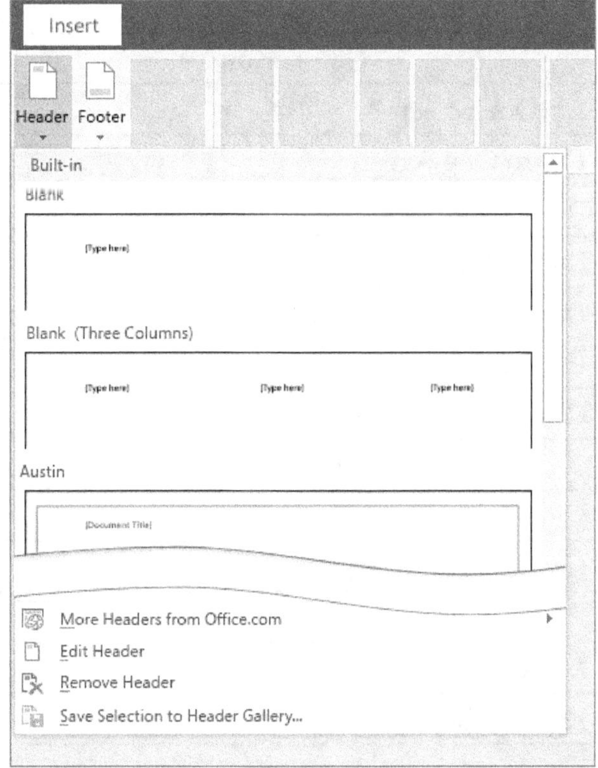

> **TRIVIA**
>
> The overall global storage is projected to reach 175 zettabytes by the end of 2025.

Text Box

To add a text box:

- On the **Insert** tab, in the **Text** group, click **Text Box**, and then click **Draw Text Box**.
- Click in the document, and then drag to draw the text box the size that you want.
- To add text to a text box, click inside the text box, and then type or paste text.

Insert a Header and Footer

1. With your cursor on the first page of your document, go to **Insert**, select **Header** or **Footer**, and then pick a built-in layout and design, or select **Edit Header** or **Edit Footer** to create your own.

2. Whatever you want repeated on the pages of your document: add it in the header or footer area on the page.

If you don't want the header or footer on the first page, select **Different First Page**.

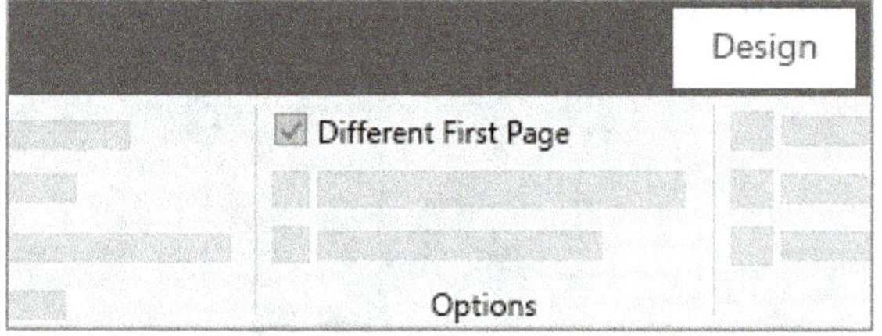

3. When you're done, select **Close Header and Footer**.

Shortcut Keys

General	To Do
Open a Document	Ctrl + O
Create New	Ctrl + N
Save a Document	Ctrl + S
Print a Document	Ctrl + P
Close a Document	Ctrl + W
Help	F1
Navigation	**To Do**
Up One Screen	Page Up
Down One Screen	Page Down
Beginning of Line	Home
End of Line	End
Beginning of Document	Ctrl + Home
End of Document	Ctrl + End
Open the Go To dialog box	F5
Editing	**To Do**
Cut	Ctrl + X
Copy	Ctrl + C
Paste	Ctrl + V
Undo	Ctrl + Z
Redo or Repeat	Ctrl + Y

Formatting	To Do
Bold	Ctrl + B
Italics	Ctrl + I
Underline	Ctrl + U
Align Left	Ctrl + L
Center	Ctrl + E
Align Right	Ctrl + R
Justify	Ctrl + J
Text Selection	**To Do**
A Word	Double-click the word
A Sentence	Press and hold **Ctrl** and click anywhere in the sentence
A Line	Click in the selection bar next to the line
A Paragraph	Triple-click the paragraph
Everything	Ctrl + A

➡ When you cut text, it is stored on the Clipboard. Information stored on the Clipboard stays there until new information is either cut or copied.

➡ *Line spacing* refers to the vertical distance between the lines within a paragraph and determines the location of each line relative to the line above it.

➡ The *indent before text* refers to the width of the additional empty space that is inserted between the margin and the text on the left-hand side of a paragraph of left-to-right text, and the indent after text refers to the width of the additional empty space that is inserted between the text and the margin on the right-hand side of a paragraph of left-to-right text.

1. Which of the following is NOT a valid version of MS Office?
   (a) Office Vista
   (b) Office XP
   (c) Office 2007
   (d) Office 2010

2. Pressing F8 key three times selects_____.
   (a) A word
   (b) A sentence
   (c) A paragraph
   (d) The Entire document

3. What does the key F12 display?
   (a) Save dialog box
   (b) Open dialog box
   (c) Close dialog box
   (d) Save As dialog box

4. What is the use of the ▣ button just above the vertical scroll bar?
   (a) To show and hide the Ribbon
   (b) To show and hide the scroll bars
   (c) To show and hide the Ruler.
   (d) To show and hide the Quick Access Toolbar.

5. What is the default font size of a new Word document based on Normal template?
   (a) 10pt   (b) 11pt
   (c) 12pt   (d) 8pt

6. Which of the following are/were Word processors?
   (a) Word Star
   (b) Word Perfect
   (c) Microsoft Write
   (d) All of these

7. Which option places the selected text slightly below the line of normal printed text?
   (a) Subscript   (b) Superscript
   (c) Small front   (d) Small caps

8. Match the following.

Column - I	Column - II
(i) Ctrl + F	(a) Replace
(ii) Ctrl + H	(b) Go to
(iii) Ctrl + C	(c) Bold
(iv) Ctrl + B	(d) Find

   (a) (i)–(d), (ii)–(a), (iii)–(b), (iv)–(c)
   (b) (i)–(a), (ii)–(b), (iii)–(c), (iv)–(d)
   (c) (i)–(d), (ii)–(c), (iii)–(a), (iv)–(b)
   (d) (i)–(a), (ii)–(d), (iii)–(b), (iv)–(c)

9. What does a ruler show?
   (a) Page width
   (b) Position of tabs, column, etc.
   (c) Length of the document
   (d) All of these

10. Which of the following is NOT a valid shortcut for setting the line spacing between lines of text?
    (a) Ctrl + 1
    (b) Ctrl + 2
    (c) Ctrl + 3
    (d) None of these

11. ¶ is used to______.
    (a) Create a new paragraph
    (b) Display or hide symbols for characters like spaces and tabs
    (c) Display or hide the title bar
    (d) Display or hide spelling and grammar errors

12. What are margins?
    (a) The amount of space between the text and the edge of the page on all four sides.
    (b) The amount of space on top.
    (c) The amount of space on sides.
    (d) The amount of space at bottom.

13. Match the following.

Column - I	Column - II
(i)	(a) Increase Indent
(ii)	(b) Align text to the right
(iii) x^2	(c) Start a bulleted list
(iv)	(d) Create small letters above the line of text
(v)	(e) Center text

(a) (i)-(a), (ii)-(e), (iii)-(d), (iv)-(b), (v)-(c)
(b) (i)-(c), (ii)-(b), (iii)-(d), (iv)-(e), (v)-(a)
(c) (i)-(c), (ii)-(b), (iii)-(a), (iv)-(e), (v)-(d)
(d) (i)-(c), (ii)-(e), (iii)-(d), (iv)-(b), (v)-(a)

14. Match the following.

Column - I	Column - II
(i) Ctrl + A	(a) Paste
(ii) Red Wavy	(b) Change Case lines
(iii)	(c) Synonyms and Antonyms
(iv) Aa	(d) Selects the entire document
(v) Thesaurus	(e) Spelling Mistakes

(a) (i)-(d), (ii)-(c), (iii)-(b), (iv)-(a), (v)-(e)
(b) (i)-(d), (ii)-(e), (iii)-(b), (iv)-(a), (v)-(c)
(c) (i)-(d), (ii)-(e), (iii)-(a), (iv)-(b), (v)-(c)
(d) (i)-(a), (ii)-(d), (iii)-(b), (iv)-(c), (v)-(e)

15. Which of the following can be used to set the size of a page?

(a)   (b)
(c)   (d)

16. How many column does a word document have by default?
(a) One   (b) Two
(c) Three   (d) Four

17. What is the shortcut to set the line spacing to 1.5?
(a) Ctrl + 1   (b) Ctrl + 2
(c) Ctrl + 3   (d) Ctrl + 5

18. If I want 3 sets of copies of a document, what option should I select to get the first set complete of the whole document?
(a) Numbers of copies
(b) Collate
(c) Scale
(d) Pages

19. From the Print Menu you can do all the following except _____.
(a) Print multiple copies
(b) Preview the document
(c) Change the document style
(d) Adjust the page margins

20. Times New Roman, Comic Sans and Calibri are _____.
(a) Fonts   (b) Styles
(c) Text patterns   (d) Font sizes

21. Which of the following is NOT a tab in MS Word 2010?
(a) File   (b) Insert
(c) Home   (d) Design

22. The operations group, illustrations, Links Heater & Footer, Text, etc. are found in which of the following tabs?
(a) Home   (b) Insert
(c) View   (d) Design

23. The Backstage view of word document is given.

To go to the document, from the Backstage view, click on _____.

(a)
(b) Exit
(c) Close
(d) Any tab on the Ribbon

24. Which of the following option is NOT present in Review tab?

(a) 
(b)
(c)
(d)

25. Identify the given icon.

(a) Create PDF
(b) Start Mail Merge
(c) Envelopes
(d) Labels

HOTS

1. The Styles task pane of MS Word 2010 is shown here. Styles have three kinds of icons next to them: ¶, a, ¶a. Which of the following statements is incorrect about ¶a icon?
   (a) It can be used either as character style or a paragraph style.
   (b) It cannot be applied only to a part of the paragraph.
   (c) It can be applied to the entire paragraph as well as to a part of the paragraph.
   (d) Both (a) and (b)

2. Find the odd one out in context to MS Word 2010.
   (a) A
   (b) abc
   (c) x^2
   (d) ¶

3. Suppose you want to type a symbol ∞ (infinity) in MS Word 2010 document, which of the following steps is correct?
   (a) File → Options → Proofing → AutoCorrect Options → Math AutoCorrect
   (b) Home → AutoCorrect Options → Math AutoCorrect
   (c) Insert → Shapes → Math AutoCorrect
   (d) View → Options → PROOFING → autocorrect

4. Word has a list of predefined typing, spelling, capitalization, and grammar errors that ____________ can detect and correct.
   (a) AutoEntry
   (b) AutoCorrect
   (c) AutoAdd
   (d) AutoSpell

5. After typing header text, how can you quickly enter footer text?
   (a) Press Page-Down key and type the text for footer
   (b) Click on Switch between Heeder & Footer then type the text
   (c) Both of these
   (d) None of these

1. **What are different alignment options in MS Word?**

Ans.

There are four alignment options:

i. **Align Left:** This option places the text towards the left margin, leaving an uneven right edge.

ii. **Center:** This option places the text in the center of the left and right margins.

iii. **Align Right:** This option places the text towards the right margin, leaving an uneven left edge.

iv. **Justify:** This option places the text in a way that the text is equally distributed between both the margins and none of the edges of the text appear uneven.

2. **How you can use line spacing in MS Word?**

Ans.

Line spacing is the amount of space between the lines of text in a paragraph of a Word document. We can increase or decrease this space by following these steps:

Step 1

Select the text or the paragraph or just place the cursor anywhere in the paragraph

Step 2

Click on the Line and Paragraph Spacing option in the Paragraph group on the Home tab. A drop-down list appears

Step 3

Select the desired spacing value from the drop-down list

3. **How you can use Paragraph spacing in MS Word?**

Ans.

To precisely specify the values for line and paragraph spacing, we can follow the given steps:

Step 1

Click on Line Spacing Options. In the Line and Paragraph Spacing drop-down list in the Paragraph group under the Home tab. The Paragraph dialog box appears.

Step 2

Choose the required settings in the Spacing section of the dialog box.

Step 3

Click OK to apply the settings.

4. **What is the use of Find feature in MS Word? How it can be used?**

Ans.

After typing a document, we may want to search a specific word or a phrase. Instead of reading and going through the entire document, we can make use of the Find feature of Word. The Find feature can be used to search all the occurrences of a given word or phrase. The steps to use this feature are:

Step 1

Click on the Home tab.

Step 2

Click on the Find option in the Editing group. The Navigation pane appears.

Step 3

Type the word that you want to find in the Search box. Word searches the text you entered and displays the results in the Navigation pane and also highlights the word in the document.

Step 4

Click on a result in the Navigation pane to see it in the document. You can look at all the results by clicking on the Next Search Result and the Previous Search Result arrows in the Navigation pane.

5. How you can set tabs in MS Word? Explain it.

Ans.

There are two ways to set tabs - by either using the Tabs Dialog Box or using the ruler

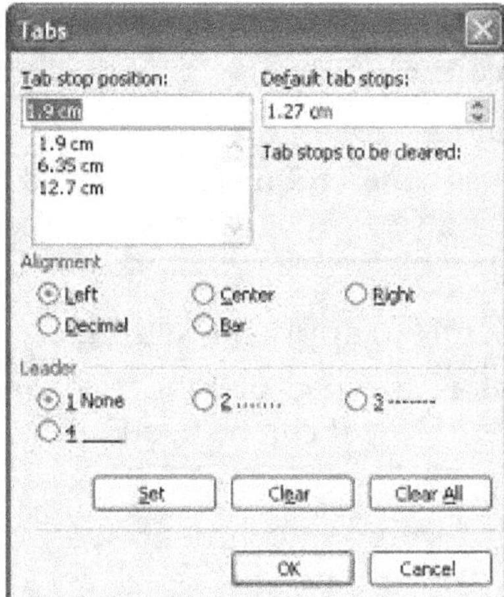

Setting tabs by using the Ruler is an easy, two-step process.

Click the Tab Alignment button on the left of the ruler to choose the type of alignment. Click the position on the ruler to set the tab.

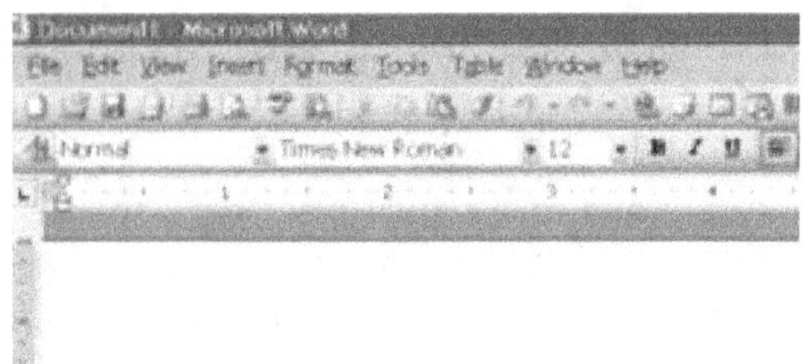

Steps to set tabs in a document by using the Tabs dialog box:

- Open Microsoft Word on your computer.
- Put the cursor in the document where you want the new tab to take place.
- Click on the Format menu.
- Click on the Tabs option in the Format menu. The Tabs dialog box appears.
- Under the Tab Stop Position, enter where you would like the tab to appear. i.e. 0.5", 1", 2" etc. The default tabs are set every 0.5".
- When you have finished making your selection, click on the OK button.

MS PowerPoint 6

Learning Objectives : In this chapter, students will learn about:
- ✓ Steps to Create a New Document
- ✓ Different Views
- ✓ Keyboard Shortcuts

CHAPTER SUMMARY

We all know that MS PowerPoint is a software that helps us make digital presentations that are effective, interesting and clear. The MS PowerPoint comes with features that help us to make our presentations easy to grasp. The opening Screen of MS PowerPoint window looks similar to this one.

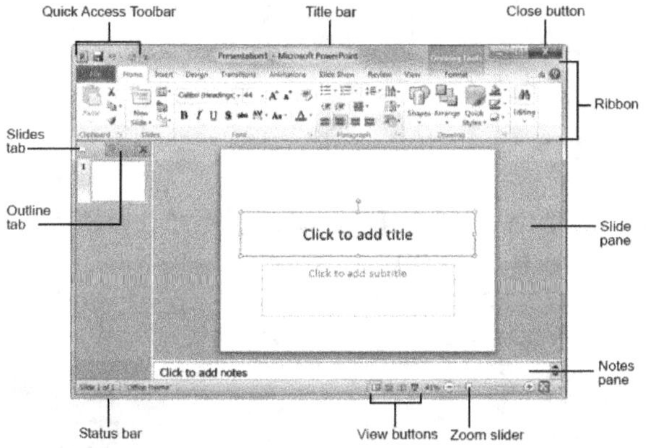

The File tab menu and Backstage view contain commands for working with a program's files, including New, Open, Save, Print and Close.

To Create a New Presentation

Click the **File** tab, click **New**, and click **Create**. Or, press **Ctrl + N**.

- **To Open a Presentation:** Click the **File** tab and click **Open**, or press **Ctrl + O**.
- **To Save a Presentation:** Click the Save button on the Quick Access Toolbar, or press **Ctrl + S**.
- **To Close a Presentation:** Click the **File** tab and click **Close**, or press **Ctrl + W**.
- **To Get Help:** Press **F1** to open the Help window. Type your question and press **Enter**.
- **To Exit PowerPoint:** Click the **File** tab and click **Exit**.
- **To Insert a New Slide:** Click the **Home** tab and click **New Slide** in the Slides group, or press **Ctrl + M**.
- **To Change the Slide Layout:** Click the **Home** tab, click the **Layout** button in the Slides group, and select a layout.
- **To Insert a Header or Footer:** Click the **Insert** tab on the Ribbon and click the **Header & Footer** button in the Text group. Select the option(s) that you want and click **Apply** or **Apply to All**.
- **To Cut or Copy Text:** Select the text you want to cut or copy and click the **Cut** or **Copy** button in the Clipboard group on the Home tab.
- **To Paste Text:** Place the insertion point where you want to paste and click the **Paste** button in the Clipboard group on the Home tab.
- **To Add a Slide Transition:** Navigate to the slide you want to add a transition to. Click the **Transitions** tab on the Ribbon, click the **More** button in the Transition to This Slide group, and select a transition effect.

- **To Add an Animation Effect to an Object:** Select the object that you want to animate, click the Animations tab on the Ribbon. Click the ▼ More button in the Animation group, and select an animation effect. The animation effect can be Fly In, Bounce, Zoom, Spin etc.

- **To Insert a Picture:** Click the **Insert** tab on the Ribbon and click the **Picture** button in the Illustrations group. Find the picture you want to insert and click **Insert**.

- **To insert an Audio File:** Click the Insert tab on the ribbon and click the audio drop down arrow and select an audio from file to insert your personal sound or audio file.

- **To Insert a Video file:** Click the Insert tab on the Ribbon and click the Video button in the Media group. Find the video you want to insert and click Insert. You can also choose what part of the video you want to appear on the screen by using the Trim video option.

Views

⊞ **Normal view:** This is the default view in MS PowerPoint. Normal view includes the Outline pane, Slide pane, and Notes pane.

⊞ **Slide Sorter view:** This view displays all the slides in the presentation as thumbnails (tiny images). Use Slide Sorter view when you want to rearrange the order of slides or add transition effects between slides.

⊞ **Reading View:** Similar to Slide Show view, it displays the presentation in a window with simple controls, making it easy to review.

⊞ **Slide Show view:** This view displays the presentation as an electronic slide show. Whenever you deliver a presentation in front of an audience, Slide Show view is definitely the view you want to use.

To Present a Slide Show: Click the **Slide Show** button on the status bar, or press **F5**.

To End a Slide Show: Press **Esc**

Wikipedia claims there are over 700 computer languages.

Inserting Clip Arts

1. On the **Insert** tab of the toolbar ribbon, in the **Images** section, select **Clip Art**. The **Clip Art** task panel appears on the right side of the application window.

2. In the **Search for** box, type keywords that describe the art you're looking for.

3. Under **Results should be**, select the types of media you want included in the search results:

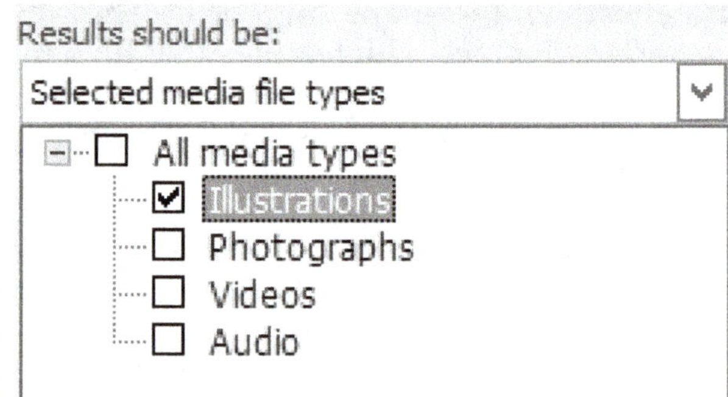

4. Ensure that **Include Bing content** is selected if you're connected to the Internet and want images from the web included in your search results.*

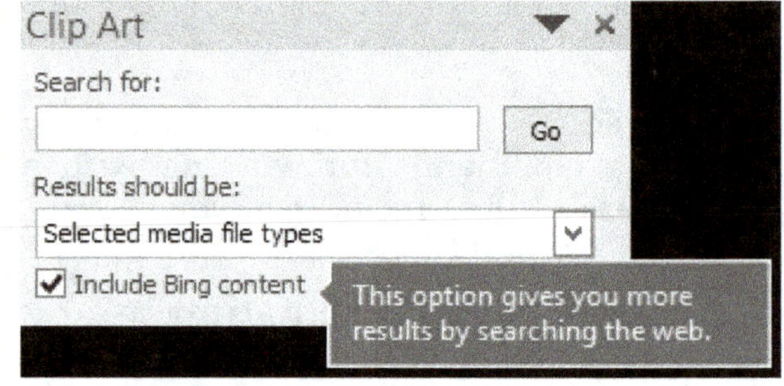

Turning on this option gives you more search results to choose from. (Otherwise, leave that box cleared, and you'll only receive search results from the pictures installed on your computer by Office.)

5. Select **Go** to start the search.

   The search results are shown in the task panel.

   - You can scroll vertically if the results don't all fit in the task pane.
   - To see a larger version of a thumbnail image in the result list, or to simply see the image if all that is shown is a small red x placeholder, right-click the thumbnail and select **Preview/Properties**.

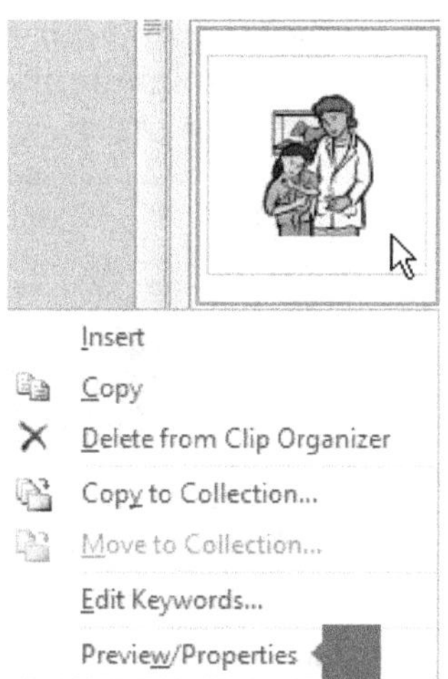

While you're in the **Preview/Properties** window, you can browse through the images by selecting **Previous** and **Next**.

6. To insert a picture in your document, right-click the thumbnail image in the task panel, and select **Insert**.

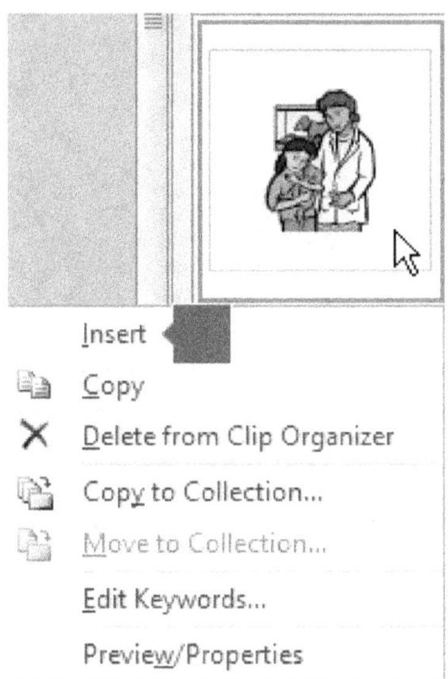

Once the image is inserted, you can adjust its placement by selecting it and dragging with the mouse.

Insert Symbol

1. Place your cursor in the file at the spot where you want to insert the symbol.
2. On the **Insert** tab, click **Symbol**.

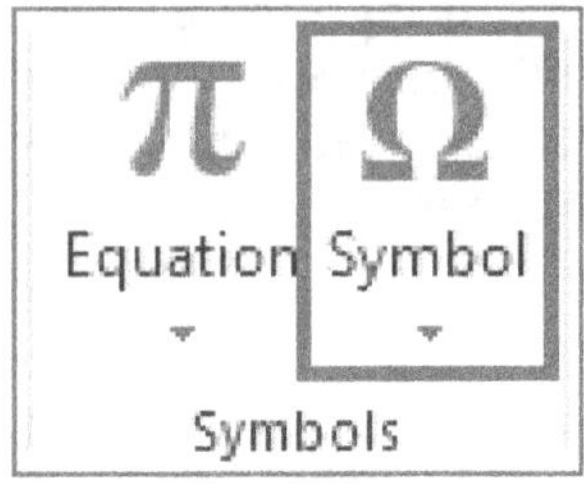

3. If you see the symbol you want listed on that gallery, just click it to insert. Otherwise, click **More Symbols** to open the **Symbol** dialog box.

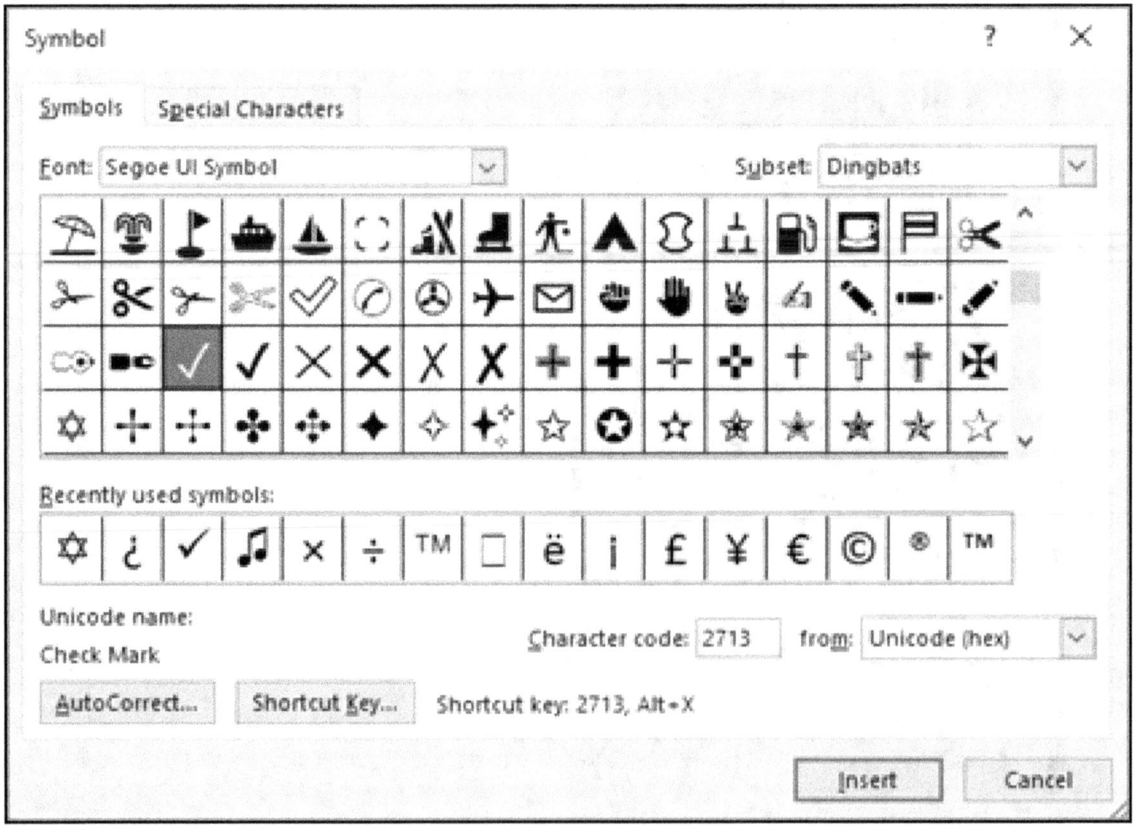

4. Scroll up or down to find the symbol you want to insert.

   Different font sets often have different symbols in them and the most commonly used symbols are in the **Segoe UI Symbol** font set. Use the **Font** selector above the symbol list to pick the font you want to browse through.

5. When you find the symbol you want, double-click it. The symbol will be inserted in your file. You can click **Close** now unless you want to insert additional symbols.

Insert a SmartArt graphic

1. On the **Insert** tab, in the **Illustrations** group, click **SmartArt**.

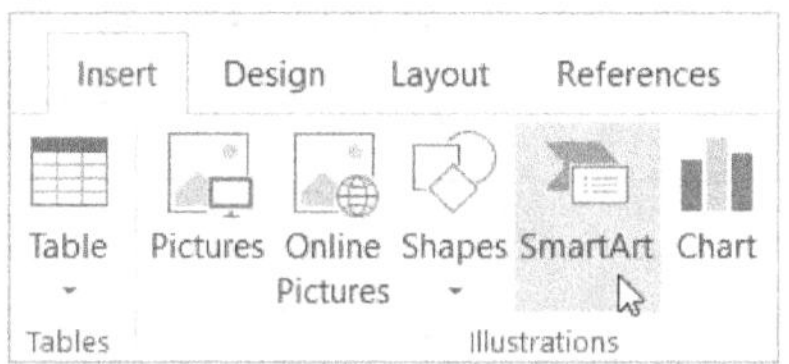

2. In the **Choose a SmartArt Graphic** dialog box, click the type and layout that you want.

3. Enter your text by doing one of the following:
   - Click **[Text]** in the Text pane, and then type your text.
   - Copy text from another location or program, click **[Text]** in the Text pane, and then paste your text.

Add or delete shapes in your SmartArt graphic

1. Click the SmartArt graphic that you want to add another shape to.

2. Click the existing shape that is located closest to where you want to add the new shape.

3. Under **SmartArt Tools**, on the **Design** tab, in the **Create Graphic** group, click the arrow next to **Add Shape**.

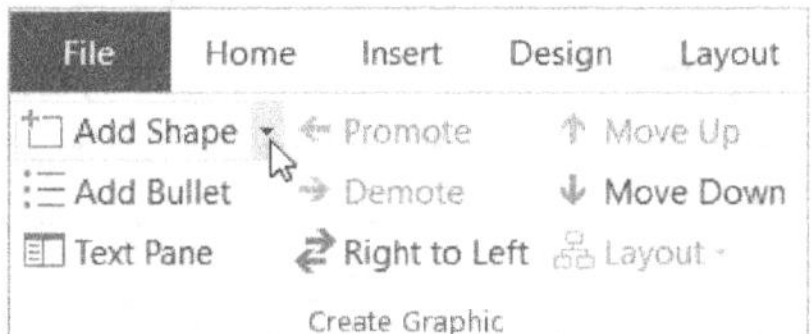

If you don't see the **SmartArt Tools** or **Design** tabs, make sure that you've selected the SmartArt graphic. You may have to double-click the SmartArt graphic to open the **Design** tab.

4. Do one of the following:
   - To insert a shape after the selected shape, click **Add Shape After**.
   - To insert a shape before the selected shape, click **Add Shape Before**.

Insert and play a video file from your computer

You can **insert an embedded video** (the default behavior) or **link to a video file** stored on your computer.

- **Inserting an embedded video** is convenient, but it increases the size of your presentation.
- **A linked video** keeps your presentation file smaller, but links can break. We recommend storing presentations and linked videos in the same folder.

Embed a video stored on your PC

1. In Normal view, click the slide in which you want to embed the video.

2. On the **Insert** tab, in the **Media** group, click the arrow under **Video**.

3. Select **Video from file**, and then browse to the location of your video, and select it.

4. On the **Insert** button, click the down arrow, and then click **Insert**.

Link to a video stored on your PC

To help prevent broken links, we recommend copying the video into the same folder as your presentation, and then linking to it there.

1. On the **Slides** tab in **Normal** view, click the slide to which you want to add a video or animated GIF file.

2. On the **Insert** tab, in the **Media** group, click the arrow under **Video**.

3. Select **Video from file**, and then browse to the location of your video, and select it.

4. On the **Insert** button, click the down arrow, and then click **Link to file**.

Keyboard Shortcuts

General	Shortcuts
Open a Presentation	Ctrl + O
Create New	Ctrl + N
Save a Presentation	Ctrl + S
Print a Presentation	Ctrl + P
Close a Presentation	Ctrl + W
Insert a New Slide	Ctrl + M
Help	F1
Editing	**Shortcuts**
Cut	Ctrl + X
Copy	Ctrl + C
Paste	Ctrl + V
Undo	Ctrl + Z
Redo or Repeat	Ctrl + Y
Find	Ctrl + F
Replace	Ctrl + H
Select All	Ctrl + A
Formatting	**Shortcuts**
Bold	Ctrl + B
Italics	Ctrl + I
Align Left	Ctrl + L
Center	Ctrl + E
Justify	Ctrl + J
Navigation	**Shortcuts**
The Next Slide	Spacebar
The Previous Slide	Backspace
Slide Show Delivery	**Shortcuts**
Begin Slide Show	F5
Resume Slide Show	Shift + F5
End Slide Show	Esc
Jump to Slide	Slide # + Enter
Toggle Screen Black	B
Toggle Screen White	W
Pause Show	S
Show/Hide Pointer	A
Change Arrow to Pen	Ctrl + P
Change Pen to Arrow	Ctrl + A
Erase Doodles	E

➡ Slide Sorter view displays all the slides in the presentation as thumbnails.
➡ Slide Show view displays the presentation as an electronic slide show.

Direction (1–4): View the PowerPoint window given below and answer the following questions.

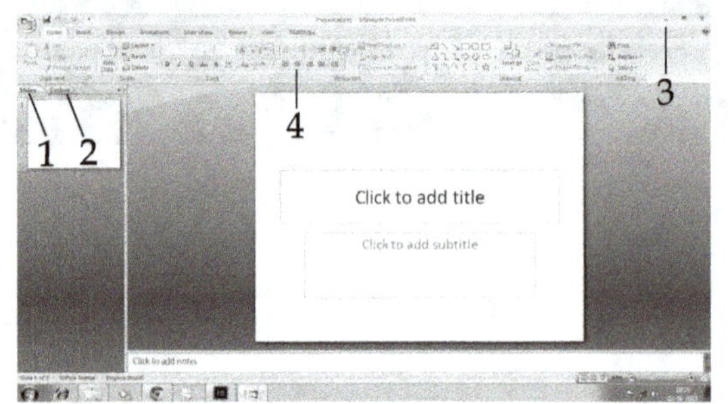

1. Area 1 displays the Slides tab. The Slides tab is used to _____.
   (a) Add and Delete slides
   (b) Duplicate slides
   (c) Rearrange slides
   (d) All of these

2. Area 2 displays the Outline tab. The outline tab is used for _____.
   (a) The text content of each slides
   (b) The presentation outline
   (c) The outline of the slide with images and text
   (d) All of these

3. Button 3 is used to _____.
   (a) Draw shape
   (b) Display scroll bar
   (c) Minimize the Ribbon
   (d) Display title bar

4. Button 4 is used to _____.
   (a) Split   (b) Justify
   (c) Align center   (d) Align left

5. A presentation is the collection of _____ arranged in a sequential manner.
   (a) Data   (b) Disks
   (c) Slides   (d) Documents

6. A _____ presentation is used to create slides with our own imagination.
   (a) Default   (b) Blank
   (c) Normal   (d) Basic

7. What is the shortcut key to create new presentation?
   (a) Ctrl + X   (b) Ctrl + N
   (c) Ctrl + A   (d) Ctrl + P

8. When you create a new presentation, the first slide will be the _____.
   (a) Blank slide
   (b) Title slide
   (c) First slide
   (d) Last slide

9. Which view displays the slides only with the buttons at the bottom?
   (a) Play slide show
   (b) Reading View
   (c) Slide Sorter View
   (d) Normal View

10. A new presentation always starts in the _____.
    (a) Normal View
    (b) Outline View
    (c) Slide Sorter View
    (d) Slide show

11. Which of the following is NOT a view in MS PowerPoint?
    (a) Zoomed View
    (b) Normal View
    (c) Slide Sorter View
    (d) Reading View

12. Which view displays smaller versions of all the slides in the presentation?
    (a) Slide View
    (b) Outline View
    (c) Slide Sorter View
    (d) Slide Show

13. Which of the following views displays the current slide and a text box for adding notes?
    (a) Slide Sorter View
    (b) Slide Show
    (c) Notes Page View
    (d) Outline View

14. In a normal view presentation, window is divided into _____ parts.
   (a) 1   (b) 2
   (c) 3   (d) 4
15. A presentation can contain which of the following objects?
   (a) Graphics   (b) Movies
   (c) Sounds   (d) All of these
16. To change the layout of a slide, you should _____.
   (a) Right click on the slide, click Layout then select the layout you want
   (b) Click Layout in the slides group of Insert tab
   (c) Click Layout in the slides group of the Home tab of the Ribbon
   (d) Both (a) and (b)
17. Which of the following should you use if you want to make changes to every slide in your presentation including ones added later to the presentation?
   (a) The Slide Layout option
   (b) Add a slide option
   (c) Outline View
   (d) Slide Master View
18. Which type of fonts are best suited for titles and headlines?
   (a) Serif fonts
   (b) Sans serif fonts
   (c) Text fonts
   (d) Picture fonts
19. ⓘ is used to _____
   (a) Close the presentation
   (b) Minimize the Ribbon
   (c) Provide Help
   (d) Close Power Point

20. To create videos, CD or handouts for your presentation, you should click on _______ in the Backstage view
   (a) Save As   (b) Save and Send
   (c) Save   (d) Options
21. Which of the following groups is NOT present in the Insert tab?
   (a) Symbols   (b) Links
   (c) Paragraph   (d) Media
22. The cursor changes into an upside–down cross as shown in the figure when you _______.
   (a) Click on the Text Box icon in the insert tab of the Ribbon
   (b) Click on Save in the Quick Access Toolbar
   (c) Insert a new slide in the presentation
   (d) Delete a slide from the presentation
23. Which of the following is NOT an animation effect?
   (a) Appear   (b) Fade
   (c) Translate   (d) Wheel
24. Identify the given icon.
   (a) Slide Number   (b) Object
   (c) Slide view   (d) Action
25. The function of given image is to _____
   (a) Reset the position of the slide
   (b) Organise the slides into sections
   (c) Change the layout of slide
   (d) Add a new slide

1. Which of the following AutoFit behavior lets the added text overflow at the bottom of the text box when Wrap Text is ON in MS PowerPoint?
   (a) Do not Autofit
   (b) Shrink Text on Overflow
   (c) Resize Shape to Fit Text
   (d) All of these

2. Which of the following steps is incorrect to turn grid lines ON or OF in MS PowerPoint?
   (a) Press Shift + F9
   (b) Insert tab → Show group → Select or deselect the Grid lines check box
   (c) Home → Drawing → Arrange → Align → View Grid lines
   (d) Both (a) and (b)

3. In MS PowerPoint presentations, the designs regulate the layout and formatting for the slide. These are commonly known as:
   (a) Blueprints   (b) Placeholders
   (c) Templates   (d) Design Plates

4. The Handout Master consists of placeholders for all of these except the:
   (a) Title   (b) Slide number
   (c) Header   (d) Footer

5. Which of these PowerPoint features would allow any user to create a given simple presentation quicker?
   (a) Animations
   (b) Chart Wizard
   (c) Transition Wizard
   (d) AutoContent Wizard

SUBJECTIVE QUESTIONS

1. What are different views in PowerPoint?

Ans.

Normal view: This is the default view in PowerPoint 2010. Normal view includes the Outline pane, Slide pane, and Notes pane.

Slide Sorter view: Displays all the slides in the presentation as thumbnails (tiny images). Use Slide Sorter view when you want to rearrange the order of slides or add transition effects between slides.

Reading view: Similar to Slide Show view, it displays the presentation in a window with simple controls, making it easy to review.

Slide Show view: Displays the presentation as an electronic slide show. Whenever you deliver a presentation in front of an audience, Slide Show view is the view you want to use.

2. How you can insert a picture in MS Powerpoint?

Ans.

Bright and colourful pictures make the presentation interesting and engaging for the audience. Let us learn how to add pictures in PowerPoint by following steps:

i. Click on the Insert tab.

ii. Click on the Pictures option in the Images group. The Insert Picture dialog box appears.

iii. Locate the appropriate drive and the folder which contains the picture file that needs to be inserted on the slide. Select the picture file and click on the Insert button. The selected picture is added to the slide in the center. You can drag the picture to the desired location on the slide.

3. How you can resize a picture that has been inserted in PowerPoint?

Ans.

After you have inserted the picture on the slide, you can resize using following steps:

i. Click to select the picture. A solid line will appear around the selected picture.

ii. Click and drag the corner sizing handles until the picture is the desired size.

4. **What is the use of WordArt? How to insert it into PowerPoint?**

Ans.

You have already learnt about the WordArt feature in Word that lets you insert text in various styles in a document. The same steps can be used to insert WordArt in PowerPoint to emphasise text.

You can also convert existing text on the slide to WordArt by following these steps:

i. Click to select the text.

ii. Click on the Format tab.

iii. Click the More drop-down arrow in the WordArt Styles group. A drop-down list of various text styles appears.

iv. Select the desired text style. You will notice that the selected text gets formatted according to the chosen style.

5. **How you can add Boxes in the Organization Chart?**

Ans.

Following are steps to add boxes:

i. Click on an existing box closest to the point where you want to add a new box.

ii. Click on the Design tab.

iii. Click the arrow next to Add Shape option in the Create Graphic group and choose one of the following options:

a. Add Shape After: To insert a box after the selected box at the same level as the selected box.

b. Add Shape Before: To insert a box before the selected box at the same level as the selected box.

c. Add Shape Above: To insert a box one level above the selected box.

d. Add Shape Below: To insert a box one level below the selected box.

6. **How one can change colour of background in PowerPoint?**

Ans.

When using themes, the background colour is already applied to the slides. However, at times you wish to apply your own background colour or add a background picture. You can also add gradient, pattern or texture to the coloured background. To change the background colour of a slide, follow the given steps:

Select the slide or slides whose background colour you wish to change.

i. Click on the Design tab

ii. Click on the Format Background option in the Customize group.

iii. The Format Background pane will appear on the right. Select the desired fill options.

a. Select the Solid fill radio button to apply a solid colour as the background to the slide.

b. Select the Picture or texture fill radio button to use a picture as a slide background

c. Select the Gradient fill radio button if you wish to apply a blend of two or more fill colours as the background.

d. Select the Pattern fill radio button if you want to apply a pattern as the background to the slide.

iv. Click on the Color drop-down arrow and then select the colour that you want. The background style of the selected slide will change accordingly.

v. If you want to apply the same background style to all the slides in the presentation, you can click the Apply to All option.

Windows 10 7

Learning Objectives : In this chapter, students will learn about:
- ✓ HomeGroup
- ✓ Pinning any program
- ✓ Jump Lists
- ✓ Windows Search

CHAPTER SUMMARY

Windows 10 is a major release of Microsoft's Windows NT operating system. It is the direct successor to Windows 8.1, which was released nearly two years earlier. Windows 10 was made available for download via MSDN and TechNet, as a free upgrade for retail copies of Windows 8 and Windows 8.1 users via the Windows Store, and to Windows 7 users via Windows Update. Windows 10 receives new builds on an ongoing basis, which are available at no additional cost to users.

Windows 10 supports universal apps, an expansion of the Metro-style first introduced in Windows 8. Universal apps can be designed to run across multiple Microsoft product families with nearly identical code—including PCs, tablets, smartphones, embedded systems, Xbox One, Surface Hub and Mixed Reality. On Windows 10, the Microsoft Store serves as a unified storefront for apps, video content, and eBooks. Windows 10 also allows web apps and desktop software (using either Win32 or .NET Framework) to be packaged for distribution on the Microsoft Store. A new iteration of the Start menu is used on the Windows 10 desktop, with a list of places and other options on the left side, and tiles representing applications on the right. The menu can be resized, and expanded into a full-screen display, which is the default option in Tablet mode. A new virtual desktop system was added by a feature known as Task View, which displays all open windows and allows users to switch between them, or switch between multiple workspaces.

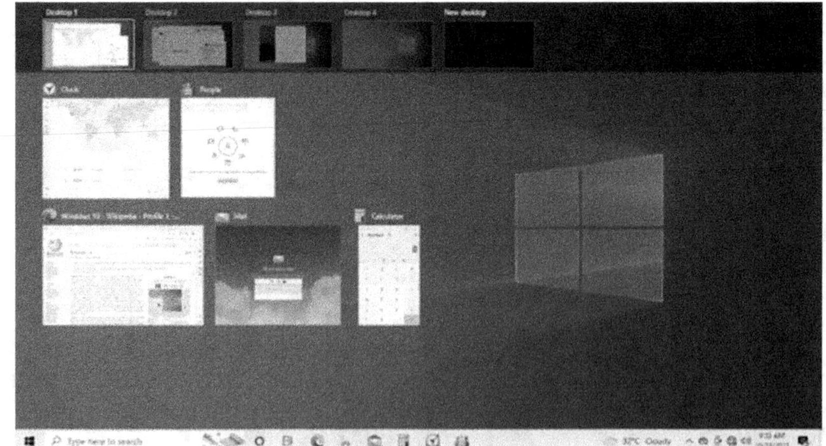

HomeGroup

A HomeGroup is a group of desktops or laptops on a home network that can share files and printers. Using a homegroup makes sharing easier. You can easily connect two or more PCs running Windows on your home network to automatically start sharing files, pictures, videos other media and printers.

You can also protect your homegroup by creating a password to restrict accessibility. You can also prevent certain files and folders from being shared.

Jump Lists

Jump Lists take you to the documents, pictures, songs, or websites you visit frequently or every day. To open a Jump List, just right-click a program button on the Windows taskbar. Jump lists do not show shortcuts to files.

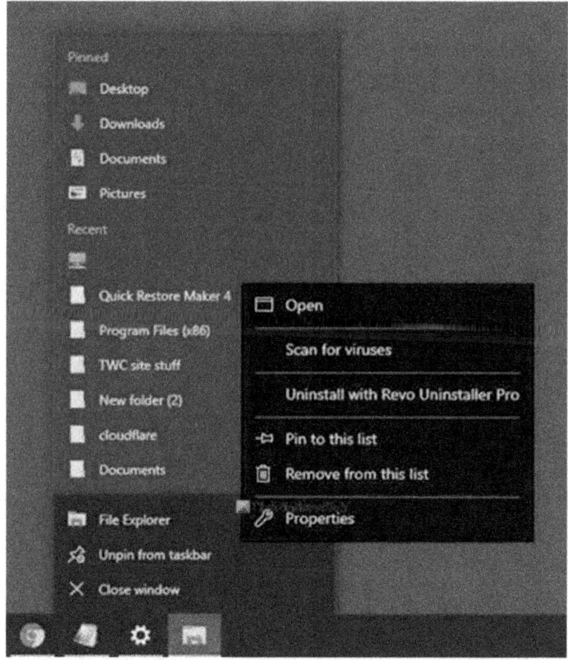

Pinning any Program

In Windows, you can pin your favorite programs or the programs that you need to use frequently anywhere on the taskbar for easy access. You can rearrange them any way you like by clicking and dragging the icons of the programs.

Windows Search

Windows Search, earlier known as Windows Desktop Search (WDS) is an indexed desktop search platform created by Microsoft. Windows Search builds a full-text index of files on a computer. Windows Search by default includes filters for Word, Excel, PowerPoint, HTML files. MP3, AVI and JPEG files.

System security

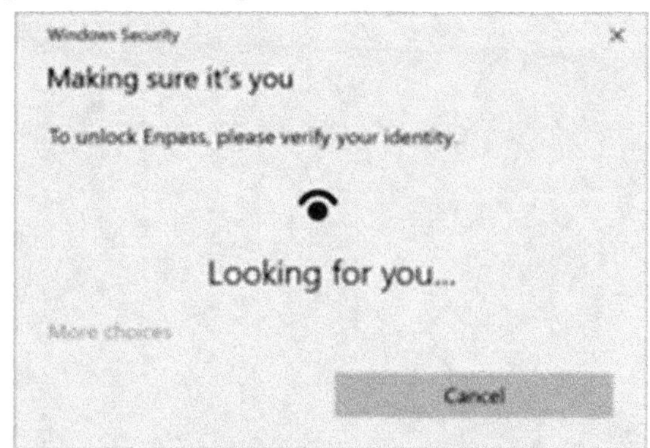

Windows Hello unlock prompt while using Enpass (a password manager). Windows 10 incorporates multi-factor authentication technology based upon standards developed by the FIDO Alliance. The operating system includes improved support for biometric authentication through the Windows Hello platform. Devices with supported cameras (requiring infrared illumination, such as Intel RealSense) allow users to log in with iris or face recognition, similarly to Kinect. Devices with supported readers allow users to log in through fingerprint recognition. Support was also added for palm-vein scanning through a partnership with Fujitsu in February 2018. Credentials are stored locally and protected using asymmetric encryption.

TRIVIA

Since 2005, no human has defeated a high-powered computer in a tournament standard chess match.

➡ A homegroup is a group of desktops or laptops on a home network that can share files and printers.

➡ Windows Search, earlier known as Windows Desktop Search (WDS) is an indexed desktop search platform created by Microsoft.

1. _____ is a program that helps in viewing and managing files and folders.
   (a) Windows Manager
   (b) Windows Explorer
   (c) File Handler
   (d) Control Panel

2. In Windows, files are stored in locations called _____.
   (a) Storage   (b) Programs
   (c) Folders   (d) Stacks

3. What does the left pane in Windows Explorer display?
   (a) Images   (b) Files
   (c) Drives and Folders (d) None of these

4. Where can you find all storage locations on a computer?

   (a)   (b)

   (c)   (d)

5. What is pinning?
   (a) On the start button, you can right-click the icon to view recently used files in a jump list.
   (b) Link to folder containing the items you see the most
   (c) To easily access programs, you can attach, or pin a program icon directly to the taskbar or Start menu.
   (d) The common center for configuring Windows settings

6. What is Windows Taskbar?
   (a) Identifies the path for the currently open folder.
   (b) The command center for configuring Windows settings.
   (c) Software that controls the basic operations of your computer.
   (d) Appears at the bottom of the screen and displays icons of programs that you can easily access.

7. _____ tell windows the type of a file and the program that would be used to open it.
   (a) Folder names   (b) Drive names
   (c) File extensions   (d) File names

8. What is address bar?
   (a) Software that control the basic operation of your computer.
   (b) Store the file you want to delete and operations your computer.
   (c) The main work area in Windows.
   (d) Identify the path for the currently open folder.

9. .wav is an extension used by _____ files.
   (a) Audio   (b) Video
   (c) Text   (d) Picture

10. What does DLL stand for?
    (a) Data Link List
    (b) Disk Link Library
    (c) Dynamic Link Library
    (d) None of these

11. How is information organized on a drive?
    (a) Files   (b) Folders
    (c) Sub-folders   (d) All of these

12. What characteristic of a file must be specified to save it?
    (a) File name   (b) File location
    (c) File extension   (d) All of these

13. Which of the following is Windows application program?
    (a) Notepad
    (b) Windows Explorer
    (c) Paint
    (d) All of these

14. A set of routines that work closely with the hardware to support the transfer of information between elements of the system, such as memory disks and the monitor is called _____.
    (a) BIUS   (b) BIOS
    (c) BOIP   (d) None of these

15. The graphical system that manages what appears on the screen and provides graphics support for printers and other output device is called _____.
    (a) DGI
    (b) IGD
    (c) GDI
    (d) GUI

16. What is the use of the Control Panel?
    (a) Identifies the path for the currently open folder.
    (b) The command center for configuration Windows settings.
    (c) Used to close a window.
    (d) To easily access programs, you can attach, or pin a program icon drectly to the taskbar or Start menu.

17. Which of the following provides important messages about critical security and maintenance components on your computer, such as the firewall, antivirus protection and spyware protection?
    (a) Pointer
    (b) Jump List
    (c) Computer Folder
    (d) Action Center

18. In this area, you can check the time and date, adjust speaker volume and access other network or system features.
    (a) Notification area
    (b) Status bar
    (c) Action Center
    (d) Start button

19. A _____ is a "mini-menu" of performance tasks for an icon on the taskbar.
    (a) Gadget
    (b) Snap
    (c) Jump List
    (d) Pin task

20. Identify the icon given here.

    (a) Computer
    (b) Network
    (c) Windows Explorer
    (d) Recycle Bin

HOTS

1. Raman has opened few programs on Windows 7 and is switching between them from time to time. Which of the following shortcut keys will let him cycle through the programs on the taskbar in the order they are accessed?
   (a) Alt + Tab + F4
   (b) ⊞ + Home
   (c) Alt + Shift + Esc
   (d) ⊞ + D

2. _____ is a set of routines that performs a variety of generalized operations such as sorting, searching, merging copying, printing and maintenance on data files.
   (a) File utilities
   (b) File organization
   (c) File management
   (d) FTP

3. Which of the following syntax should be typed in the search box of start menu to search picture files in any indexed format such as JPEG, GIF, Bitmap, PNG, as well as icons and shortcuts to image files?
   (a) Kind/pic
   (b) Kind = pic
   (c) Kind//pic
   (d) Kind: = pic

4. _____ is a Window utility program that locates and eliminates unnecessary fragments and rearranges files and unused disk space to optimize operations.
   (a) Disk Defragmenter
   (b) Restore
   (c) Disk Cleanup
   (d) Backup

5. File ___ shrinks the size of a file so it requires less storage space.
   (a) Compression
   (b) Defragmenting
   (c) Synthesizing
   (d) Scanning

1. What is a restore point?

Ans.

A restore point is a representation of a stored state of your computer's system files. You can use a restore point to restore your computer's system files to an earlier point in time. Restore points are automatically created by System Restore weekly.

2. Explain briefly about Windows 10 feature – Cortana and Multiple Desktops.

Ans.

Cortana is a virtual assistant just like Siri, Google, and Alexa, provided by Microsoft. It can help with multiple tasks like opening files, reading and sending mails and messages, weather details, etc.

Also, Windows 10 offers a feature of multiple virtual desktops and an easy task view to switch between tabs and avoid clustering of multiple windows. This can be accessed with the use of (Windows + Tab) button.

3. What is Tablet Mode in Windows 10?

Ans.

Windows 10 offers its users to switch between Tablet mode and Desktop mode for devices that offer touch screen. Users can switch between these modes very easily. Windows 10 automatically detects if the device is attached with a keyboard and a mouse, and it works in a desktop mode.

4. What role does Icons play in Windows 10?

Ans.

Icons are the tools that allow the users to open apps for various operations. These are small picture-like shortcuts that are used to start apps. These icons can be selected with a single mouse-click and can be opened by either selecting and then pressing enter or by double-clicking the icon.

5. What is Windows 10 Pro edition?

Ans.

Windows 10 Pro is a desktop edition for PCs, tablets and 2-in-1s. Building upon both the familiar and innovative features of Windows 10 Home, it has many extra features to meet the diverse needs of small businesses. Windows 10 Pro helps to manage their devices and apps, protect their sensitive business data, support remote and mobile productivity scenarios and take advantage of cloud technologies effectively and efficiently. Windows 10 Pro devices are a great choice for organizations supporting Choose Your Own Device (CYOD) programs and prosumer customers. Windows 10 Pro also lets customers take advantage of the new Windows Update for Business, which will reduce management costs, provide controls over update deployment, offer quicker access to security updates, and provide access to the latest innovation from Microsoft on an ongoing basis.

6. What are different Windows search options?

Ans.

When you do a search, a series of tabs appears across the top of the screen:

- All displays all search results.
- Apps shows any app-related matches.
- Documents shows documents on your PC that match the search.
- Web displays results from the web.

More shows results from other places, including individual folders, email and apps including Music, People, Photos, Settings, and Videos. You'll have to click the down arrow next to *More* to see them all.

Network 8

Learning Objectives : In this chapter, students will learn about:

- ✓ LAN
- ✓ Intranet
- ✓ Network Interface Cards
- ✓ IP Addressing
- ✓ WAN
- ✓ MAN

CHAPTER SUMMARY

A network is any collection of independent computers that communicate with one another over a shared network medium. A computer network is a collection of two or more connected computers. When these computers are joined in a network, people can share files and peripherals such as modems, printers, tape, backup drives or CD-ROM drives.

Every network includes:

- At least two computer servers or client workstation.
- Networking Interface Card's (NIC)
- A connection medium, usually a wire or cable, although wireless communication between networked computers and peripherals is also possible.
- Network Operating system software, such as Microsoft Windows NT or 2000, Novell NetWare, Unix and Linux.

TRIVIA

To communicate and run a program, the first computers could only comprehend 0s and 1s.

Types of Networks

LAN (Local Area Network)

This network is any collection of independent computers that communicate with one another over a shared network medium. LANs are networks usually confined to a small geographical area, such as a single building or a college campus.

WAN (Wide Area Network)

Wide area networking accomplished by connecting the different LANs. It combines multiple LANs that are geographically separate over the long distance. This is done using services such as dedicated leased phone lines, dial-up phone lines (both synchronous and asynchronous), satellite links and data packet carrier services.

Intranet

An Intranet is a private network utilizing Internet-type tools, but available only within that organization. For large organizations, an intranet provides an easy access mode to access information for employees.

MAN (Metropolitan Area Network)

This refers to a network bigger than the LAN. It covers the network of computers with in a city.

Network Interface Cards

In the initial days of computing, each computer operated as stand-alone system. The earliest personal computer did not have an option to connect to other computers. To transfer files between computers, a floppy disk was used. However, in modern day computers, connecting to a network is essential and has been made easy. For example, you need it to use e-mail, access information on the Internet, share documents within a corporate network.

Network Interface Cards, commonly referred to as NICs or network interface controller, are used to connect a PC to a network. A network interface card gives full-time connection to a network. Personal computers connected through local area network typically have a network interface card specifically designed for the LAN transmission technology.

IP Addressing

An IP (Internet Protocol) address is a unique identifier for a node or host connection on an IP network. An IP address is a 32 bit binary number usually represented as 4 decimal values, each representing 8 bits, in the range 0 to 255 (known as octets) separated by decimal points. This is known as "dotted decimal" notation.

Example: 123.167.222.500

- ➡ A network is any collection of independent computers that communicate with one another over a shared network medium.
- ➡ LANs are networks usually confined to a small geographical area, such as a single building or a college campus.
- ➡ An intranet is a private network utilizing Internet-type tools, but available only within that organization.
- ➡ An IP (Internet Protocol) address is a unique identifier for a node or host connection on an IP network.

1. A computer network is _____.
   (a) A collection of hardware components and computers
   (b) Computers which are connected to each other
   (c) Computers which share resources and information
   (d) All of these

2. A device or a system connected to a network is also called _____ .
   (a) Branch
   (b) Leaf
   (c) Node
   (d) Block

3. What is the benefit of networking?
   (a) Sharing files and data among connected computers.
   (b) Easy access to all resources like internet and printers over the network.
   (c) Earlier and faster backup of valuable data
   (d) All of these

4. Which of the following is a networking device?
   (a) Gateway
   (b) Router
   (c) Firewall
   (d) All of these

5. A device that encodes digital computer signals into anolog telephone signals and vice versa.
   (a) ISP
   (b) Web browser
   (c) Telephone Line
   (d) Modem

6. When computers in a computer laboratory in a school are connected, then such a connection of computers is called _____.
   (a) Internet
   (b) Local Area Network
   (c) Wide Area Network
   (d) Metropolitan Area Network

7. What does a protocol define in a network?
   (a) It defines what data is communicated.
   (b) It defines how data is communicated.
   (c) It defines when data is communicated.
   (d) All of these

8. Which of the following device is NOT essential to connect to the internet?
   (a) Modem
   (b) ISP
   (c) Telephone Line
   (d) Web Camera

9. What unit of measurement was used to describe dial-up modem speeds?
   (a) Kbps
   (b) Gbps
   (c) KHz
   (d) GHz

10. While browsing the internet, when you get the message "Web page cannot be displayed", what should you do?
    (a) Close the Browser
    (b) Click on the Favorite button
    (c) Click on the Stop button
    (d) Click on the Refresh button

11. What is the use of Ping command?
    (a) To test if the device on a network is reachable or not
    (b) To test a computer fault
    (c) To test a fault in the power supply
    (d) To test the quality of a painter

12. What is firewall in a network?
    (a) It is the physical boundary of a network.
    (b) A network operating system
    (c) A system preventing unauthorized access to a network
    (d) It is a web browsing software.

13. Radio waves and microwaves are used in which of the following communications?
    (a) Voice over
    (b) IP Telephony
    (c) Wireless
    (d) Office

14. A large number of computers in a wide geographical area can be efficiently connected by _____.
    (a) Cables
    (b) Magnetic rays
    (c) Twisted pair lines
    (d) Communication Satellites

15. A wireless network is also known as _____.
    (a) Wi-Fi network   (b) Internet
    (c) Intranet   (d) None of these

16. What protocol sends encrypted data over the Internet?
    (a) HTTP   (b) SSL
    (c) SMPT   (d) FTP

17. Which of the following statements is NOT netiquette?
    (a) You should tell your parents right away if you come across any information that make you feel uncomfortable.
    (b) Send anyone your picture or share any other personal information on the Internet without first consulting your parents.
    (c) Do not respond to any messages that in anyway make you feel uncomfortable.
    (d) Always talk to your parents so that together you can set up rules for going online.

18. A company that provides Internet access to a large number of users is called _____.
    (a) Website   (b) Web Host
    (c) ISP   (d) Web Server

19. A _____ is a computer program that browses the World Wide Web website that helps methodical and automated manner to create an information based on websites that help search engines in providing faster results to queries.
    (a) Web crawler   (b) Website
    (c) Windows   (d) Wallpaper

20. What is the search engine that searches multiple search engines called?
    (a) Metasearch Engine
    (b) Universal Search Engine
    (c) Search Portal
    (d) Search Station

21. Business done over the Internet is also called _____.
    (a) Web-business
    (b) E-commerce
    (c) Selling Internet
    (d) Online sales

22. What is the user name/password combination often called?
    (a) Passcode
    (b) Security Key
    (c) User account
    (d) Login

23. P2P is used for what type of Internet service?
    (a) Online Browsing
    (b) File Sharing
    (c) Online Gaming
    (d) Online Selling

24. What protocol is used to deliver web page to web browsers?
    (a) SMPT   (b) HTTP
    (c) FTP   (d) UDP

25. What is the purpose of an extranet?
    (a) It shares information within organization.
    (b) It extends an interact over the Internet.
    (c) It provides a backup network connection.
    (d) It adds extra network security.

1. 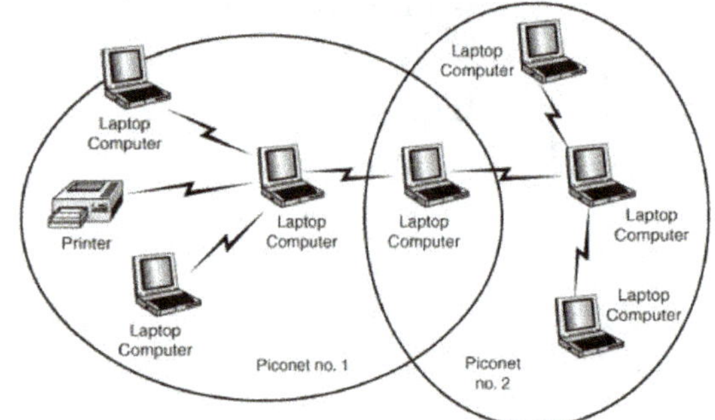

When different piconets are combined together in a way such that one serves as a primary station and another serves as a secondary station, what kind of network would be formed?

(a) Scatnet
(b) Dishnet
(c) Scatternet
(d) Segmentednet

2. Choose the port number of FTP.
(a) 23 (b) 21
(c) 10 (d) 25

3. What is the term used when the main server sends mail to another mail server?
(a) SMTP (b) FTP
(c) TCP (d) WWW

4. Identify the device used to boost up a weak signal.
(a) Modem (c) Switch
(b) Repeater (d) Router

5. Who keeps the private key in asymmetric key cryptography?
(a) Receiver
(b) Sender
(c) Both Sender and Receiver
(d) None

1. Differentiate between LAN and WAN.

Ans.

LANs are networks usually confined to a geographic area, such as a single building or a college campus. Wide area networking or WAN combines multiple LANs that are geographically separate. This is accomplished by connecting the different LANs using services such as dedicated leased phone lines, dial-up phone lines (both synchronous and asynchronous), satellite links, and data packet carrier services.

2. What is Hyperlink? What is its usage?

Ans.

It is an element in an electronic document that links to another place in the same document or an entirely different document, or another resource.

Hyperlinks usually appear as underlined text and in a different color, but they may also appear as graphics, such as buttons to click.

Hyperlinks may be used to link another place in the same place, or another page, to play an audio or video file, to download file, to set up a message to an e-mail address, and to link to other Internet resources.

3. Name three governing groups of the Internet.

Ans.

The Internet is an interconnection of a number of computers with different types of networks across the globe. Thus, no one actually owns it. But there are three volunteer groups that were formed to help, coordinate and guide the technical parts of the Internet. These are:

(i)   Internet Activities Board (IAB)

(ii) Internet Engineering Task Force (IETF)

(iii) Internet Research Task Force (IRTF)

4. List any three rules of Netiquette.

Ans.

When you interact with people, you follow some rules to make the interaction pleasant. This set is known as etiquette. Similarly, you have to follow some rules of behaviour when you interact with people on the internet. This set of rules is known as Netiquette. It guides you on how you should interact over networks, ranging from net surfing and mailing lists to chats and forums. Three rules of netiquette are -

(i)   Use simple electronic signatures.

(ii) Avoid revealing personal information while chatting.

(iii) Do not use objectionable language while mailing or chatting.

5. Write a short note on IP Address.

An IP (Internet Protocol) address is a unique identifier for a node or host connection on an IP network. An IP address is a 32 bit binary number usually represented as 4 decimal values, each representing 8 bits, in the range 0 to 255 (known as octets) separated by decimal points. This is known as "dotted decimal" notation.

Internet   9

CHAPTER SUMMARY

In the early days, most people used the Internet to search for information only. Today's Internet is a constantly evolving tool that not only contains an amazing variety of information but that also provides new ways of accessing, interacting and connecting with people and content. As a result, new terms are constantly appearing.

World Wide Web

When most people think of the Internet, the first thing they think about is the World Wide Web. Nowadays, the terms "Internet" and "World Wide Web" are often used interchangeably—but they are actually not the same thing.

- The Internet is the physical network of computers all over the world.
- The World Wide Web is a virtual network of websites connected by hyperlinks (or "links"). Websites are stored on servers on the Internet, so the World Wide Web is a part of the Internet.

The World Wide Web was created in 1989 by **Tim Berners-Lee**, a software engineer. Before then, computers could communicate over the Internet, but there were no web pages.

HTML

The backbone of the World Wide Web is made of HTML files, which are specially formatted documents that can contain links, as well as images and other media. All web browsers can read HTML files.

URL

To get to a web page, you can type the URL (Uniform Resource Locator) into a browser. The URL, also known as the web address, tells the browser exactly where to find the page. However, most of the time, people get to a web page by following a link from a different page or by searching for the page using a search engine.

Web Browser

A web browser is the tool used to access the World Wide Web. Chrome, Firefox, Internet Explorer, Safari, and Opera are the most popular web browsers. Each one has its own look and feel, but they have the same goal: to display web pages correctly. For most web pages, any well-known browser will work.

Following are some key combinations used in Internet Explorer:

- **To Open a New Tab:** Press **Ctrl + T**, or click the New Tab button to the right of the most recently opened tab.
- **To Open a Duplicate Tab:** Press **Ctrl + K**, or right-click the tab you wish to duplicate and select Duplicate Tab from the contextual menu.
- **To Open a Link in a New Tab:** Press and hold the Ctrl key and click the link you want to open. Or, click the link with the middle mouse button (the mouse wheel).

- **To Open Search Results in a New Tab:** Press **Alt** + **Enter** from the Search box to open search results in a new tab.
- **To Open Quick Tabs View:** Press **Ctrl** + **T**, or click the New Tab button to the right of the most recently opened tab.
- **To Close a Tab:** Click the ☒ Close Tab button on the tab. Or, press **Ctrl** + **W**. Or, click a tab with the middle mouse button (the mouse wheel).
- **To Close All Tabs:** Press **Alt** + **F4** and click the **Close all** button.
- **To Close All Other Tabs:** Press **Ctrl** + **Alt** + **F4**, or right-click a tab and select Close other tabs from the contextual menu.
- **To Reopen a Closed Tab:** Press **Ctrl** + **Shift** + **T**, or right-click a tab and select Recently closed tabs and select a web page from the list.
- **To Switch Between Tabs:** Click the tab you want to view. Or, press **Ctrl** + **Tab** to move to the next tab. **Press Ctrl** + **Shift** + **Tab** to move to the previous tab.
- **To Show Tabs on a Separate Row:** Right-click a tab and select Show tabs on a separate row from the contextual menu.

Home and Tools

To Go to the Home Page: The home web page(s) appears when the Internet Explorer is launched. Click the Home Page button. Or, press **Alt** + **Home**.

To Add or Change the Home Page: Make sure the web site(s) is open in the browser. Click the Tools button list arrow and select Internet options. When the web page appears in the Home page section, click the Use current button. Click OK.

To Remove a Home Page: Click the Tools button list arrow and select Internet options. Delete the web page you want to remove from the Home page section and click OK.

To Pin a Web Page to the Taskbar: Click and drag the web page tab onto the Windows taskbar.

To Launch a Web Page Pinned to the Taskbar: Click the web page icon on the taskbar. The web page appears in the Internet Explorer window.

To Get Help: Press F1 to open the Help window, type your question and press Enter.

To Zoom In or Out on a Web Page: Click the Tools button, select Zoom, and select a zoom percentage from the menu. Or, press **Ctrl + to zoom in**, press **Ctrl – to zoom out**.

To View the Page at 100%: Click the Tools button, select Zoom, and select 100% from the menu. Or, press **Ctrl + 0**.

To Increase Text Size: Click the Page button on the Command Bar, point to Text Size and select an option from the list.

To View Internet Explorer in Full Screen: Click the Tools button and select File Full screen from the menu. Or, press **F11**.

To View the Menu Bar: Press the Alt key. The Menu Bar appears below the Address Bar. To keep the menu bar displayed, right-click an empty area of a toolbar and select Menu Bar from the contextual menu.

To Print a Web Page: Click the Tools button and select Print → Print from the menu. Or, press **Ctrl + P**.

To Print Preview: Click the Tools button and select Print → Print Preview from the menu.

To Find Text on a Page: Click the Tools button and select File → Find on this page from the menu. Or, press **Ctrl + F**.

Favorites, Feeds and History

To View and Open Favorites: Click the View favorites, feeds, and history button, or press **Alt** + **C**. If necessary, click the Favorites tab. Select a favorite. Click the right button on the mouse and click open from the list of options displayed.

To Add a Favorite: Open the page you want to add as a favorite. Click the View favorites, feeds, and history button and click Add to Favorites. Or, press **Ctrl** + **D**.

To Add a Tab Group to Favorites: Click the View favorites, feeds, and history button, click the Add to Favorites button list arrow, and select Add current tabs to favorites from the list. Enter a folder name for the tabs and click Add.

To Organize Favorites: Click the View favorites, feeds, and history button, click the Add to Favorites button list arrow, and select Organize favorites from the list.

To Subscribe to an RSS Feed: Open the page from which you want to access feeds. (If a feed is available on the page, the Feeds button on the Command Bar will appear orange.) Click the View feeds on this page button. Click the Subscribe to this feed link.

To View RSS Feeds: Click the View favorites, feeds, and history button and click the Feeds tab. Click a feed to view its updates.

To View History: Click the View favorites, feeds, and history button and click the History tab. Or, press **Ctrl** + **Shift** + **H**. Click a time frame or click the View By list arrow to change how history is viewed.

To Clear History: Click the Tools button and select Internet options. Click Delete under Browsing history. Or, click the Tools button and select Safety → Delete browsing history from the menu.

To Pin the Favorites Center to the Window: Click the View favorites, feeds and history button and click the [icon]. Pin the Favorites Center button in the menu.

TRIVIA

It was in 1971 that the first-ever computer virus emerged.

Top websites

Alexa ranks websites based on a combined measure of page views and unique site users. Alexa creates a list of "top websites" based on this data surveyed over three-month periods and only accounts for the top level domain names. Here is the list of top 20 websites.

Domain	Alexa Rank
Google.com	1
YouTube.com	2
Baidu.com	3
Bilibili.com	4
Facebook.com	5
Bing.com	6
Qq.com	7
Twitter.com	8
Wikipedia.org	9
Amazon.com	10
Zhihu.com	11
Instagram.com	12
Linkedin.com	13
ReddIt.com	14
WhatsApp.com	15
Yahoo.com	16
OpenAi.com	17
MicroSoft.com	18
Zoom.us	19
Yandex.ru	20

- The Internet is the physical network of computers all over the world.
- The World Wide Web is a virtual network of websites connected by hyperlinks.
- The World Wide Web was created in 1989 by Tim Berners-Lee.
- A web browser is the tool used to access the World Wide Web.

1. The tools which help us to find information on the internet is called _______.
   (a) Find engine
   (b) Search engine
   (c) Search pot
   (d) Find station

2. Search engines search for websites based on _____.
   (a) File
   (b) Information
   (c) Keywords
   (d) Data

3. What is an advantage of e-mail?
   (a) Speedy message spending process
   (b) Can be used to multiple people at the same time
   (c) Variety of media that can be sent
   (d) All of these

4. How many parts does an e-mail address have?
   (a) 2   (b) 1
   (c) 3   (d) 4

5. Which of the following are the parts of an e-mail?
   (a) Username
   (b) @
   (c) Host server name
   (d) All of these

6. The domain name "org" is derived from _______.
   (a) Organization
   (b) Orbit
   (c) Non-profit organization
   (d) None of these

7. Application through which chatting can be done is called _______.
   (a) Chat box
   (b) Chat messenger
   (c) Instant messenger
   (d) Instant chat

8. Which of the following is NOT an Instant Messenger?
   (a) skype   (b) talk
   (c) icq   (d) Piriform

9. What can you search in a search engine?
   (a) Articles, Stories and News
   (b) Images and Pictures
   (c) Games, Videos and Software
   (d) All of these

10. Where do you type the URL in a browser?
    (a) Title bar
    (b) Scroll bar
    (c) Address bar
    (d) None of these

11. If you want to send e-mail to more than one person, you can type multiple e-mail addresses separated by _______
    (a) Colon   (b) Comma
    (c) Hyphen   (d) Slash

12. When chatting publicly, what should you NOT do?
    (a) Talk to strangers
    (b) Give your personal information
    (c) Reveal your identities
    (d) All of these

13. _______ is a software that is installed on a PC to take partial control over the user's interaction without user consent.
    (a) Docware   (b) Spyware
    (c) Softspy   (d) Spy

14. Obtaining unauthorized access to other systems in a network is called _______.
    (a) Access   (b) Stealing
    (c) Forging   (d) Hacking

15. How can you get rid of Pop-ups?
    (a) Pop up remover
    (b) Pop up saver
    (c) Pop up blocker
    (d) None of these

16. ________ is a system that prevents unauthorized use and access to your computer.
   (a) Protect   (b) Firewall
   (c) Healwall   (d) Heal

17. ________ program are used to remove spyware.
   (a) Adware
   (b) Pop up blocker
   (c) Firewall
   (d) Anti Spyware

18. What company devolved the Chrome web browser?
   (a)    (b) Microsoft
   (c) Google   (d) mozilla FOUNDATION

19. What language is also known as the language of the web?
   (a) Java
   (b) C++
   (c) XML
   (d) HTML

20. What is the difference between Cc and Bcc in an e-mail?
   (a) Bcc supports attachments, while Cc does not.
   (b) Cc data is sent unencrypted, while Bcc is sent over a secure connection.
   (c) Bcc hides the sender's e-mail address, while Cc does not.
   (d) Bcc hides all of the recipient e-mail addresses, while Cc does not

21. What is the name for Microsoft's search engine?
   (a) Google   (b) altavista
   (c) bing   (d) metacrawler SEARCH THE SEARCH ENGINES!®

22. Pick the odd one out.
   (a)    (c)
   (c)   (d)

23. Along with Sabeer Bhatia, who was the co-founder of the famous e-mail software technology Hotmail?
   (a) Jack Smith
   (b) Bill Gates
   (c) Larry Page
   (d) Tim Berners-Lee

24. What type of webpage provides an overview of all the pages on a website?
   (a) Home Page
   (b) About Page
   (c) Contact Us Page
   (d) Site Map

25. Which of the following statement is NOT true for a hyperlink?
   (a) You can have only one hyperlink on one web page.
   (b) When a hyperlink is clicked, you are connected to other pages on the web.
   (c) Hyperlink are highlighted by underlining the text or displaying them in different colors or both.
   (d) It is highlighted text on a web page.

1. Servers are computers that provide resources to other computers connected to a
   (a) Client
   (b) Mainframe
   (c) Supercomputer
   (d) Network

2. A program that is used to view websites is called a
   (a) Browser
   (b) Web viewer
   (c) Spreadsheet
   (d) Word processor

3. Which of the following is not a type of broadband internet connection?
   (a) Satellite
   (b) DSL
   (c) Dial up
   (d) Cable

4. A typical modern computer uses
   (a) Valves
   (b) LSI chips
   (c) Vacuum tubes
   (d) All of these

5. What is the term for unsolicited Email?
   (a) Spam
   (b) Backbone
   (c) Usenet
   (d) News group

SUBJECTIVE QUESTIONS

1. **Write a short note on IP Address.**

Ans.

An IP (Internet Protocol) address is a unique identifier for a node or host connection on an IP network. An IP address is a 32 bit binary number usually represented as 4 decimal values, each representing 8 bits, in the range 0 to 255 (known as octets) separated by decimal points. This is known as "dotted decimal" notation.

2. **Define World Wide Web.**

Ans.

The World Wide Web is a virtual network of websites connected by hyperlinks (or "links"). Websites are stored on servers on the Internet, so the World Wide Web is a part of the Internet.

3. **What is a web browser? Define URL.**

Ans.

A web browser is the tool you use to access the World Wide Web. Chrome, Firefox, Internet Explorer, Safari, and Opera are the most popular web browsers. Each one has its own look and feel, but they have the same goal: to display webpages correctly. For most webpages, any well-known browser will work.

To get to a webpage, you can type the URL (Uniform Resource Locator) into a browser. The URL, also known as the web address, tells the browser exactly where to find the page.

4. **List some uses of Internet.**

Ans.

Uses of internet are as follows:
- We can send birthday greeting cards through the internet.
- We can earn online by doing freelancing jobs, selling online, completing surveys, etc.
- We can sell old items that are of no use to us.
- It contains a huge amount of information on different fields.
- Internet is an entertainment hub.
- The Internet also provides e-business which can also enhance business.
- We can listen to music, watch movies or play video games on it.

- The students can get the academic information they require.
- We can read online news websites.

5. What are Hardware and Software Requirements for the Internet?

Ans.

The hardware and software needed for connecting to the internet will involve five basic items:

- Computer
- Modem
- An internet connection
- Cable for connecting the modem to the internet connection
- Special software

6. Explain any two uses of Internet.

Ans.

Two uses or the Internet are -

(i) Information exchange: The Internet is a virtual treasure trove of information. There is a huge amount of information available on the Internet about every subject. It may range from government laws and services, trade fairs and conferences, market information and new ideas for technical support.

The 'search engines' on the Internet can help you to find data on any subject that you need. Google, Yahoo and Bing are examples of such search engines.

(ii) Buy and Sell Products: You can buy and sell products all over the world through the Internet. This is called online shopping. There are many online stores and sites that can be browsed to see the products that can be bought. You need not leave your house, and can do your shopping from the convenience of your home.

7. Discuss the importance of Internet Explorer.

Ans.

Internet Explorer is a series of graphical web browser developed by Microsoft. It was included as part of the Microsoft Windows line of operating systems in 1995. It has been one of the most widely used web browsers since then. Internet Explorer opens just like any other software window.

8. State the difference between a Computer Virus and an Internet Virus.

Ans.

A computer virus is a program or piece of code that is loaded onto your computer without your knowledge. It makes the computer run against your instructions. Viruses can also replicate themselves that is, they can multiply, in numbers. All computer viruses are man-made.

A simple virus that can make a copy of it over and over again is relatively easy to produce. Even a simple virus is dangerous because it will quickly use all the available memory and bring the system to a halt. An even more dangerous type of virus is one capable of transmitting itself across networks and bypassing security systems.

An internet virus is a program that is sent to different people through the Internet in the form of emails or links. These are sent to harm computer systems. At times, you may receive an email with subject 'Very Important', the moment you open it, the system will crash. These computer viruses behave the same way as biological viruses by contaminating any computer systems they come in contact with. These self-executing programs are generally very small and work at damaging the way your computer works.

Learning Objectives : In this chapter, students will learn about:
- ✓ Amoled
- ✓ PIM
- ✓ iPad Air

CHAPTER SUMMARY

Nothing in today's world grows as fast as the technology. We can say technology has been sprinting over the last few decades providing us with better accessibility, interaction and development. Here are some of the latest additions to the technology field.

AMOLED

AMOLED (Active-Matrix Organic Light-Emitting Diode) is a display technology in mobile devices and television. It supports low-power, low-cost and large-size (for example, 40-inch) applications.

It contains active matrix of pixels that generate light on being electrically activated. The active matris is suported by a thin film transistor which acts as as witch to control the flow of pixels. AMOLED also offer higher refresh rates. Super AMOLED is the term Samsung uses for an AMOLED display with an integrated digitizer. The layer that detects touch is integrated into the screen, rather than being places on top of it.

TRIVIA

The first webcam was used to monitor a coffee maker, allowing users to save returns to an empty pot.

PIM

A Personal Information Manager or PIM is a type of application software that functions as a personal organizer. As an information management tool, it facilitates the recording, tracking, and management of certain types of personal information.

iPad Air

The iPad Air is the fifth-generation tablet computer designed and manufactured by Apple Inc. It was was released in space gray and silver colors on November 1, 2013. The iPad Air features a thinner design with 64-bit Apple A7 processor with M7 coprocessor. The iPad Air is available in 16, 32, 64 or 128 GB.

Technology never fails to surprise us in a pleasant way. It is very much a boon to mankind if utilized in the proper way.

- ➡ AMOLED (Active-Matrix Organic Light-Emitting Diode) is a display technology in mobile devices and television. It supports low-power, low-cost and large-size (for example, 40-inch) applications.
- ➡ A personal information manager or PIM is a type of application software that functions as a personal organizer.

1. Apple iPad air runs on _______ operating system.
   - (a) Android
   - (b) iOS 7.0.4
   - (c) iOS 6
   - (d) iOS 6.4.5

2. Which of the latest version of Apple's immensely popular mobile smart phone released on September 16, 2022?
   - (a) iPhone 10
   - (b) iPhone 4
   - (c) iPhone 14
   - (d) iPhone 6

3. Identify the popular note-making software.

   - (a) Evernote
   - (b) NotePad
   - (c) Notice Board
   - (d) Note Taker

4. Which of the following is also known as a Recommendation Engine?
   - (a) Wikepedia
   - (b) Meta Crawler
   - (d) Google
   - (d) Stumble Upon

5. The Aakash tablet from Datawind runs on which operating system?
   - (a) iOS
   - (b) Windows Mobile
   - (c) Android
   - (d) Maebo

6. A series of e-book readers produced by Barner and Noble. Name them.
   - (a) Nook
   - (b) Kindle
   - (c) Cybook
   - (d) eDGe

7. Nexus 5 smartphone contains similarities of _________.
   - (a) LG G2
   - (b) Nokia Lumia 820
   - (c) Samsung Galaxy Core
   - (d) Samsung Wave 3

8. Arrange the android versions in ascending order (From earliest release to latest release)
   - (a) Donut, Cupcake, Éclair, Gingerbread, Froyo, Honeycomb, IceCream Sandwitch, Jelly Bean, Kitkat
   - (b) Cupcake, Donut, Éclair, Froyo, Ginger Bread, Honeycomb, Ice CreamSandwich, Jelly Bean, Kitkat
   - (c) Jelly Bean, Kitkat, Honeycomb, IceCream Sandwich, Froyo, Donut, Cupcake, Gingerbread, Éclair
   - (d) Donut, Eelair, Gingerbread, Froyo, Honeycomb, Ice Cream Sandwich, JellyBean, Kitkat

9. A personal cloud storage service is NOT provided by _________.
   - (a) MediaFire
   - (b) Google Nexus
   - (c) Google Drive
   - (d) Dropbox

10. AMOLED is a _______ for mobile devices.
    - (a) Wireless technology
    - (b) Touch technology
    - (c) Display technology
    - (d) None of these

11. The Xbox 360 successor which released on November 22, 2013 is _________.
    - (a) Xbox 2010
    - (b) Xbox One
    - (c) Xbox 360S
    - (d) Xbox 360 E

12. A PIM (Personal Information Management) application from Microsoft.
    - (a) One Note
    - (b) Two Note
    - (c) Sky Drive
    - (d) All of these

13. Mozilla launched a __________ version of its touch enable Firefox browser for Windows 8 and Windows 8.1 in February 2014.
    - (a) Alpha
    - (b) Eama
    - (c) Beta
    - (d) SIGMA

14. A touch screen device from Google that run's the company's Chrome OS.
    (a) Chromebook   (b) Retina Display
    (c) Surface Pro   (d) Nexus
15. Google Goggles was a downloadable image recognition application used for searches based on images taken by hand-held devices. They are examples of _______ technology.
    (a) Handheld
    (b) Wearable
    (c) Real life
    (d) Secret storage
16. A feature that enables Google Android-based smartphones, tablets and similar mobile devices to share content with other near-field communication-capable devices by simply touching the devices together and pressing a button on the device sending the content.
    (a) Android App
    (b) Android Launcher
    (c) Android Beam
    (d) Android wall
17. The smallest device in Apple's line up digital portable music players.
    (a) ipod Touch   (b) iPod Nano
    (c) iPod Mini   (d) iPod Shuffle
18. A supercomputer developed at Oak Ridge National Laboratory, funded by the U.S. Department of Energy which is capable of petaflops, or 20,000 trillion calculations per second.
    (a) iWarp   (b) Mosaic
    (c) Titan   (d) Titanic
19. A mobile commerce strategy that focuses on designing and developing e-commerce websites and related processes to improve the browsing and shopping experience on tablet devices.
    (a) Wi-Fi commerce
    (b) Tablet commerce
    (c) iCommerce
    (d) Mobile commerce

20. Samsung Galaxy Grand 2 runs on which of the following operating systems?
    (a) Android 4.2
    (b) Android 4.4
    (c) Android 4.3
    (d) iOS
21. The following statements refer to which social networking platform?
    ■ It is social networking service owned by Specific Media LLC and popstar Justin Timberlake.
    ■ Its founders are Chris De Wolfe and Tom Anderson.
    (a) Twitter   (b) Orkut
    (c) MySpace   (d) Facebook
22. The Chinese company, who sued Facebook claiming, "Timeline as their feature" is _______.
    (a) Cubic Network
    (b) Cuboidal Network
    (c) Square Network
    (d) Central Network
23. The given N-Marked logo is of _______ enabled device.

    (a) CFN   (b) NFC
    (c) FNC   (d) BBM
24. Thunderbolt (interface) was brought to the marked by Intel with technical collaboration from _______.
    (a) Microsoft   (b) Apple
    (c) Toshiba   (d) Acer
25. Which of the following is NOT a social networking site?
    (a) Ning   (b) Tagged
    (c) Hi5   (d) My Year

1. ________ is Sony's name for digital rights management, a copy protection technology.
   (a) Magic Gate   (b) Magic data
   (c) Magic code   (d) Pro

2. An internet-based 3D virtual world where you move through the world as a 3D-Avatar is known as ______.
   (a) Google-Maps   (b) Second-Life
   (c) Del.icio.us   (d) Twitter

3. Pick the odd one out.
   (a) **CARBONITE**
   (b) **BACKBLAZE**
   (c) CRASH**PLAN**
   (d) twitter

4. SSL stands for ________
   (a) Secure Socket Layer
   (b) Secure Secret Level
   (c) Secure System Level
   (d) Section Security Layer

5. Full form of W3C is ________
   (a) World Wide Websites community
   (b) World Wide Web community
   (c) World Wide Websites consortium
   (d) World Wide Web consortium

SECTION 2
LOGICAL REASONING

Patterns 1

Learning Objectives : In this chapter, students will learn about:
- ✓ Series
- ✓ Figure Pattern
- ✓ Figure Matrix

CHAPTER SUMMARY

There are many patterns in our everyday world. For example, see the pattern of bricks on a wall. Patterns can also be in number forms. For example, first you sell one chocolate for ₹5 and then two chocolates for price ₹10. In this example, the pattern increases by 5.

Series

The well-arranged order of a number/letter placed in a special group is called Series. This includes the completion of incomplete series of numbers, letters, figures and their combination. A particular place is left blank in the series. These terms follow a certain pattern. You are required to recognize this pattern and complete the series or identify the wrong member of that series.

Identify the next number in the series given in the following examples.

Example 1: 4, 6, 9, 13, ...

    (a) 17   (b) 18

    (c) 21   (d) 25

Sol. (b)

The difference between the two consecutive numbers is increasing in the order of 2,3,4,5, etc. Hence, answer is 18.

Example 2: 120, 99, 80, 63, 48, ?

    (a) 34   (b) 36

    (c) 35   (d) 25

Sol. (c)

The pattern is –21, –19, –17, –15, ... Hence the answer is 48 – 13 = 35.

Example 3: 1, 1, 2, 6, 24, ?, 720

    (a) 108   (b) 100

    (c) 10   (d) 120

Sol. (d)

The pattern is × 1, × 2, × 3, × 4, ... Hence, missing term = 24 × 5 = 120.

Figure pattern

In this type of pattern, a figure is given and you are required to identify the missing part. You have to select the best among four options given to complete the pattern.

Example 1: Which of the following is the missing figure?

Problem Figure

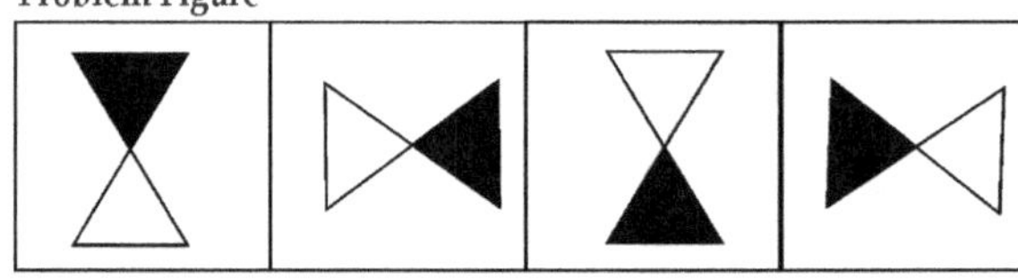

Answer Figure

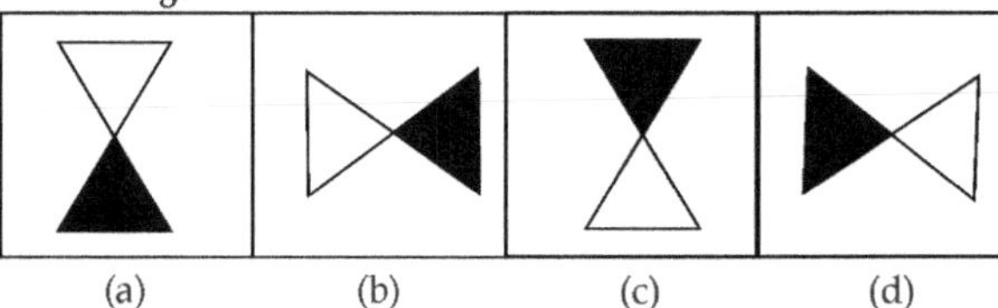

  (a)   (b)   (c)   (d)

Sol. (c)

In this example, the question figure is rotated clockwise through 90 degrees each time. The answer is therefore option (c) which represents the last shape rotated through a further 90 degrees.

Finding the missing pattern in a sequence

Here a set of terms following a certain pattern is given. You are required to identify the relation or pattern followed in the given terms and find the missing character. Determine if the order of numbers is ascending (getting larger in value) or descending (becoming smaller in value). Also find the difference between the numbers that are next to each other. You can also use the difference between numbers to find the missing number.

Example 1: Find the missing number: 15, 13, ?, 9

    (a) 14   (b) 12
    (c) 10   (d) 11

Sol. (d)

The order of numbers is going down or descending.

The difference between numbers is 15 − 13 = 2

Since the order is descending, subtract 2 from 13

The missing number is 11 since it is 2 more than the last number 9.

Figure matrix

In this type of pattern, the picture and number figures or shapes or activities are given. Here sets of figures follow the same rule either row-wise or column-wise. You have to analyse the set of figures and identify the rule and then find the missing figure from the set of alternatives.

Example 1: Select a suitable figure from the four alternatives that would complete the figure matrix.

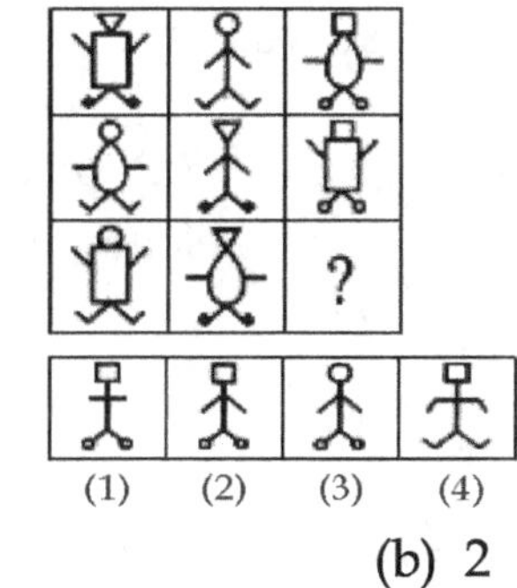

    (a) 1   (b) 2
    (c) 3   (d) 4

Sol. (a)

In each row, the second figure is obtained from the first figure by increasing the number of smaller elements by one and the third figure is obtained from the second figure by increasing the number of smaller elements by one.

Example 2: Select a suitable figure from the four alternatives that would complete the figure matrix.

    (a) 1   (b) 2
    (c) 3   (d) 4

Sol. (b)

There are 3 types of faces, 3 types of bodies, 3 types of hands and 3 types of legs, each of which is used only once in a single row. So, the features which have not been used in the first two figures of the third row would combine to produce the missing figure.

➡ The well-arranged order of a number/letter placed in a special group is called series. This includes the completion of incomplete series of numbers, letters, figures and their combination.

1. Complete the series _op _ mo _ n _ _ pnmop _
   (a) mnpmon   (b) mpnmon
   (c) mpnmop   (d) mnompn

2. Complete the series ba_ba_bac_acb_cbac
   (a) aacb   (b) bbca
   (c) ccba   (d) cbac

3. Complete the series m _ nm _ n _ an _ a _ ma _
   (a) aamnan   (b) ammanm
   (c) aammnn   (d) amammn

4. Complete the series adb_ac_da_cddcb_dbc_cbda
   (a) bccba   (b) cbbaa
   (c) ccbba   (d) bbcad

5. Complete the series bca_b_aabc _a_caa
   (a) acab   (b) bcbb
   (c) cbab   (d) ccab

6. Find the next two elements in series: A/2, B/4, C/6, D/8
   (a) E/8, F/10
   (b) E/12, F/14
   (c) E/10, F/12
   (d) D/10, E/10

7. Find the missing element: Q1F, S2E, U6D, W21C, ?
   (a) Z88B   (b) Y66B
   (c) Y44B   (d) Y88B

8. Find the missing element: 2Z5, 7Y7, 14X9, 23W11, 34V13, ?
   (a) 27U24   (b) 47U15
   (c) 45U15   (d) 47V14

9. Find the missing element: P3C, R5F, T8I, V12L, ?
   (a) Y17O   (b) X17M
   (c) X17O   (d) X16O

10. Find the missing element: J2Z, K4X, 17V, ?, H16R, M22P
    (a) L11S   (b) L12T
    (c) L11T   (d) L12S

11. Find the missing element: 3F, 6G, 11I, 18L, ?
    (a) 21O   (b) 25N
    (c) 27P   (d) 27Q

12. Find the missing element: D-4, F-6, H-8, J-10, ?
    (a) K-12, M-13
    (b) L-12, M-14
    (c) L-12, N-14
    (d) K-12, M-14

13. Find the missing element: 2A11, 4D13, 12G17, ?
    (a) 36I19   (b) 48J21
    (c) 36J21   (d) 48J23

14. Find the missing element: C4X, F9U, 116R, ?
    (a) K25P   (b) Y44B
    (c) Y88B   (d) Z88B

15. Find the missing element: B, D, F, I, L, P, ?
    (a) R   (b) S
    (c) T   (d) U

16. Find the missing element: BAZ, DCY, FEX, ?
    (a) FXW   (b) EFX
    (c) FEY   (d) HGW

17. Find the missing element: FLP, INS, LPV, ?
    (a) ORY   (b) UXZ
    (c) VXY   (d) SVW

18. Find the missing element: M, N, O, L, R, I, V, ?
    (a) A   (b) E
    (c) F   (d) H

19. Find the missing element: BAS, ?, DCQ, DDP, FEO
    (a) CBT   (b) ABR
    (c) BCT   (d) BBR

20. Find the missing element: DEF, HIJ, MNO, ?
    (a) STU   (b) RTV
    (c) SRQ   (d) TUV

21. Identify the figure that completes the pattern.

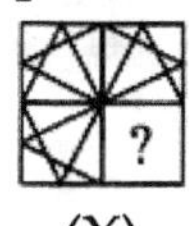 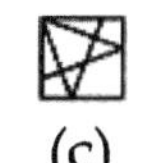

(X)   (a)   (b)   (c)   (d)

22. Identify the figure that completes the pattern.

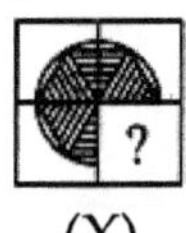    

(X)   (a)   (b)   (c)   (d)

23. Identify the figure that completes the pattern.

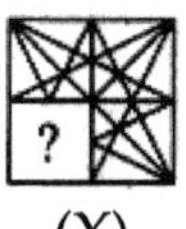 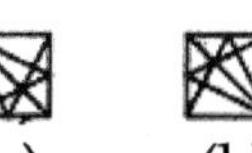 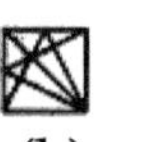 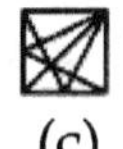 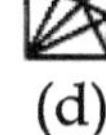

(X)   (a)   (b)   (c)   (d)

24. Identify the figure that completes the pattern.

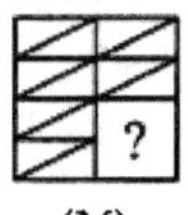

(X)   (a)   (b)   (c)   (d)

25. Identify the figure that completes the pattern.

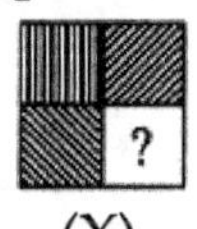  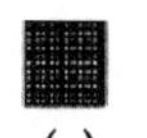

(X)   (a)   (b)   (c)   (d)

Learning Objectives : In this chapter, students will learn about:
- ✓ Analogy
- ✓ Classification

CHAPTER SUMMARY

Analogy

Analogy means similarity. Analogy specifies a relationship between given words, events, objects or alphabet sets which has to be recognised. In these type of questions, two terms/figures related in some way are given and you have to choose the third terms/figures among the four or five alternatives. It is the process of reasoning on the basis of parallel events or objects.

Example 1: 'Nun' is related to 'Convent' in the same way as 'Hen' is related to

  (a) Nest   (b) Shed

  (c) Cell   (d) Cote

Sol. (d)

As dwelling place of 'Nun' is 'Convent' similarly the dwelling place of 'Hen' is 'Cote'.

Example 2: 'Flower' is related to 'Bud' in the same way as 'Fruit' is related to

  (a) Seed   (b) Tree

  (c) Flower   (d) Stem

Sol. (c)

As 'Flower' is made from 'Bud' similarly 'Fruit' is made from 'Flower'.

Example 3: Calf : Piglet :: Shed : ?

  (a) Prison   (b) Nest

  (c) Pigsty   (d) Den

Sol. (c)

Calf is the young one of the cow and piglet is the progeny of Pig. Shed is the dwelling place of cow. Similarly, std-pigsty is the dwelling place of pig.

Example 4: ABC : ZYX :: CBA : ?

  (a) XYZ   (b) BCA

  (c) YZX   (d) ZXY

Sol. (a)

CBA is the reverse of ABC similarly XYZ is the reverse of ZYX.

Classification

In classification, a set of terms/figures is given in which all (except one) follow similar properties. You have to identify the pattern followed in the set and find the odd one out.

Example 1: Malaria : Mosquito :: ? : ?

  (a) Poison : Death

  (b) Cholera : Water

  (c) Rat : Plague

  (d) Medicine : Disease

Sol. (b)

As malaria is caused due to mosquito, similarly cholera is cause due to water.

Example 2: Lawyer : Court :: ? : ?

    (a) Chemist : Laboratory

    (b) Businessman : Office

    (c) Labour : Factory

    (d) Athlete : Olympics

Sol. (a)

As the working field of lawyer is Court, similarly the working field of chemist is laboratory.

Example 3: Lively : Dull:: ? : ?

    (a) Employed : Jobless

    (b) Flower : Bud

    (c) Factory : Labour

    (d) Happy : Gay

Sol. (a)

First word is opposite to the second word.

➡ Analogy is the process of reasoning on the basis of parallel events or objects.

➡ In classification, a set of terms/figures is given in which all (except one) follow similar properties.

1. Anthropology is related to Man in the same way as Anthology is related to
   (a) Nature   (b) Trees
   (c) Apes   (d) Poems

2. People is related to Chatter in the same way as Leaves is related to
   (a) Whistle   (b) Ripple
   (c) Rustle   (d) Cackle

3. Lion is related to Prowl in the same way as Bear is related to
   (a) Frisk   (b) Lumber
   (c) Stride   (d) Bound

4. Mirror is related to Reflection in the same way as Water is related to
   (a) Conduction
   (b) Dispersion
   (c) Immersion
   (d) Refraction

5. Firm is related to Flabby in the same way as Piquant is related to
   (a) Bland   (b) Salty
   (c) Pleasant   (d) Small

6. Happiness is related to Sorrow in the same way as Comfort is related to
   (a) Hardship   (b) Rest
   (c) Poverty   (d) Difficulty

7. Appreciation is related to Reward in the same way as Disgrace is related to
   (a) Crime   (b) Guilt
   (c) Allegation   (d) Punishment

8. Naphthalene is related to Woollen in the same way as Antibiotics is related to
   (a) Germs   (b) Immunity
   (c) Diseases   (d) Body

9. Retirement is related to Service in the same way as Dismissal is related to
   (a) Agreement
   (b) Communication
   (c) Employment
   (d) Ad

10. Drummer is related to Orchestra in the same way as Minister is related to
    (a) Voter   (b) Constituency
    (c) Cabinet   (d) Department

11. Physiology is related to Biology in the same way as Metaphysics is related to
    (a) Physics
    (b) Statistics
    (c) Mathematics
    (d) Philosophy

12. Highbrow is related to Cultivated in the same way as Suave is related to
    (a) Elegant   (b) Urbane
    (c) Stylish   (d) Broad-minded

13. Affirm is related to Hint in the same way as Charge is related to
    (a) Insinuate   (b) Reject
    (c) Convince   (d) Deny

14. Author is related to Book in the same way as Choreographer is related to
    (a) Drama   (b) Ballet
    (c) Masque   (d) Opera

15. Thick is related to Thin in the same way as Idle is related to
    (a) Virtuous   (b) Business
    (c) Industrious   (d) Activity

16. Coherent is related to Consistent in the same way as Irate is related to
    (a) Unreasonable
    (b) Unhappy
    (c) Irritated
    (d) Angry

17. Book is related to Magazine in the same way as Newspaper is related to
    (a) Journal   (b) News
    (c) Article   (d) Headline

18. Tungsten is related to Filament in the same way as Bronze is related to
    (a) Copper   (b) Ships
    (c) Tin   (d) Ornaments

19. Claymore is related to Sword in the same way as Beretta is related to
    (a) Club (b) Axe
    (c) Knife (d) Gun

20. Indolence is related to Work in the same way as Taciturn is related to
    (a) Observe (b) Speak
    (c) Cheat (d) Act

21. Gill is related to Lamellae in the same way as Lung is related to
    (a) Ribs (b) Trachea
    (c) Alveoli (d) Pharynx

22. Dwell is related to Denizen in the same way as Inherit is related to
    (a) Acquire (b) Successor
    (c) Outcast (d) Heir

23. Solicitous is related to Concern in the same way as Verbose is related to
    (a) Tiredness (b) Wordiness
    (c) Speech (d) Deafness

24. Mouse is related to Cat in the same way as Fly is related to
    (a) Animal (b) Horse
    (c) Spider (d) Rat

25. Brain is related to Cranium in the same way as Pearl is related to
    (a) Box (b) Oyster
    (c) Sand (d) Shore

26. Horse is related to Hay in the same way as Cow is related to
    (a) Leaves (b) Fodder
    (c) Milk (d) Straw

27. Abduction is related to Kidnapping in the same way as Larceny is related to
    (a) Theft (b) Crime
    (c) Blackmail (d) Sin

28. Street is related to Lane in the same way as Road is related to
    (a) Footpath (b) Junction
    (c) Avenue (d) Highway

29. Concert is related to Theatre in the same way as Banquet is related to
    (a) Hotel (b) Party
    (c) Feast (d) Supper

30. Statue is related to Shape in the same way as Song is related to
    (a) Beauty (b) Sing
    (c) Tune (d) Poetry

Learning Objectives : In this chapter, students will learn about:
- ✓ Letter Coding
- ✓ Number Coding

CHAPTER SUMMARY

Here, you will understand the concept of coding and decoding. A code is a 'system of signals'. Therefore, coding is a method of transmitting a message between the sender and the receiver without a third person knowing it. Decoding is a process to understand a code language.

The coding and decoding test is set up to judge the candidate's ability to decipher the rule that codes a particular word/message and breaks the code to decipher the message.

Letter Coding

In letter coding type of questions, the real letters in a word are replaced by other letters according to a specific rule to form its code. You are required to detect the common rule and answer the questions accordingly.

Example 1: If in a code language, COULD is written as BNTKC and MARGIN is written as LZQFHM, how will MOULDING be written in that code?

    (a) CHMFINTK   (b) LNKTCHMF
    (c) LNTKCHMF   (d) NITKHCMF

Sol. (c)

Each letter in the word is moved one step backward to obtain the corresponding letter of the code.

Example 2: In a certain code, MONKEY is written as XDJMNL. How will TIGER be written in that code?

    (a) QDFHS   (b) SDFHS
    (c) SHFDQ   (d) UJHFS

Sol. (a)

The letter of the word is written in a reverse order and then each letter is moved one step backward to obtain the code.

Number Coding

In Number coding type of questions, either numerical code values are assigned a word or alphabetical code letters are assigned to the numbers. You are required to analyse the code as per the directions.

Example 1: If DELHI is coded as 73541 and CALCUTTA as 82589662, how is CALICUT coded?

    (a) 5279431   (b) 5978213
    (c) 8251896   (d) 8543691

Sol. (c)

The letters are coded as follows:

D	E	L	H	I	C	A	U	T
7	3	5	4	1	8	2	9	6

So, in CALICUT,
C is coded as 8,
A as 2,
L as 5,
I as 1,
U as 9 and
T as 6.
Thus, the code for CALICUT is 8251896.

Example 2: In a certain code, RIPPLE is written as 613382 and LIFE is written as 8192. How is PILLER written in that code?

    (a) 318826   (b) 318286

    (c) 618826   (d) 338816

Sol. (a)

The letters are coded as follows:

R	I	P	L	E	F
6	1	3	8	2	9

So, in PILLER,

P is coded as 3,

I as 1,

L as 8,

E as 2 and

R as 6.

Thus, the code for PILLER is 318826.

Example 3: If in a certain code, TWENTY is written as 863985 and ELEVEN is written as 323039, how is TWELVE written in that code?

    (a) 863203   (b) 863584

    (c) 863903   (d) 863063

Sol. (a)

The letters are coded as follows

T	W	E	N	Y	L	V
8	6	3	9	5	2	0

So, in TWELVE,

T is coded as 8,

W as 6,

E as 3,

L as 2,

V as 0.

Thus, the code for TWELVE is 863203.

Number to Letter Coding

Sometimes numbers/symbols are assigned to words.

Example 1: In a certain code, 15789 are written as EGKPT and 2346 is written ALUR. How is 23549 written in that code?

    (a) ALEUT   (b) ALGTU

    (c) ALGUT   (d) ALGRT

Sol. (c)

In the given codes, the numbers are coded as follows:

1	5	7	8	9	2	3	4	6
E	G	K	P	T	A	L	U	R

i.e., 2 as A,

3 as L,

5 as G,

4 as U and

9 as T.

So, 23549 is coded as ALGUT.

Example 2: The number in each question below is coded as follows:

Digit	7	2	1	5	3	9	8	6	4
Letter	W	L	M	S	I	N	D	J	B

How is 879341 coded?

    (a) DWNIBS   (b) DWNBIM

    (c) DWNIBM   (d) NDWBIM

Sol. (c)

As given, 8 is coded as D,

7 as W,

9 as N,

3 as I,

4 as B and

1 as M.

So, 879341 is coded as DWNIBM.

➡ The coding and decoding test is set up to judge the candidate's ability to decipher the rule that codes a particular word/message and breaks the code to decipher the message.

1. If GIVE is coded as 5137 and BAT is coded as 924. how is GATE written in that code?
   (a) 5427   (b) 2547
   (c) 5247   (d) 5724

2. If LUTE is written as MUTE and FATE is written as GATE, how is BLUE be written in that code?
   (a) CLUE   (b) GLUE
   (c) FLUE   (d) SLUE

3. If INSTITUTION is written as NOITUTITSNI, how is PERFECTION written in that code?
   (a) NOICTEFREP
   (b) NOITCEFERP
   (c) NOITCEFREP
   (d) NOITCEFPER

4. If GANTIC is written as GIGTANCI, how is MIRACLES written in that code?
   (a) MIRLCAES
   (b) MIRLACSE
   (c) RIMCALSE
   (d) RIMLCAES

5. If GOODNESS is written as HNPCODTR. How is GREATNESS written in that code?
   (a) HQFZUODTR
   (b) HQFZUMFRT
   (c) HQFZSMFRT
   (d) FSDBSODTR

6. If EXPLAINING is written as PXEALNIGNI, how is PRODUCED written in that code?
   (a) ORPBUDEC
   (b) ROPUDECD
   (c) ORPUDECD
   (d) None of these

7. If MADRAS is coded as NBESBT, how is BOMBAY written in that code?
   (a) CPNCBZ   (b) CPNCPZ
   (c) CPOCBZ   (d) CQOCBZ

8. If FISH is written as EHRG, how is JUNGLE be written in that code?
   (a) ITMFKD   (b) ITNFKD
   (c) KVOHMF   (d) TIMFKD

9. If TWINKLE is written as SVHOJKD, how is FILTERS be written in that code?
   (a) EHKSDQR   (b) EHKUDQR
   (c) EGKUDQR   (d) GJMSFSR

10. If ROAD is written as URDG, how is SWAN written in that code?
    (a) VXDQ   (b) VZDQ
    (c) VZCP   (d) UXDQ

11. If OPERATION is written as NODQBUJPO, how is INVISIBLE written in that code?
    (a) JOWJTJCMF
    (b) JOWJTHAKD
    (c) HMUHTJCMF
    (d) HMUHTHAKD

12. If FAVOUR is written as EBUPTS, how is DANGER written in that code?
    (a) CBFFDS   (b) CBMHDS
    (c) EBFHDS   (d) EBHHFS

13. If SUMMER is coded as RUNNER, how is WINTER written in that code?
    (a) SUITER   (b) VIOUER
    (c) WALKER   (d) SUFFER

14. If PRODUCTIONS is written as QQPCVEUHPMT, how is ORIENTATION written in that code?
    (a) PQJDOVBSJNO
    (b) PQJDOUBUJPO
    (c) PSJFOVBSJNO
    (d) NSHFMVBSJNO

15. If MIND is KGLB and ARGUE is YPESC, how is DIAGRAM written in that code?
    (a) BGYEPYK
    (b) BGYPYEK
    (c) GLPEYKB
    (d) LKBGYPK

16. If BASIC is written as DDULE, how is LEADER written in that code?
   (a) NGCFGT   (b) NHCGGU
   (c) OGDFHT   (d) OHDGHU

17. If SIGHT is written as FVTUG, how is REVEAL written in that code?
   (a) YNRIRE   (b) DQHQMX
   (c) FSJSOZ   (d) ERIRNY

18. If MIRACLE is coded as NKUEHRL, how is GAMBLE written in that code?
   (a) JDOCMF   (b) CLEMNK
   (c) HCPFQK   (d) AELGMN

19. If BELIEF is written as AFKKDI, how is SELDOM written in that code?
   (a) RDKCNL   (b) RFKENM
   (c) RFKFNP   (d) TFKENP

20. If TRIPPLE is written as SQHOOKD, how is DISPOSE written in that code?
   (a) CHRONRD   (b) DSOESPI
   (c) ESJTPTF   (d) ESOPSID

21. If COULD is written as BNTKC and MARGIN is written as LZQFHM, how is MOULDING written in that code?
   (a) CHMFINTK
   (b) LNKTCHMF
   (c) LNTKCHMF
   (d) NITKHCMF

22. If COMPUTER is written as RFUVQNPC, how is MEDICINE written in the same code?
   (a) EOJDJEFM   (b) EOJDEJFM
   (c) MFEJDJOE   (d) MFEDJJOE

23. If VICTORY is coded as YLFWRUB, how is SUCCESS written in that code?
   (a) VXEEIVV   (b) VXFFHVV
   (c) VYEEHVV   (d) VYEFIVV

24. If TOGETHER is written as RQEGRJCT, how is PAROLE written in that code?
   (a) NCPQJG   (b) NCQPJG
   (c) RCPQJK   (d) RCTQNC

25. If BOMBAY is written as MYMYMY, how is TAMIL NADU written in that code?
   (a) TIATIATIA
   (b) MNUMNUMNU
   (c) IATIATIAT
   (d) ALDALDALD

26. If FRIEND is coded as HUMJTK, how is CANDLE written in that code?
   (a) EDRIRL   (b) DCQHQK
   (c) ESJFME   (d) FYOBOC

27. If COUNSEL is coded as BITIRAK, how is GUIDANCE written in that code?
   (a) EOHYZKBB   (b) FOHYZJBB
   (c) FPHZZKAB   (d) HOHYBJBA

Learning Objectives : In this chapter, students will learn about:
- ✓ Ranking Test
- ✓ Alphabet Test

CHAPTER SUMMARY

Ranking test

In ranking-based problems, usually the ranks of one or two persons from the top and from the bottom are mentioned. A candidate is required to compute either the total number of persons or the rank of a particular person.

Logical sequence of words

In such type of problems, some words are given. These words have some relationship with one another or have a specific sequence. A candidate is asked to determine this relationship or sequence and to put these words in a logical sequence. This sequence may be according to size, age, happening, need, etc.

Alphabet test

In alphabet test, the questions are based on the understanding of the position of letters in the English alphabet. In a dictionary, the words are arranged in the alphabetical order. The words beginning with the same letter are again arranged alphabetically with respect to the second letter in the word and so on. In order to solve questions on order arrangement, we may have to compare all the letters sequentially.

Alphabetical order of words

In this type of question, certain words are given. The candidate is required to arrange them in the order in which they would be arranged in a dictionary and then state the word which is placed in the desired place. For such questions, the candidate requires basic knowledge of 'Dictionary Usage'. In a dictionary, the words are put in alphabetical order with respect to the second alphabet of the words and so on.

Example 1: Aarti scored more than Golu. Yash scored as much as Asha. Latika scored less than Manju. Golu scored more than Yash. Manju scored less than Asha. Who scored the lowest?

    (a) Manju   (b) Yash
    (c) Latika   (d) Golu

Sol. (c)

Students scored in ascending order as follows:

Aarti > Golu > Yash = Asha > Manju > Latika

Example 2: Arrange the given words in alphabetical order and choose the one that comes first.

    (a) Wasp   (b) Waste
    (c) War   (d) Wrinkle

Sol. (c)

War, Wasp, Waste, Wrinkle, Wrist.

Example 3: Arrange the given words in alphabetical order and choose the one that comes first.

    (a) Nature   (b) Native
    (c) Narrate   (d) Nascent

Sol. (c)

    Narrate, Nascent, Native, Nature, Naughty

Letter-Word Problems

Example 1: How many pairs of letters are there in the word 'BUCKET' which have as many letters between them in the word as in the alphabet?

    (a) One   (b) Two

    (c) Three   (d) Four

Sol. (a)

Letters in the word	Letters in the alphabet
C K E	C D E

Example 2: Two letters in the word 'PRESENCE' have as many letters between them in the word as in the alphabet and in the same order. Which one of the two letters comes earlier in the alphabet? (Hint: Do not count the pair EC, because as mentioned in the question, the letters should be in the same order.)

    (a) C   (b) E

    (c) R   (d) P

Sol. (d)

Letters in the word	Letters in the alphabet
P R E S	P Q R S

Example 3: How many letters are there in the word 'CREATIVE' which have as many letters between them in the word as in the alphabet?

    (a) 1   (b) 2

    (c) 3   (d) 4

Sol. (c)

Letters in the word	Letters in the alphabet
C R E	C D E
A T I V E	A B C D E
T I V	T U V

1. Arrange the given words in alphabetical order and choose the one that comes first.
   (a) Praise   (b) Practical
   (c) Prank   (d) Prayer

2. Arrange the given words in alphabetical order and choose the one that comes first.
   (a) Animate   (b) Animosity
   (c) Anguish   (d) Ankle

3. Arrange the given words in alphabetical order and choose the one that comes first.
   (a) Probe   (b) Proclaim
   (c) Proceed   (d) Probate

4. Arrange the given words in alphabetical order and choose the one that comes first.
   (a) Guarantee   (b) Group
   (c) Grotesque   (d) Groan

5. Arrange the given words in alphabetical order and choose the one that comes first.
   (a) Signature   (b) Sight
   (c) Shrine   (d) Shrill

6. Arrange the given words in alphabetical order and choose the one that comes first.
   (a) Prominent   (b) Prohibit
   (c) Promise   (d) Programme

7. Arrange the given words in alphabetical order and choose the one that comes first.
   (a) Heredity   (b) Hesitate
   (c) Heavy   (d) Hedge

8. Arrange the given words in alphabetical order and choose the one that comes first.
   (a) Partition   (b) Passion
   (c) Parlour   (d) Participate

9. Arrange the given words in alphabetical order and choose the one that comes first.
   (a) Exhilarate   (b) Ephemeral
   (c) Entrench   (d) Enterprise

10. Arrange the given words in alphabetical order and choose the one that comes first.
    (a) Filter   (b) Homage
    (c) Chastise   (d) Certify

11. Arrange the given words in alphabetical order and choose the one that comes first.
    (a) Tenacious
    (b) Terminate
    (c) Temperature
    (d) Temple

12. Arrange the given words in alphabetical order and choose the one that comes first.
    (a) Slander   (b) Skeleton
    (c) Stimulate   (d) Similar

13. Arrange the given words in alphabetical order and choose the one that comes first.
    (a) Blast   (b) Bottle
    (c) Bondage   (d) Boisterous

14. Arrange the given words in alphabetical order and choose the one that comes first.
    (a) Grind   (b) Growth
    (c) Great   (d) Grease

15. Arrange the given words in alphabetical order and choose the one that comes first.
    (a) Length   (b) Lenient
    (c) Legacy   (d) Legal

16. How many pairs of letters are there in the word 'HORIZON' which have as many letters between them in the word as in the English alphabet?
    (a) One   (b) Two
    (c) Three   (d) More than 3

17. How many pairs of letters are there in the word 'DONATE' which have as many letters between them as there are in the English alphabet?
    (a) Nil   (b) One
    (c) Two   (d) Three

18. How many pairs of letters in the word 'CHAIRS' have as many letters between them in the word as in the English alphabet?
    (a) None   (b) One
    (c) Two   (d) Three

19. Two letters in the word 'LEMON' have as many letters between them in the word as in the alphabet. Which one of the two letters comes earlier in the English alphabet?
    (a) E   (b) L
    (c) M   (d) N

20. How many pairs of letters are there in the word 'CLANGOUR' which have as many letters between them in the word as in the English alphabet?
    (a) One   (b) Two
    (c) Three   (d) None of these

21. How many pairs of letters are there in the word 'LANGUISH' which have as many letters between them in the word as in the English alphabet?
    (a) Nil   (b) One
    (c) Two   (d) Three

22. How many pairs of letters are there in the word 'PENCIL' which have as many letters between them in the word as in the English alphabet?
    (a) Nil   (b) One
    (c) Two   (d) Three

23. How many pairs of letters in the word 'BRIGHTER' have as many letters between them in the word as in the English alphabet?
    (a) 1   (b) 2
    (c) 3   (d) 4

24. How many pairs of letters are there in the word 'CARROT' which have as many letters between them in the word as in the English alphabet?
    (a) 1   (b) 2
    (c) 3   (d) 4

25. How many pairs of letters in the word 'CATASTROPHE' have as many letters between them in the word as in the English alphabet?
    (a) One   (b) Two
    (c) Three   (d) Four

Direction Sense Test 5

Learning Objectives : In this chapter, students will learn about:
- ✓ Main Directions
- ✓ Intermediate Directions

CHAPTER SUMMARY

Here you will understand the concept of different directions and their usage in maths. There are four main directions - East, West, North and South as shown below. These are called cardinal directions.

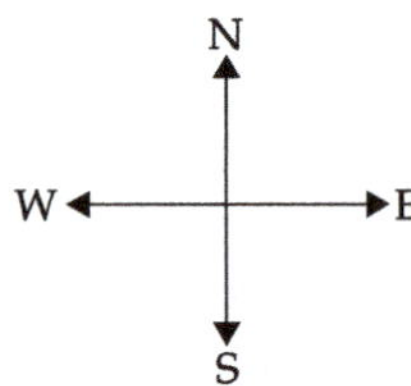

Intermediate Directions

There are four intermediate directions - North-East (N-E), North-West (N-W), South-East (S-E), and South-West (S-W) as shown below:

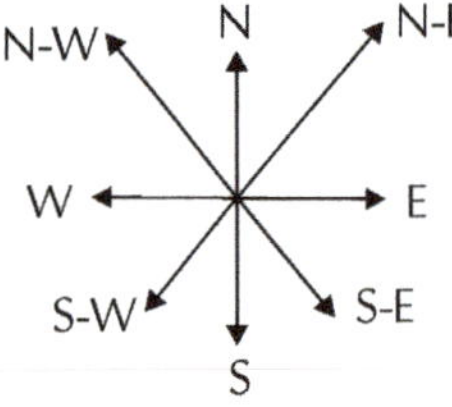

Solution:

Important Points

1. At the time of sunrise, if a man stands facing the east, his shadow will be towards the West.
2. At the time of sunset, the shadow of an object is always in the East.
3. If a man stands facing the North, at the time of sunrise his shadow will be towards his left and at the time of sunset it will be towards his right.
4. At 12:00 noon, the rays of the sun are vertically downward hence there will be no shadow.

There are four main types of questions based on directions. Let us see each type with examples.

Type 1:

Shraddha started walking from her house and walked 5 km towards the East, then she turned to her left and walked 4 Km. Finally she turned left and walked 5 Km. How far is she from her house and in what direction?

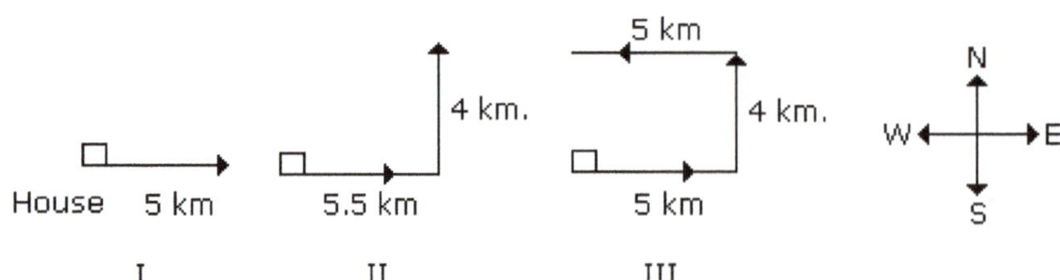

From the third position it is clear she is 4 Km from her house and she is in the North direction.

Type 2:

Sanjiv started walking from his house and walked 4 Km towards the East, then he turned to his right and walked 3 Km. What minimum distance will have to be covered by him to come back to his house?

Solution:

Sanjiv's movement

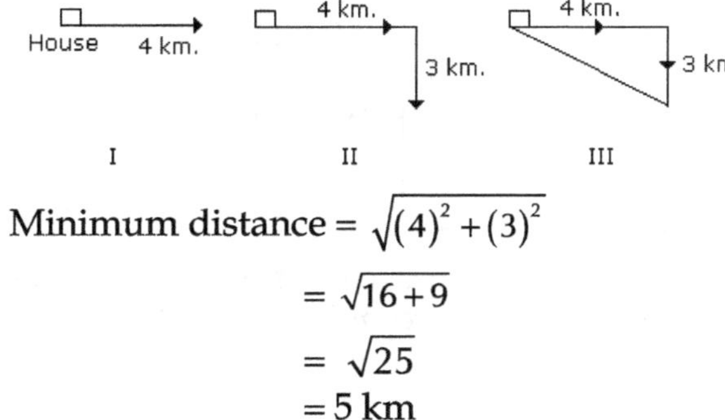

Minimum distance $= \sqrt{(4)^2 + (3)^2}$

$$= \sqrt{16 + 9}$$

$$= \sqrt{25}$$

$$= 5 \text{ km}$$

Type 3:

One morning after sunrise, Ashima while going to school met Shraddha at the road crossing. Shraddha's shadow was exactly to Ashima's right. If they were face to face, which direction was Shraddha facing?

Solution: In the morning, sunrises in the East.

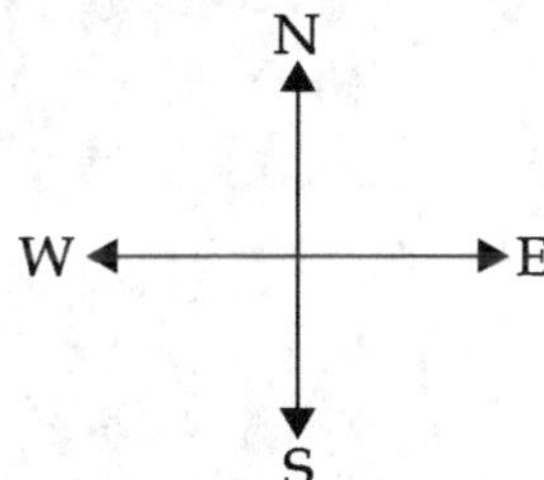

So in morning the shadow falls towards the West.

Now Shraddha's shadow falls to the right of the Ashima. Hence Ashima is facing Shraddha.

Type 4:

Shraddha starting from her house and walked 2 Km to reach the Children's Park. The road opposite to this direction goes to shopping mall. The road to the right goes to Barber Shop. If the road which goes to station is just opposite to the road with the Ice Cream Shop, then in which direction is Shraddha to the road which goes to Ice Cream Shop?

Solution:

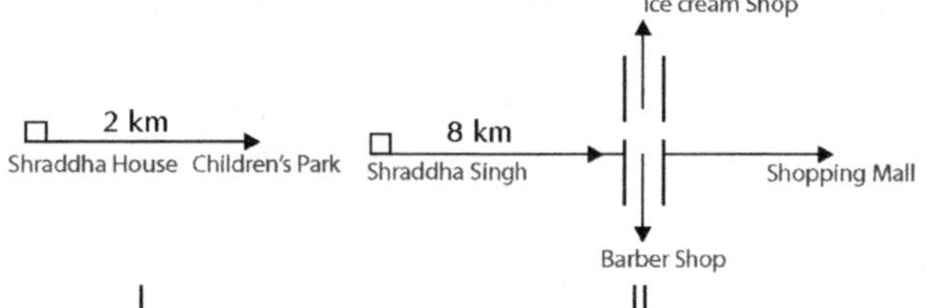

From here, it is clear that the road which goes to IT-Park is left to Shraddha.

Example 1: Ayushi walks 1 Km towards East and then she turns South and walks 5 Km. Again she turns towards East and walks 2 Km. After this, she turns towards the North and walks 9 Km. Now, how far is she from her starting point?

Sol. Ayushi's Movement

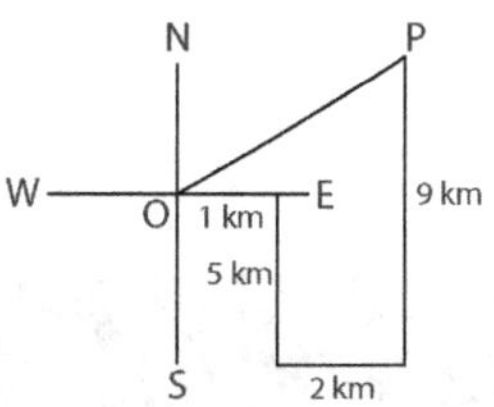

The last position of Ayushi is P and OEP is a Right angled triangle in which EP = 3 Km and OE = 4 Km

Thus,

$$OP = \sqrt{(32 + 42)}$$

$$OP = \sqrt{25}$$

$$OP = 5 \text{ Km}$$

Example 2: Shraddha walks 30 metres in the North-West direction from her house and from there 30 metres in the South-West direction. After this, she walks 30 metres in the South-East direction. Now, she turns to her house, in which direction is she going?

Sol. Movements are as follows:

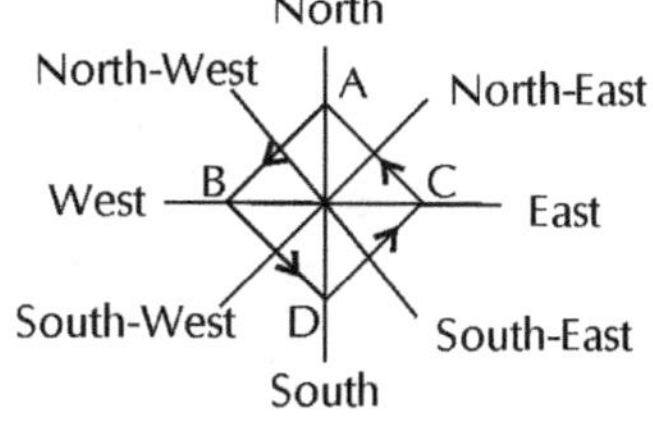

Now, Shraddha is going in North-East Direction.

Example 3: Golu was facing East. He walked 4 Km forward and then turned to his right and walked 3 Km. Again he turned to his right and walked 4 Km. After this, he turned back. Which direction was he facing at that time?

Sol. Golu's Movement

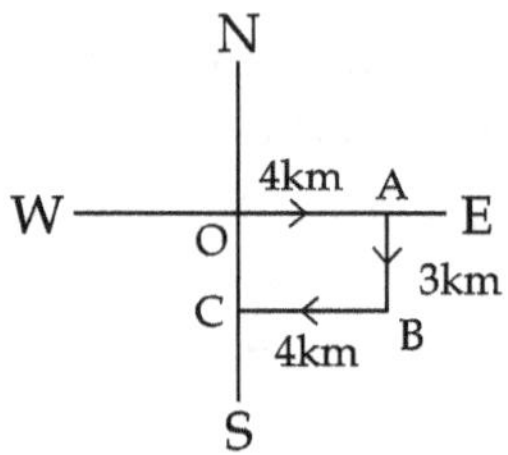

If Golu turned back from final position he must be facing in the direction of **East**.

Example 4: A cyclist travelled 30 Km towards North and then turning East, he travelled 40 Km ahead. Again he turned to his right and travelled 20 Km. After this he turned right and travelled 40 Km. How far is he from his starting point?

Sol. Cyclist's Movement

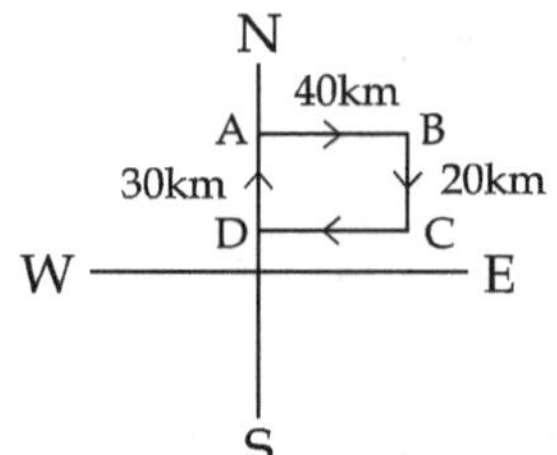

Distance of the cyclist from his starting Point O to end point D = 30 − 20 = 10 Km

➡ There are four main directions - East, West, North and South as shown below. These are called cardinal directions.

➡ There are four intermediate directions - North-East (N-E), North-West (N-W), South-East (S-E), and South-West (S-W).

➡ At the time of sunrise, if a man stands facing the east, his shadow will be towards the West.

➡ At the time of sunset, the shadow of an object is always in the East.

➡ If a man stands facing the North, at the time of sunrise his shadow will be towards his left and at the time of sunset it will be towards his right.

➡ At 12:00 noon, the rays of the sun are vertically downward hence there will be no shadow.

Direction (1-2): Dev, Kumar, Nilesh, Ankur and Pintu are standing facing North in a playground in positions as given below:

- Kumar is at 40 m to the right of Ankur.
- Dev is 60 m to the South of Kumar.
- Nilesh is at a distance of 25 m to the West of Ankur.
- Pintu is at a distance of 90 m to the North of Dev.

1. Who is in the North-East direction of the person who is to the left of Kumar?
   (a) Dev
   (b) Nilesh
   (c) Ankur
   (d) Pintu

2. If a boy started walking from Nilesh's position, met Ankur and then Kumar and Dev and then to Pintu. How much total distance did he cover while walking from one person to another?
   (a) 215 m
   (b) 155 m
   (c) 245 m
   (d) 185 m

Direction (3–6): Each of the following questions is based on the following information.

- Six flats on a floor in two rows facing North and South are allotted to P, Q, R, S, T and U.
- Q gets a North facing flat and is not next to S.
- S and U get diagonally opposite flats.
- R next to U, gets a south facing flat and T gets North-facing flat.

3. If the flats of P and T are interchanged, then who's flat will be next to that of U?
   (a) P
   (b) Q
   (c) R
   (d) T

4. Which of the following combination gets the South-facing flats?
   (a) QTS
   (b) UPT
   (c) URP
   (d) Data is inadequate

5. The flats of which of the pair other than SU, is diagonally opposite to each other?
   (a) QP
   (b) QR
   (c) PT
   (d) TS

6. Whose flat is between Q and S?
   (a) T
   (b) U
   (c) R
   (d) P

Direction (7–9): Each of the following questions is based on the following information.

- 8-trees → mango, guava, papaya, pomegranate, lemon, banana, raspberry and apple are in two rows, 4 in each, facing North and South.
- Lemon is between mango and apple but opposite to guava.
- Banana is at one end of the line and is next to the right of guava or either banana tree is after guava tree.
- Raspberry tree which is at one end of a line, is diagonally opposite to mango tree.

7. Which of the following statements is definitely true?
   (a) Papaya tree is near to apple tree.
   (b) Apple tree is next to lemon tree.
   (c) Raspberry tree is either left to the Pomegranate or after.
   (d) Pomegranate tree is diagonally opposite to the banana tree.

8. Which tree is opposite to raspberry tree?
   (a) Papaya
   (b) Pomegranate
   (c) Papaya or Pomegranate
   (d) Data is inadequate

9. Which tree is opposite to the banana tree?
   (a) Mango
   (b) Pomegranate
   (c) Papaya
   (d) Data is inadequate

Direction (10–12): Each of the following questions is based on the following information.

- A # B means B is at 1 metre to the right of A.
- A $ B means B is at 1 metre to the North of A.
- A * B means B is at 1 metre to the left of A.
- A @ B means B is at 1 metre to the South of A.
- In each question, first person from the left is facing North.

10. According to X @ B * P, P is in which direction with respect to X?
    (a) North   (b) South
    (c) North-East   (d) South-West

11. According to M # N $ T, T is in which direction with respect to M?
    (a) North-West   (b) North-East
    (c) South-West   (d) South-East

12. According to P # R $ A * U, in which direction is U with respect to P?
    (a) East   (b) West
    (c) North   (d) South

Direction: Find the correct answer for the following question based on related details given.

13. Golu starts from his house towards West. After walking a distance of 30 m, he turned towards right and walked 20 m ahead. He then turned left and moving a distance of 10 m, turned to his left again and walked 40 m. He then turned to the left and walked 5 m. Finally he turned to his left. In which direction is he walking now?
    (a) North   (b) South
    (c) East   (d) South-West

14. A rat runs towards East and turns right twice, runs and then turns to left, runs and then turns left, runs and finally turns left and runs. Now, in which direction is the rat running now?
    (a) East   (b) West
    (c) North   (d) South

15. Suraj walks 10 m towards South. Turning to the left, he walks 20 m and then turns right. After moving a distance of 20 m, he turns right and walks another 20 m. Finally, he turns right and moves a distance of 10 m. How far and in which direction is he from the starting point?
    (a) 10 m North   (b) 20 m South
    (c) 20 m North   (d) 10 m South

16. I am facing South. I turn right and walk 20 m. Then I turn right again and walk 10 m. Then I turn left and walk 10 m and then turning right walk 20 m. Then I turn right again and walk 60 m. In which direction am I from the starting point?
    (a) North
    (b) North-West
    (c) East
    (d) North-East

17. Anil went 15 Km West from his house, then turned left and walked 20 Km. He then turned East and walked 25 Km and finally turning left covered 20 Km. How far was he from his house?
    (a) 5 Km   (b) 10 Km
    (c) 40 Km   (d) 80 Km

18. Rashmi walks 20 m North. Then she turns right and walks 30 m. Then she turns right and walks 35 m. Then she turns left and walks 15 m. Then she again turns left and walks 15 m. In which direction and how many metres away is she from her original position?
    (a) 15 m West   (b) 30 m East
    (c) 30 m West   (d) 45 m East

19. The door of Adi's house faces East. From the back of his house, he walks straight 50 metres, then turns to the right and walks 50 metres again. Finally, he turns towards left and stops after walking 25 m. Now, Adi is in which direction from the starting point?
    (a) South-East   (b) North-East
    (c) South-West   (d) North-West

20. If A is to the south of B and C is to the east of B, in what direction is A with respect to C?

(a) North-East   (b) North-West

(c) South-East   (d) South-West

21. P, Q, R and S are playing a game of carom. P, R and S, Q are partners. S is to the right of R who is facing West. Then, Q is facing

(a) North   (b) South

(c) East   (d) West

22. The post office is to the east of the school while my house is to the south of the school. The market is to the north of the post office. If the distance of the market from the post office is equal to the distance of my house from the school, then in which direction is the market with respect to my school?

(a) North   (b) East

(c) North-East   (d) South-West

23. A watch reads 4.30. If the minute hand points east, in what direction does the hour hand point?

(a) North   (b) North-West

(c) South-East   (d) North-East

24. If you are facing north-east and move 10 m forward, turn left and move 7.5 m, then you are

(a) North of your initial position

(b) South of you initial position

(c) East of your initial position

(d) 12 m from your initial position

25. One morning after sunrise, Suresh and Ramesh were standing on the lawn with their backs towards each other. Suresh's shadow fell exactly towards his left hand side. Which direction was Ramesh facing?

(a) East   (b) West

(c) North   (d) South

Learning Objectives : In this chapter, students will learn about:
- ✓ Mirror Images of Capital and Small Letters
- ✓ Water Images of Capital and Small Letters
- ✓ Mirror and Water Images of Numbers

CHAPTER SUMMARY

Here, you will understand the concept of mirror and water images.

Mirror images

The image of an object, as seen in a mirror, is called its mirror reflection or mirror image. Mirror image is also known as Horizontal Plane.

Lateral inversion

In such an image, the right side of the object appears on the left side and vice-versa. A mirror-image is therefore said to be laterally inverted and the phenomenon is called Lateral Inversion.

Mirror images of capital letters

Letter	Mirror Image	Letter	Mirror Image	Letter	Mirror Image
A	A	J	ᒐ	S	Ƨ
B	ᙠ	K	ꓘ	T	T
C	Ɔ	L	⅃	U	U
D	ᗡ	M	M	V	V
E	Ǝ	N	И	W	W
F	ꟻ	O	O	X	X
G	Ɔ	P	ꟼ	Y	Y
H	H	Q	Ọ	Z	Ƨ
I	I	R	Я	-	-

Mirror images of small letters

Letter	Mirror Image	Letter	Mirror Image	Letter	Mirror Image
a	ɒ	j	ꞁ	s	ƨ
b	d	k	ʞ	t	ƚ
c	ɔ	l	l	u	u
d	b	m	m	v	v
e	ɘ	n	n	w	w
f	ꟻ	o	o	x	x
g	ϱ	p	q	y	γ
h	ʜ	q	p	z	ƨ
i	i	r	ꞁ	-	-

Mirror images of numbers

Letter	Mirror Image	Letter	Mirror Image	Letter	Mirror Image
1	Ɩ	4	ᔭ	7	ᒣ
2	Ƨ	5	Ƽ	8	8
3	Ɛ	6	ə	9	e

Water Images

The reflection of an object, as seen on the surface of water, is called its water image. It is the inverted image obtained by turning the object upside down.

Water images of Capital Letters

Letter	Water Image	Letter	Water Image	Letter	Water Image
A	∀	J	˥	S	Ƨ
B	B	K	K	T	⊥
C	C	L	Γ	U	∩
D	D	M	W	V	Λ
E	E	N	И	W	M
F	Ŀ	O	O	X	X
G	C	P	b	Y	⅄
H	H	Q	Ό	Z	Σ
I	I	R	ᴚ	-	-

Water images of Small Letters

Letter	Water Image	Letter	Water Image	Letter	Water Image
a	ɐ	j	ɾ	s	ƨ
b	p	k	ʞ	t	ʇ
c	c	l	l	u	n
d	q	m	ɯ	v	ʌ
e	ə	n	u	w	ʍ
f	ɟ	o	o	x	x
g	ƃ	p	b	y	ʎ
h	ɥ	q	d	z	Σ
I	I	r	ʟ	-	-

Water images of Numbers

Letter	Water Image	Letter	Water Image	Letter	Water Image
1	⇂	4	ᔭ	7	⅃
2	Ƨ	5	ᘕ	8	8
3	3	6	e	9	∂

1. Choose the correct mirror image of the given figure (X) from amongst the four alternatives.

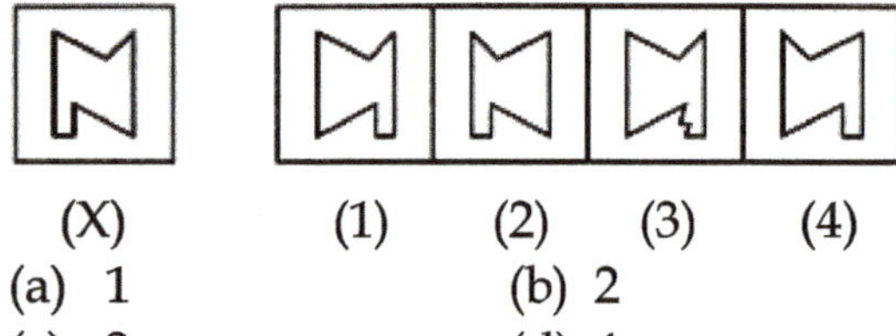

(X) (1) (2) (3) (4)
(a) 1   (b) 2
(c) 3   (d) 4

2. Choose the correct mirror image of the given figure (X) from amongst the four alternatives.

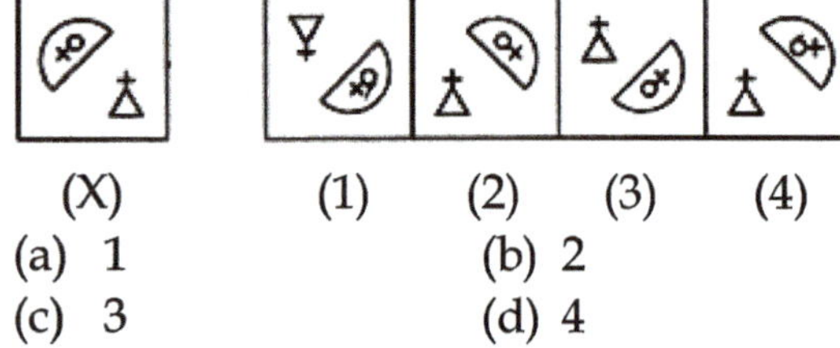

(X) (1) (2) (3) (4)
(a) 1   (b) 2
(c) 3   (d) 4

3. Choose the correct mirror image of the given figure (X) from amongst the four alternatives.

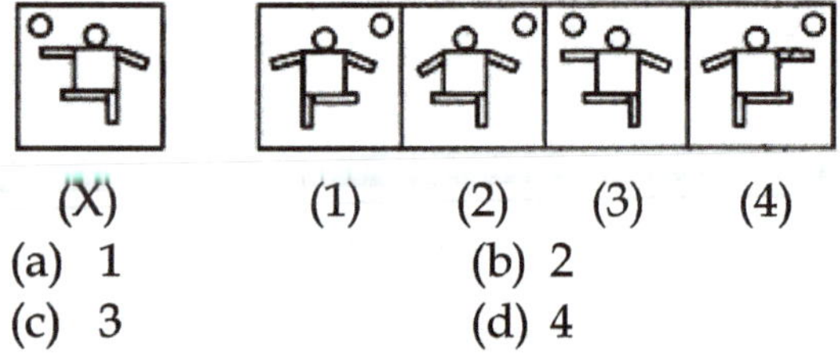

(X) (1) (2) (3) (4)
(a) 1   (b) 2
(c) 3   (d) 4

4. Choose the correct mirror image of the given figure (X) from amongst the four alternatives.

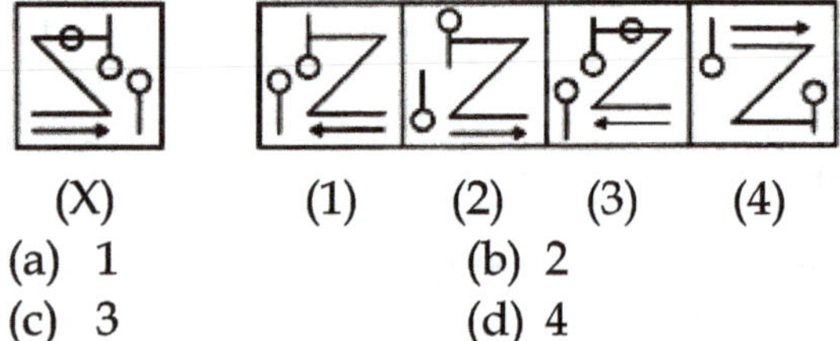

(X) (1) (2) (3) (4)
(a) 1   (b) 2
(c) 3   (d) 4

5. Choose the correct mirror image of the given figure (X) from amongst the four alternatives.

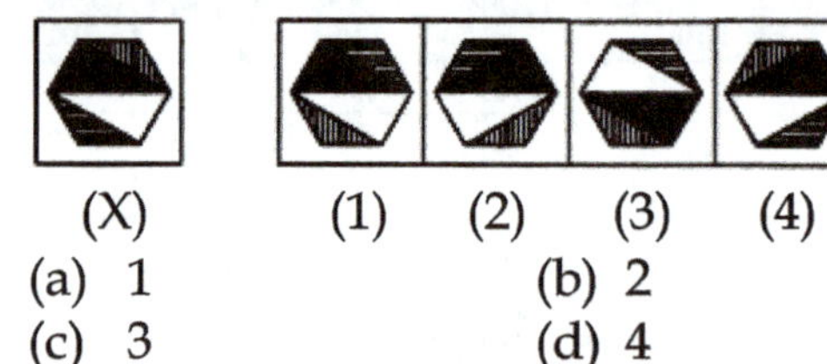

(X) (1) (2) (3) (4)
(a) 1   (b) 2
(c) 3   (d) 4

6. Choose the correct mirror image of the given figure (X) from amongst the four alternatives.

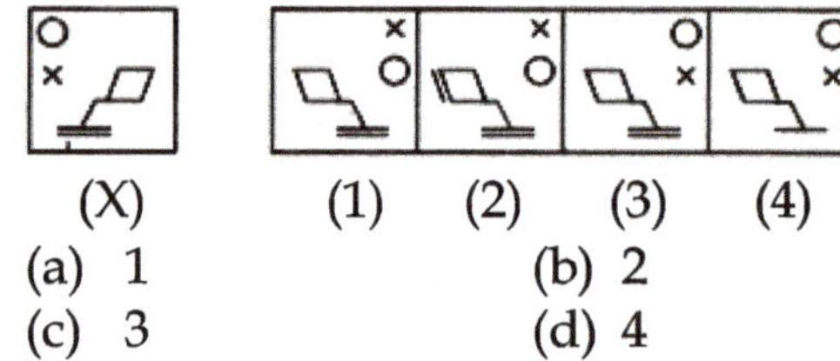

(X) (1) (2) (3) (4)
(a) 1   (b) 2
(c) 3   (d) 4

7. Choose the correct mirror image of the given figure (X) from amongst the four alternatives.

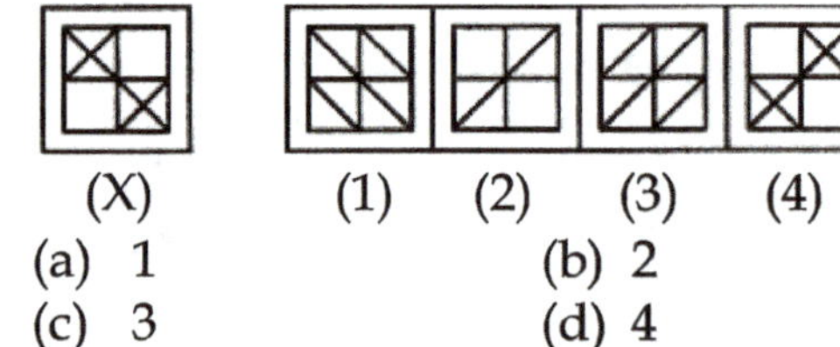

(X) (1) (2) (3) (4)
(a) 1   (b) 2
(c) 3   (d) 4

8. Choose the correct mirror image of the given figure (X) from amongst the four alternatives.

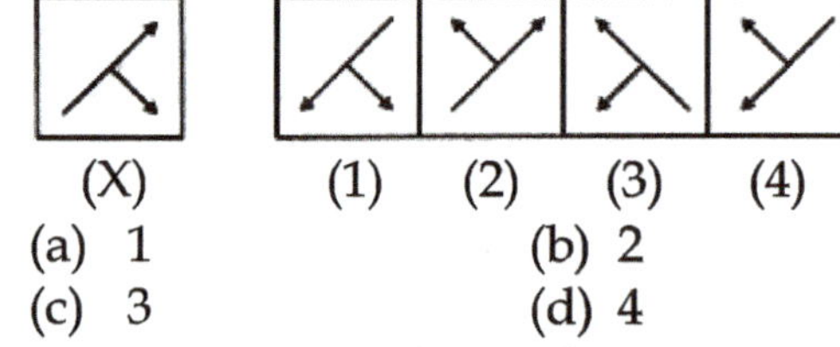

(X) (1) (2) (3) (4)
(a) 1   (b) 2
(c) 3   (d) 4

9. Choose the correct mirror image of the given figure (X) from amongst the four alternatives.

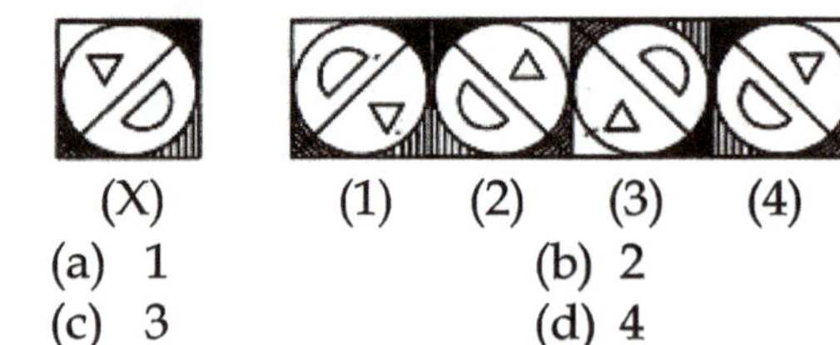

(X) (1) (2) (3) (4)
(a) 1   (b) 2
(c) 3   (d) 4

10. Choose the correct mirror image of the given figure (X) from amongst the four alternatives.

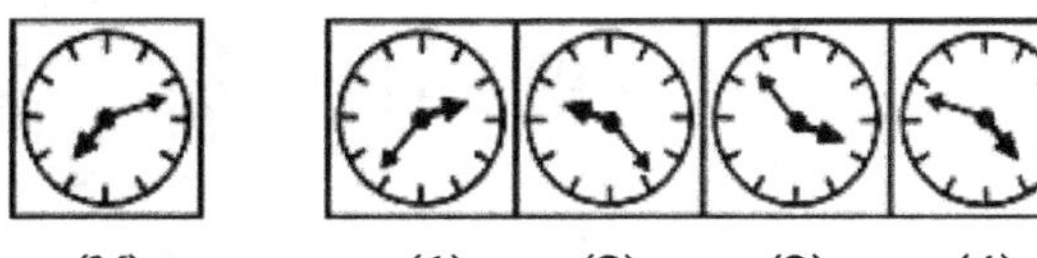

   (X)   (1)   (2)   (3)   (4)

(a) 1   (b) 2
(c) 3   (d) 4

11. Choose the correct mirror image of the given figure (X) from amongst the four alternatives.

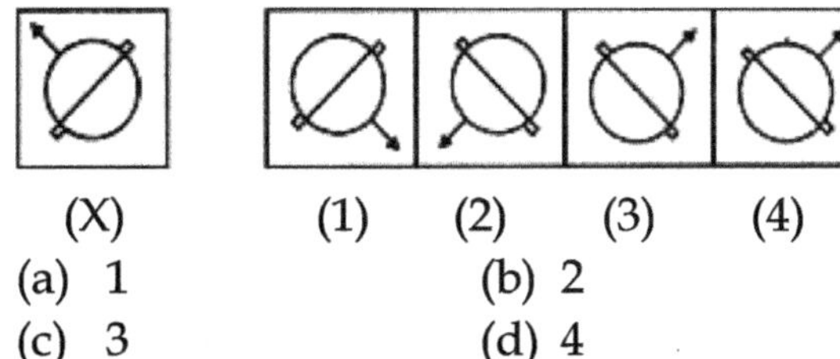

   (X)   (1)   (2)   (3)   (4)

(a) 1   (b) 2
(c) 3   (d) 4

12. Choose the correct mirror image of the given figure (X) from amongst the four alternatives.

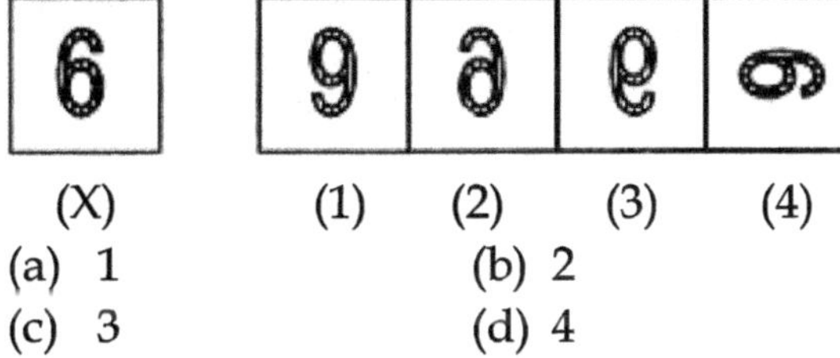

   (X)   (1)   (2)   (3)   (4)

(a) 1   (b) 2
(c) 3   (d) 4

13. Choose the correct mirror image of the given figure (X) from amongst the four alternatives.

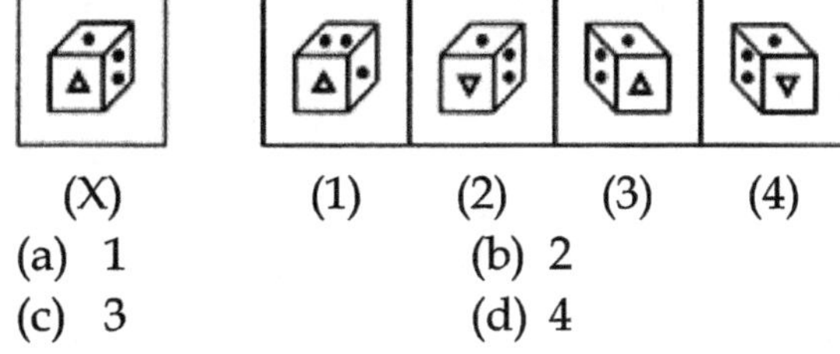

   (X)   (1)   (2)   (3)   (4)

(a) 1   (b) 2
(c) 3   (d) 4

14. Choose the correct mirror image of the given figure (X) from amongst the four alternatives.

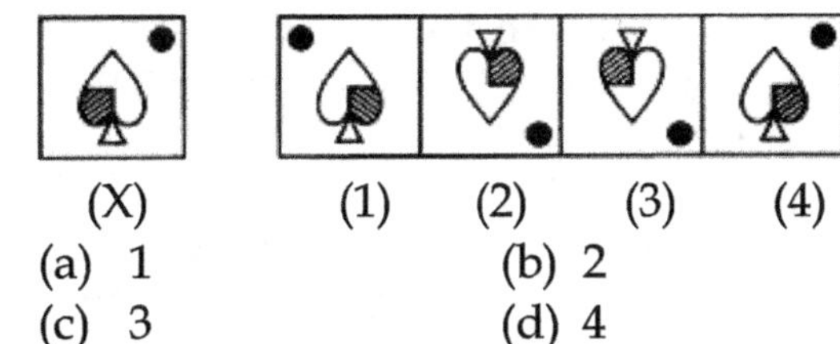

   (X)   (1)   (2)   (3)   (4)

(a) 1   (b) 2
(c) 3   (d) 4

15. Choose the correct mirror image of the given figure (X) from amongst the four alternatives.

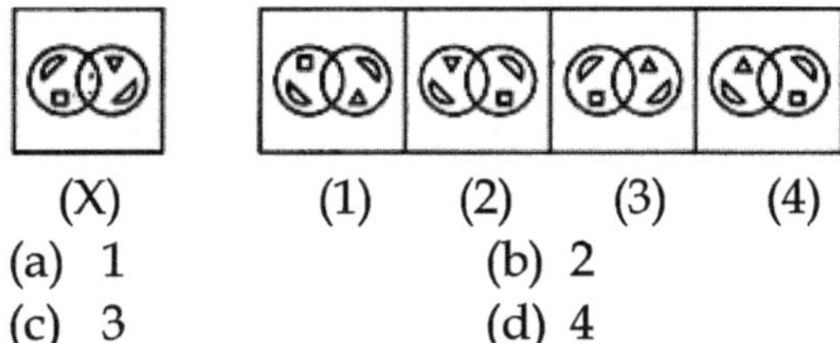

   (X)   (1)   (2)   (3)   (4)

(a) 1   (b) 2
(c) 3   (d) 4

16. Choose the correct mirror image of the given figure (X) from amongst the four alternatives.

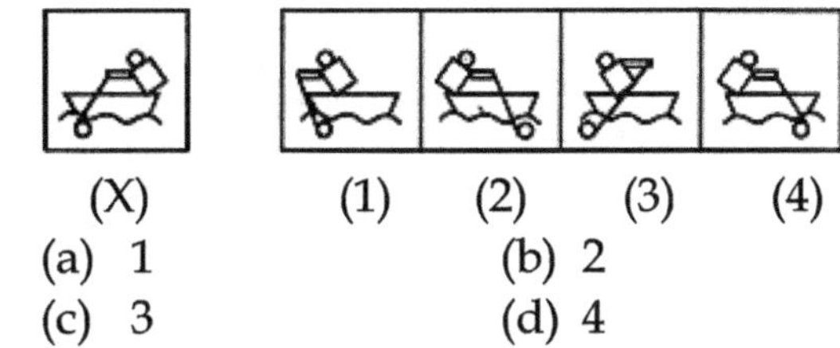

   (X)   (1)   (2)   (3)   (4)

(a) 1   (b) 2
(c) 3   (d) 4

17. Choose the correct mirror image of the given figure (X) from amongst the four alternatives.

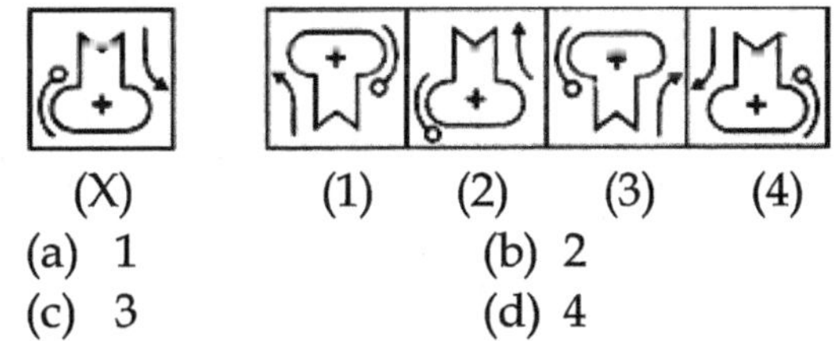

   (X)   (1)   (2)   (3)   (4)

(a) 1   (b) 2
(c) 3   (d) 4

18. Choose the correct mirror image of the given figure (X) from amongst the four alternatives.

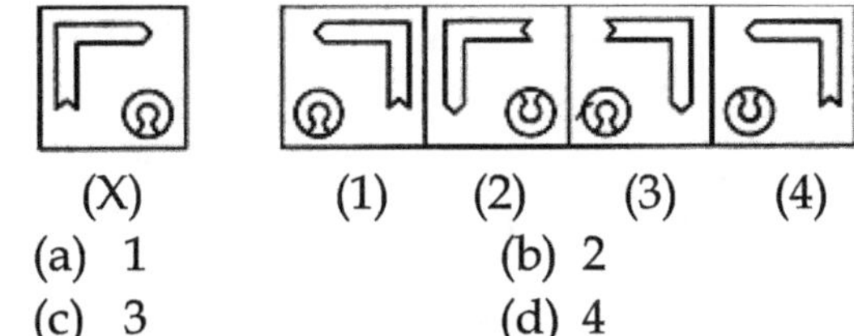

   (X)   (1)   (2)   (3)   (4)

(a) 1   (b) 2
(c) 3   (d) 4

19. Choose the correct mirror image of the given figure (X) from amongst the four alternatives.

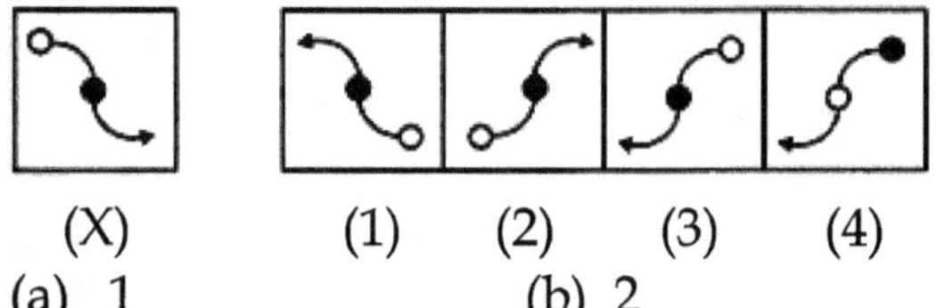

   (X)   (1)   (2)   (3)   (4)

(a) 1   (b) 2

(c) 3   (d) 4

20. Choose the correct mirror image of the given figure (X) from amongst the four alternatives.

   (X)   (1)   (2)   (3)   (4)

(a) 1   (b) 2

(c) 3   (d) 4

Learning Objectives : In this chapter, students will learn about:
- ✓ Geometry
- ✓ Classification of Angles
- ✓ Reflection
- ✓ Labeling Angles
- ✓ Types of Triangle
- ✓ Symmetry

CHAPTER SUMMARY

Geometry

It is the study of angles, lines and their relationship with each other.

Point: Point is represented by a dot on which length, breadth and height cannot be measured.

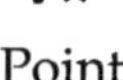

Point

Line: The distance between two points is called a line. It is represented by $\overline{XY}$.

Line

Line segment: A portion of a line having two end points is called a line segment.

Line Segment

Angle: A figure consisting of two rays with common initial point is called an angle.

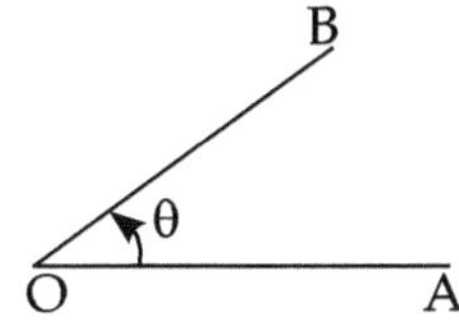

$\theta \rightarrow$ Angle = $\angle$BOA.

It is measured in degrees. *e.g.*, 30°, 45° etc.

Labeling Angles

There are two main ways to label angles:

(i) Give the angle a name, usually a lower-case letter like a or b, or sometimes a Greek letter like α (alpha) or θ (theta).

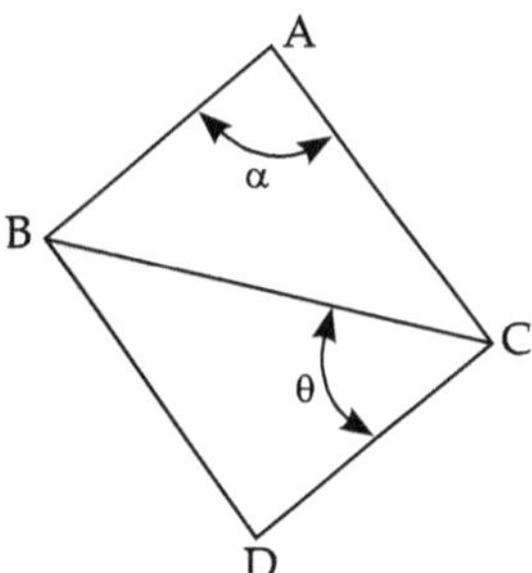

Example: Angle 'α' is $\angle$BAC, and angle 'θ' is $\angle$BCD

(ii) Or by the three letters on the shape that define the angle, with the middle letter being where the angle actually is (its vertex).

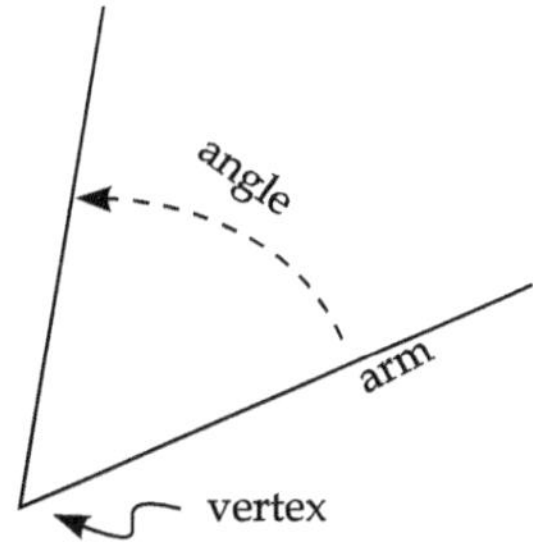

Parts of an Angle

The corner point of an angle is called the Vertex and the two straight sides are called Arms.

The angle is the amount of turn between each arm.

Positive and Negative Angles

When measuring from a line:

- a positive angle goes counter clockwise (opposite direction that clocks go)
- a negative angle goes clockwise

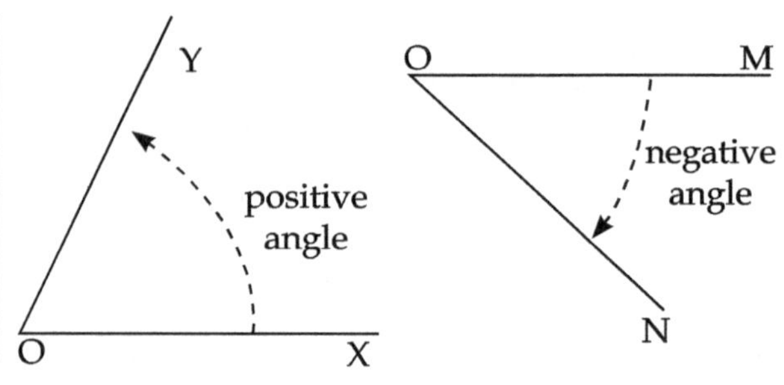

Classification of angles

Type of angle	Description
Acute Angle	an angle measures less than 90°
Right Angle	an angle measures exactly 90°
Obtuse Angle	an angle measures more than 90° but less than 180°
Straight Angle	an angle measures exactly 180°
Reflex Angle	an angle measures more than 180°

Acute angle

An Acute Angle measures less than 90°.

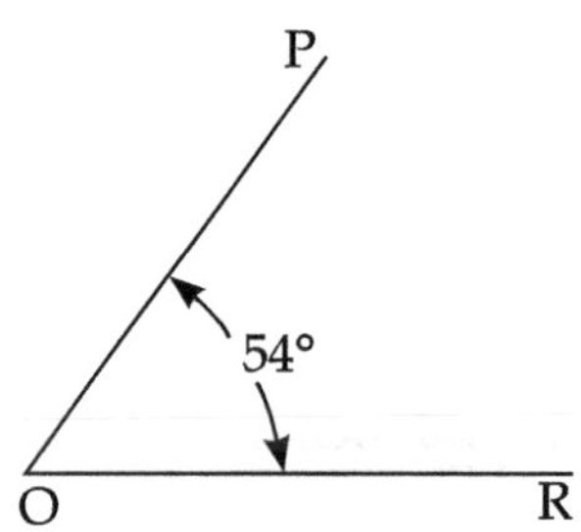

Here ∠POR is an acute angle. All the angles below are acute angles:

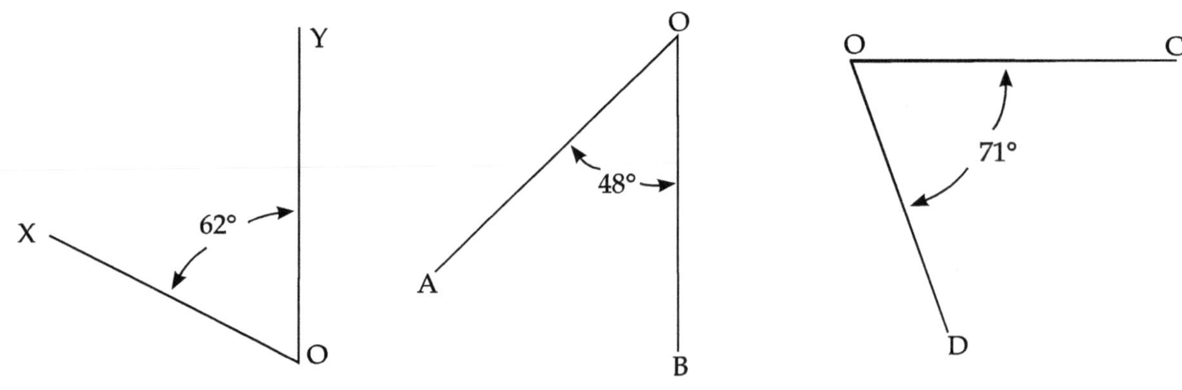

Right angle

A right angle measures 90°

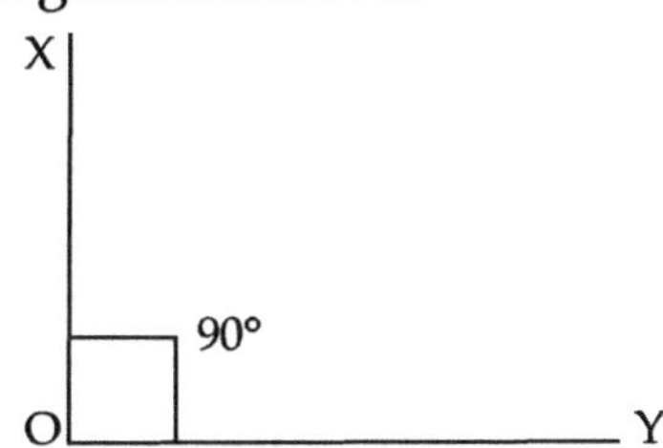

Here ∠XOY is a right angle.

All the angles below are right angles:

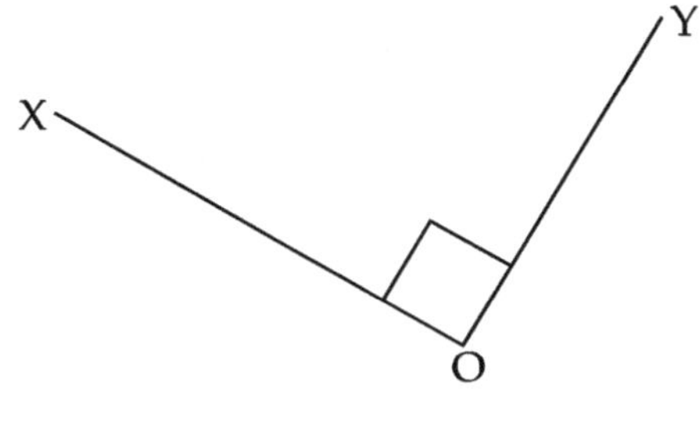

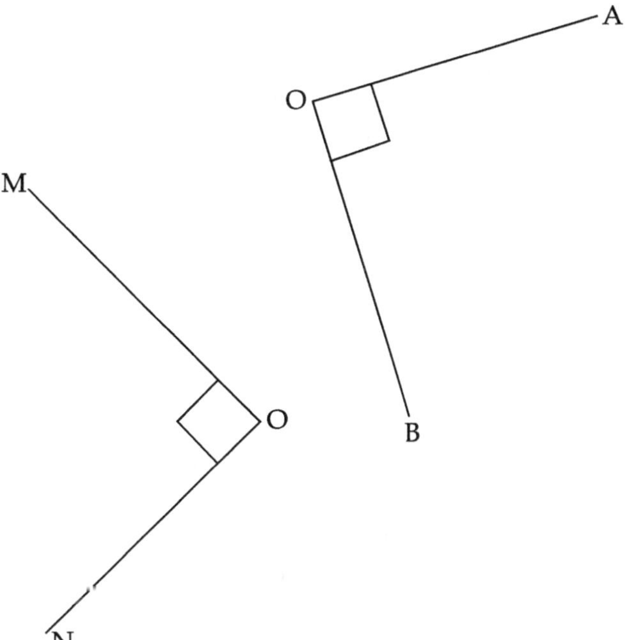

A right angle can be in any orientation or rotation as long as the internal angle is 90°

The intersection of four roads on a traffic signal is an example of right angle.

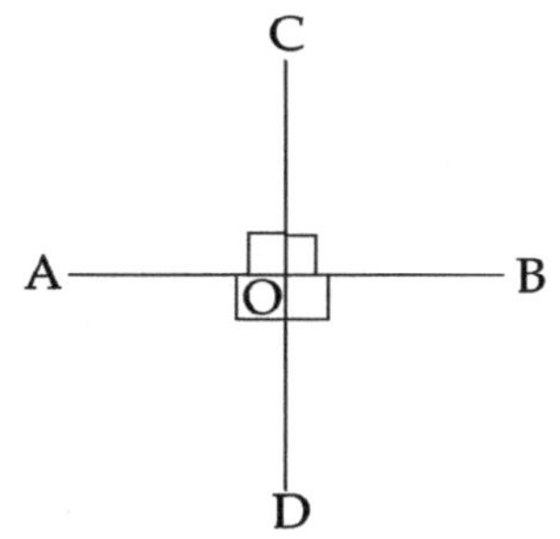

Obtuse angle

An Obtuse Angle is more than 90° but less than 180°.

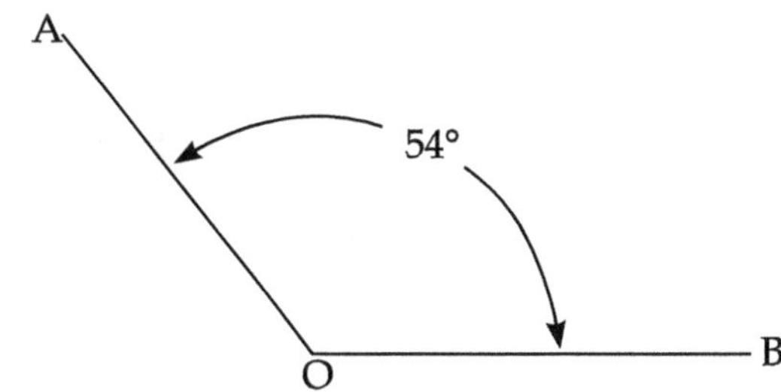

Here ∠AOB is an obtuse angle.

All the angles below are obtuse angles:

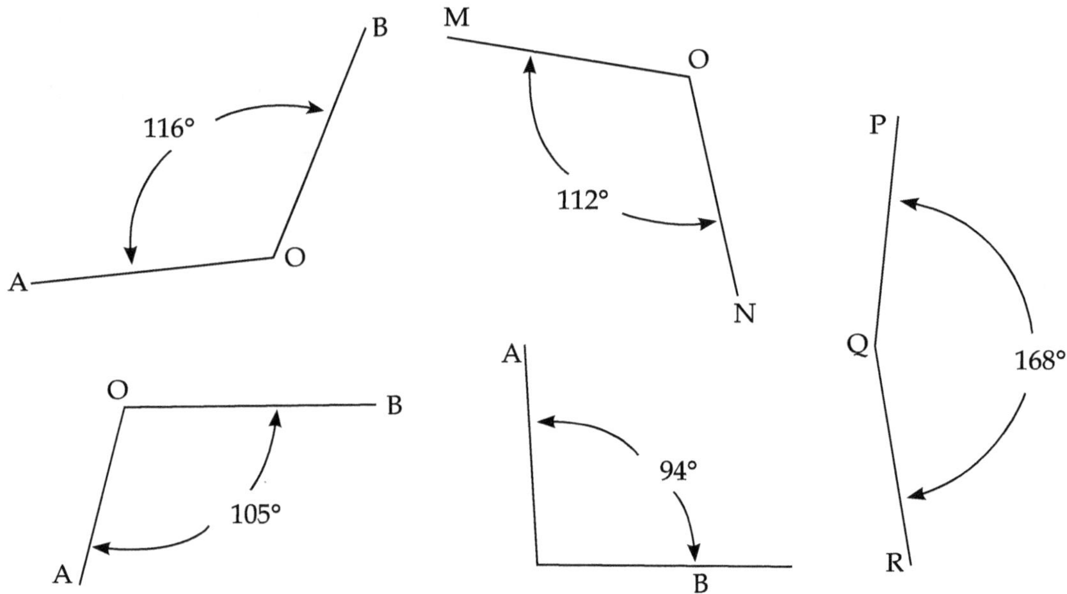

Straight Angle

A straight angle measures 180 degrees.

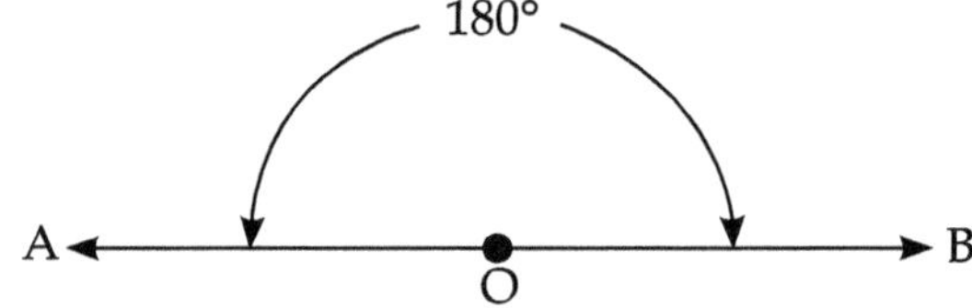

Here ∠AOB is a straight angle.

A straight angle changes the direction to point the opposite way.

All the angles below are straight angles:

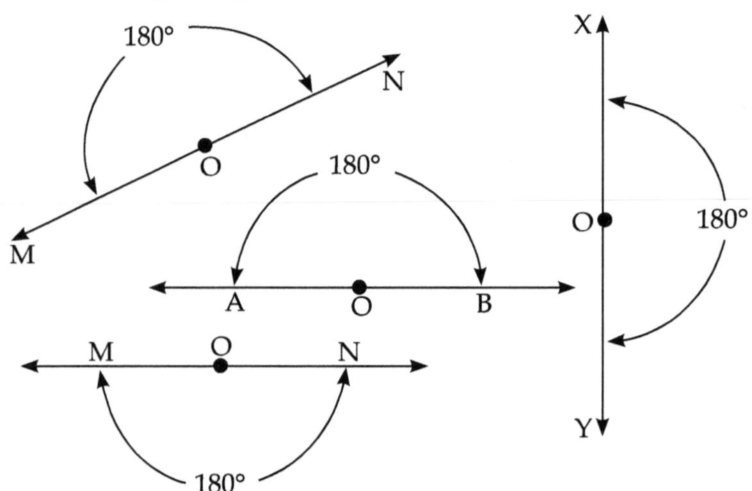

Reflex angle

A Reflex Angle measures more than 180° but less than 360°.

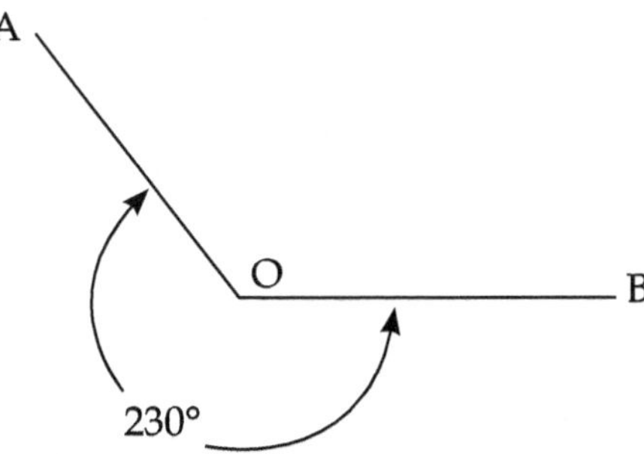

Here ∠AOB is a reflex angle.

All the angles below are reflex angles:

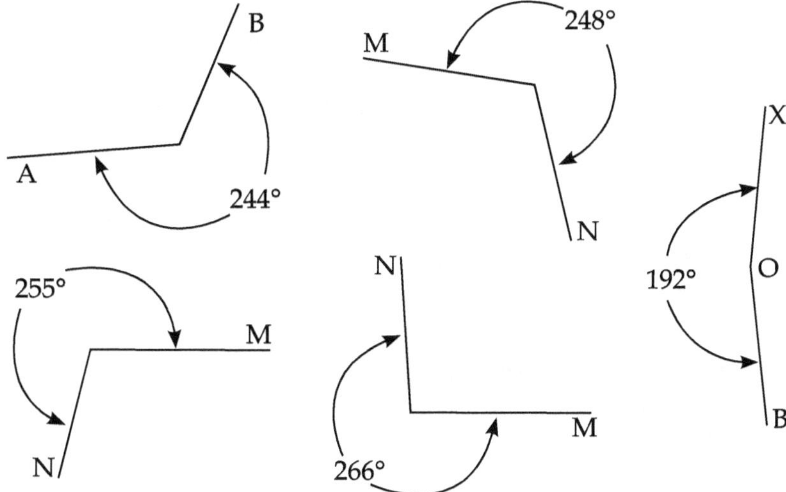

In One Diagram

This diagram might make it easier to remember:

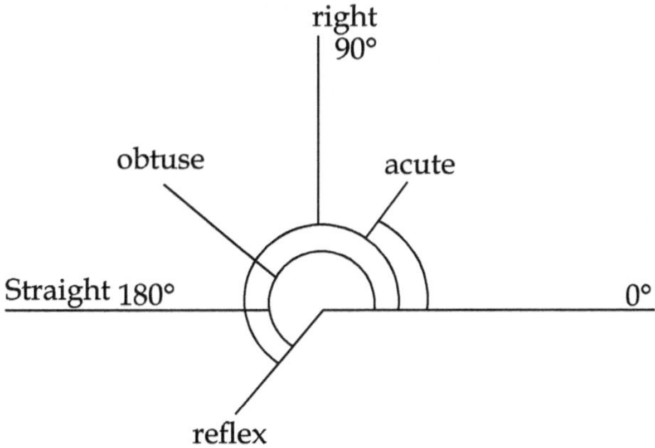

Note: Acute, Obtuse and Reflex are in alphabetical order.

Be careful what you measure.

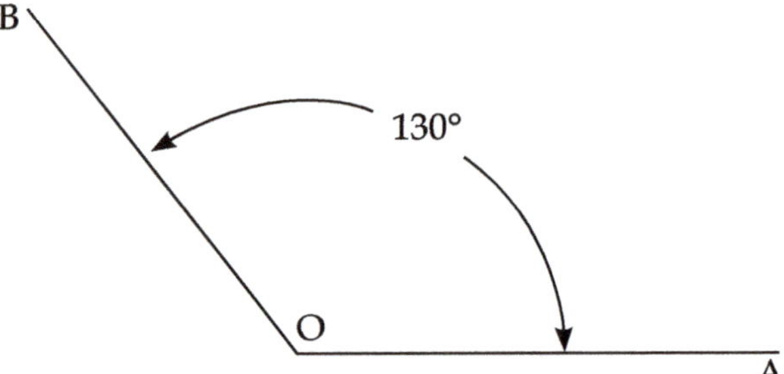

The above angle is an Obtuse Angle

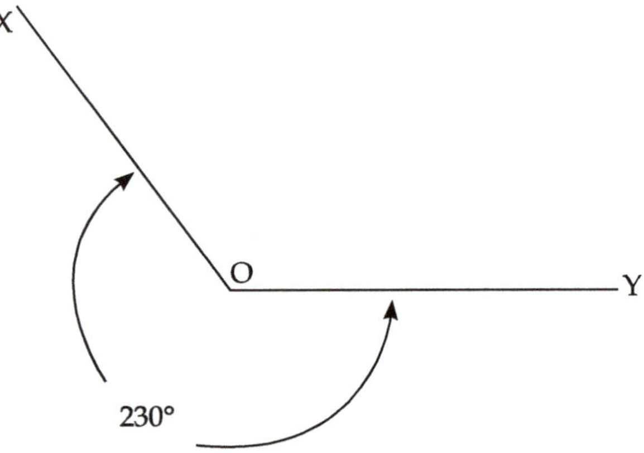

The above angle is a Reflex Angle.

But the lines are the same, so when naming the angles make sure that you know which angle is being asked for!

Triangle

A closed figure consisting of three line segments linked end to end.

Parts of a triangle

(i) Vertex   (ii) Base   (iii) Altitude

(iv) Median

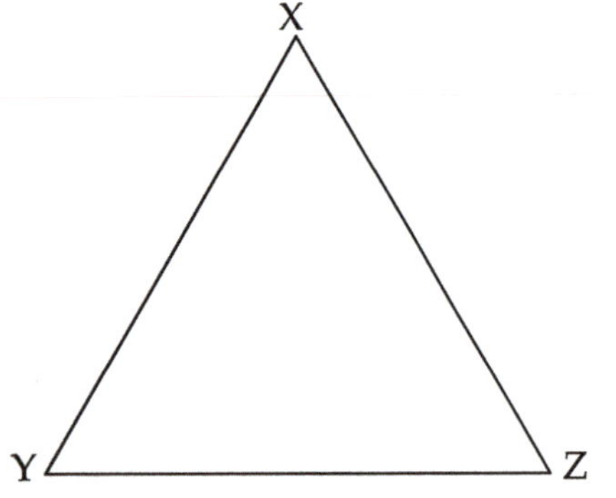

Types of triangle

There are seven types of triangles listed below: Note that a given triangle can be more than one type at the same time.

Scalene Triangle: A triangle where all three sides are different in length.

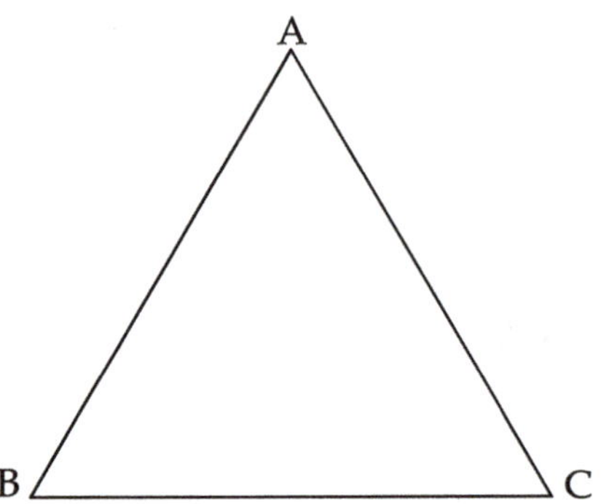

Isosceles Triangle: A triangle which has two of its sides equal in length.

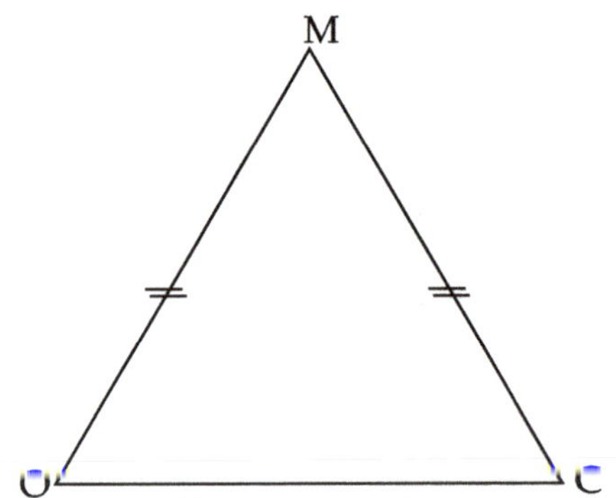

Equilateral Triangle: A triangle which has all three of its sides equal in length.

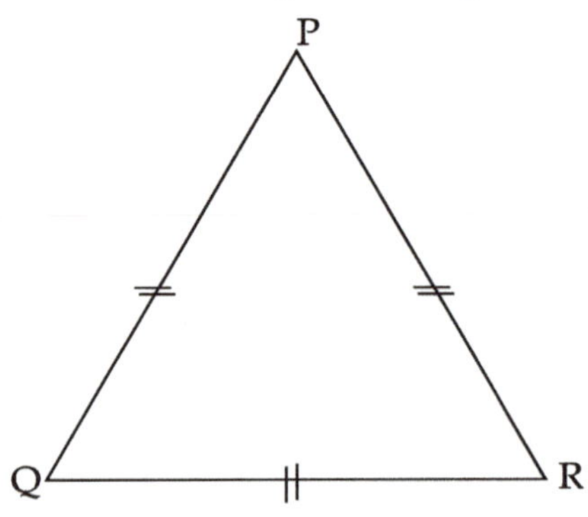

Right Triangle: A triangle where one of its interior angle is a right angle. (90°).

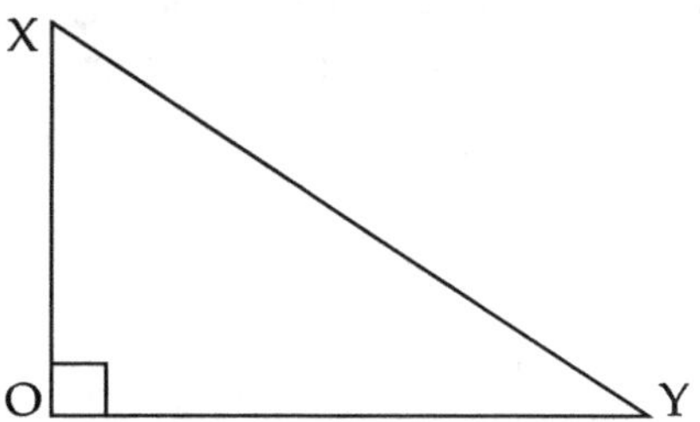

Obtuse Triangle: A triangle where one of the internal angles is greater than 90°.

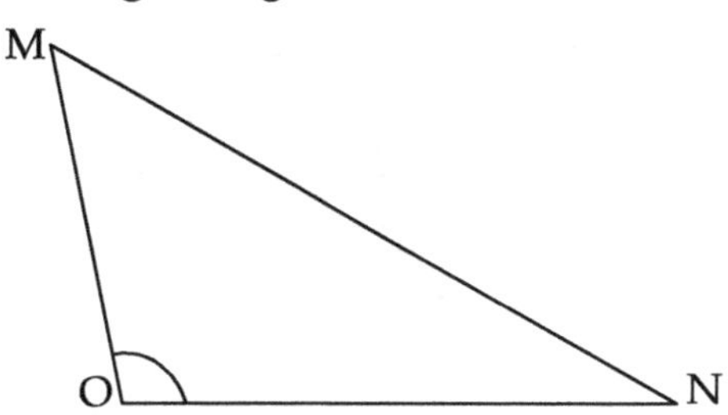

Acute Triangle: A triangle where all three internal angles are acute (less than 90°).

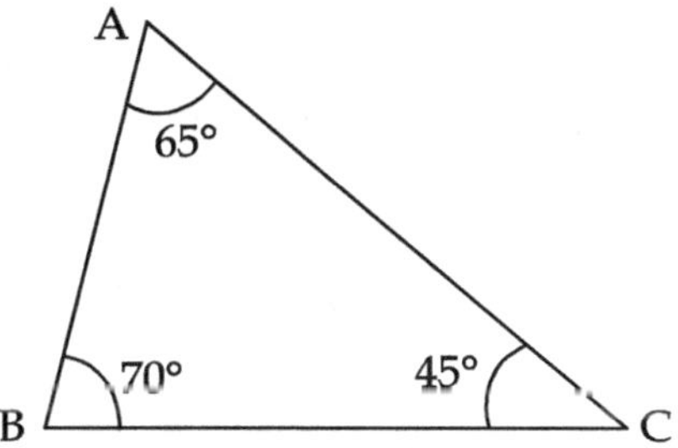

Two types of right angled triangles

There are two types of right angled triangle:

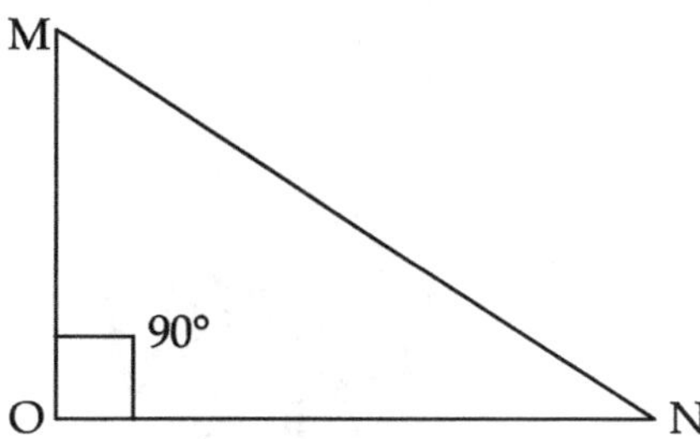

Scalene right angled triangle

- One right angle
- Two other unequal angles
- No equal sides

Isosceles right angled triangle

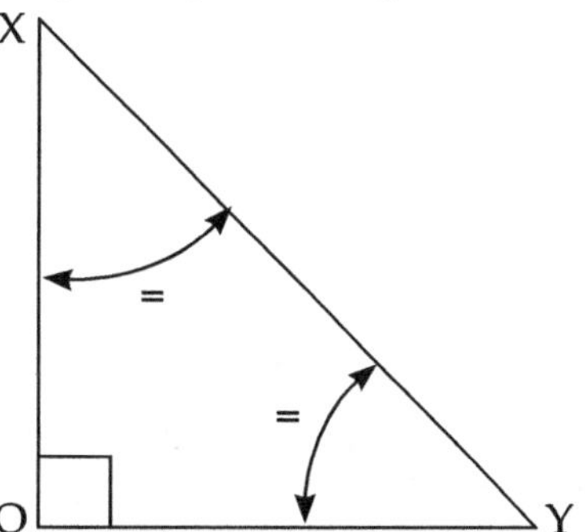

- One right angle
- Two other equal angles always of 45°
- Two equal sides

Example: The 3, 4, 5 Triangle

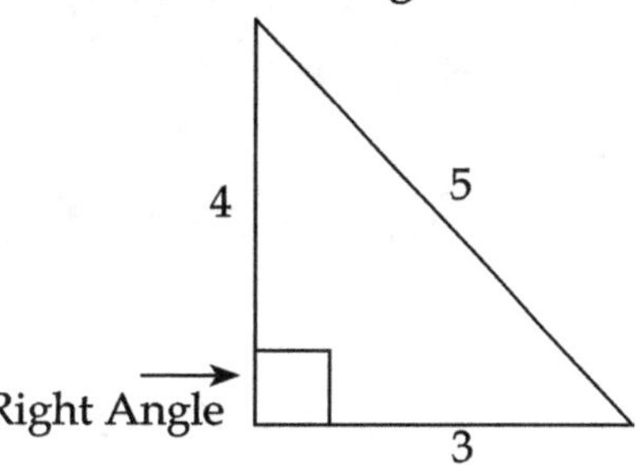

The "3, 4, 5 Triangle" has a right angle in it. It has no equal sides so it is a scalene right angled triangle.

Do you know?

ARCHITECTURE is based on angles and lines. It uses the concept of angles to design buildings.

Reflection

When we see our image in a plane mirror, we find:

(i) The distance of image behind the mirror is same as the distance of object in front by us.

(ii) The line joining the image and object is always perpendicularly bisected by the mirror.

In the below diagram, AB is a plane mirror and P′ is the image of P in the mirror AB. Clearly OP = OP′. and ∠AOP = 90°.

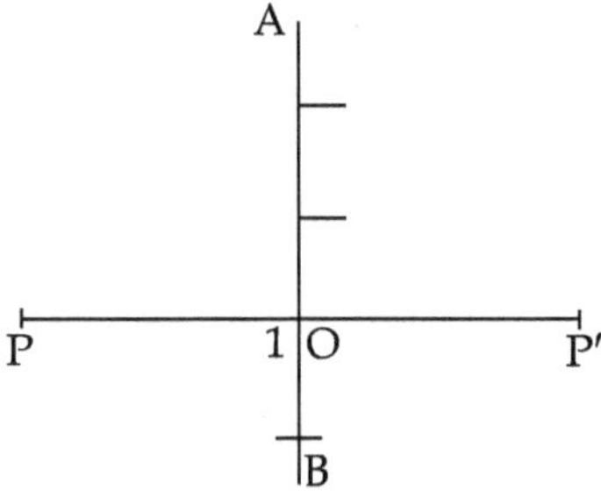

Reflections are everywhere ... in mirrors, glass, and here in a lake.

The reflection has the same size as the original image.

The central line is called the Mirror Line. Every point is the same distance from the central line.

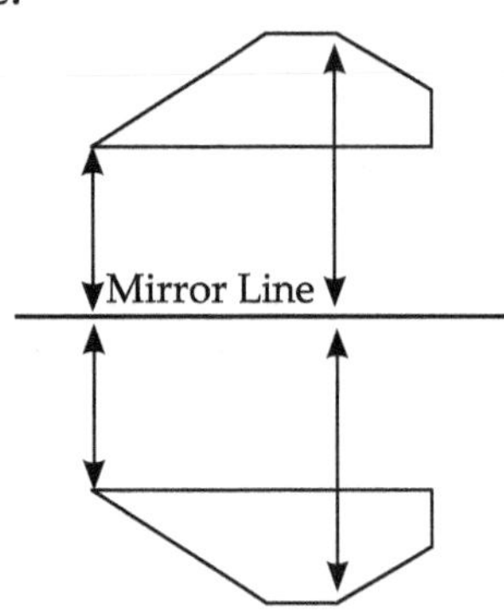

In fact Mirror Lines can be in any direction. Imagine turning the photo at the top in different directions. The reflected image is always the same size; it just faces the other way:

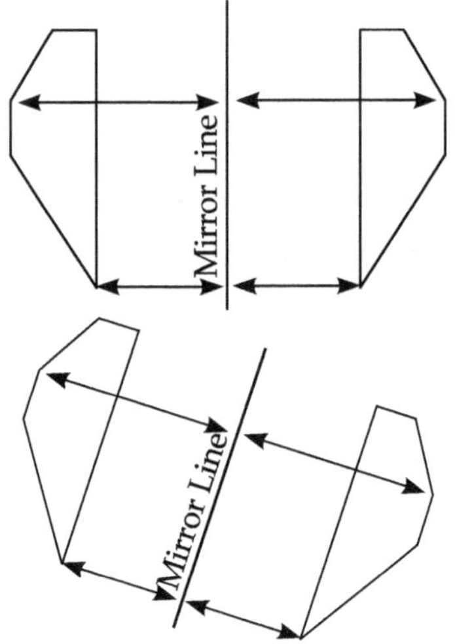

A reflection is a flip over a line.

Rotation

"Rotation" means turning around a center. The distance from the center to any point on the shape stays the same. Every point makes a circle around the center.

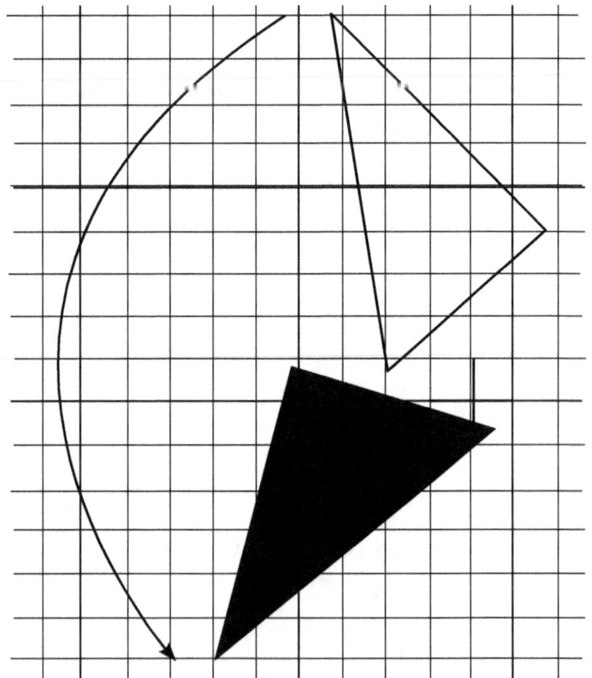

Here a triangle is rotated around the point marked with a "+".

Symmetry

Symmetry is when one shape becomes exactly like another if you flip, slide or turn it. 3D shapes have faces (sides), vertices and edges (corners). A net of a 3D shape is a figure which folds up to form 3D shape.

The exception is the sphere which has no edges or vertices.

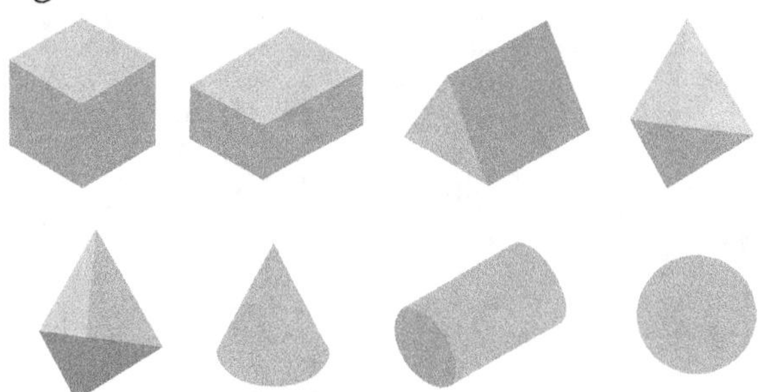

The net of a 3D shape is what it looks like if it is opened out flat. A net can be folded up to make a 3D shape.

There may be several possible nets for one 3D shape.

Here are some examples:

Net of a cube

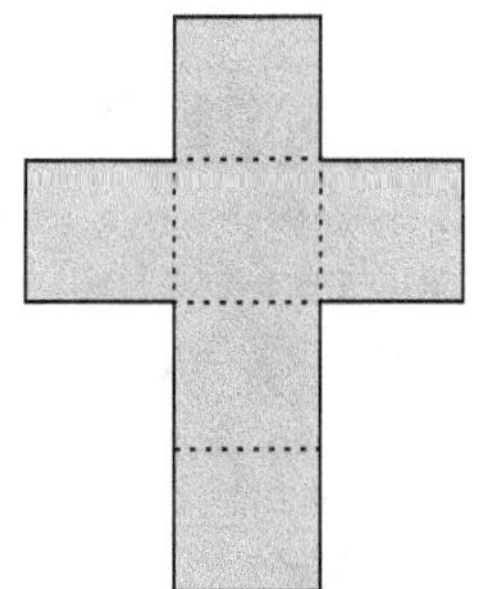

Net of a cuboid

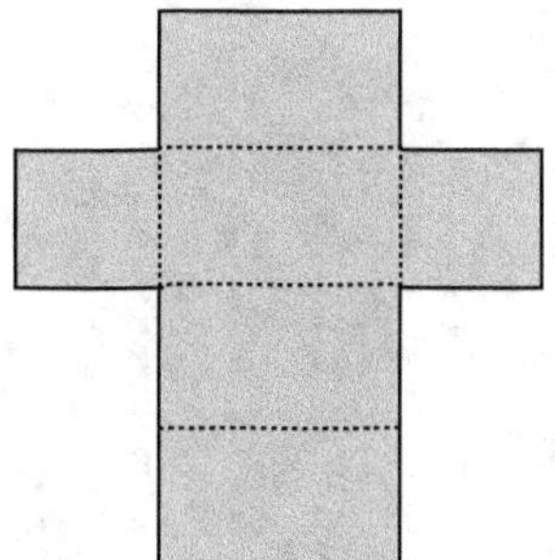

Net of a square-based pyramid

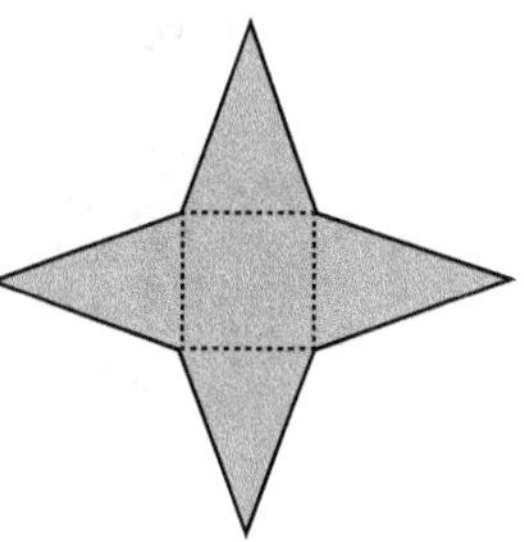

Net of a triangle-based pyramid

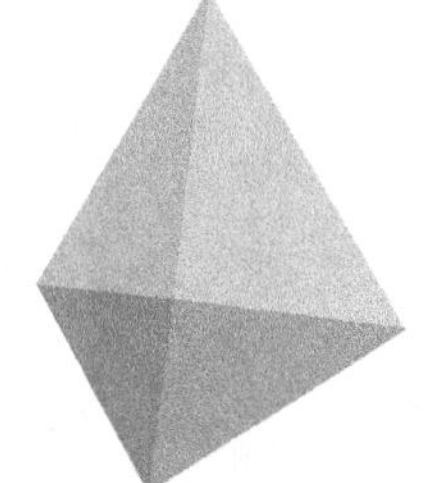
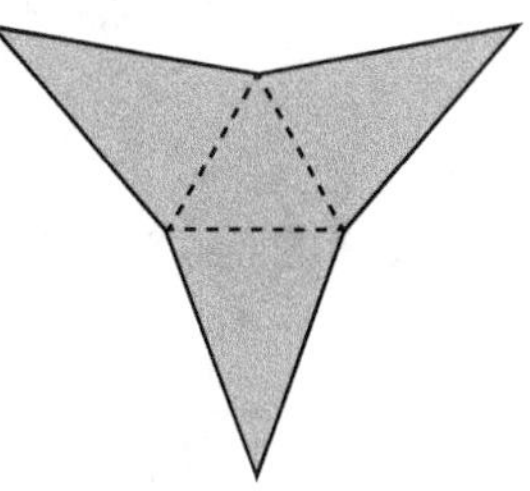

Reflection Symmetry

The simplest symmetry is Reflection Symmetry (sometimes called Line Symmetry or Mirror Symmetry). It is easy to see, because one half is the reflection of the other half.

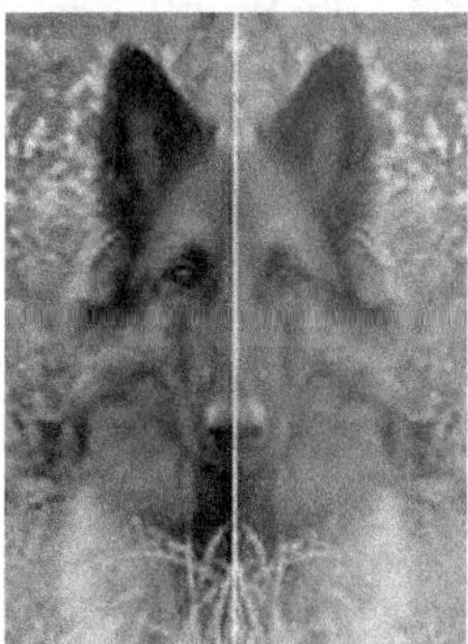

Here a dog has her face made perfectly symmetrical with a bit of photo magic. The white line down the center is the Line of Symmetry.

The Line of Symmetry does not have to be up-down or left-right, it can be in any direction.

Rotational Symmetry

With Rotational Symmetry, the image is rotated (around a central point) so that it appears 2 or more times. How many times it appears is called the Order.

Here are some examples.

Order	Example Shape	Artwork
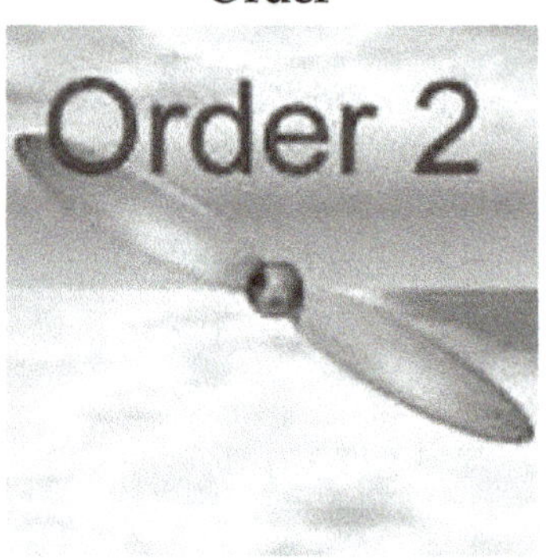	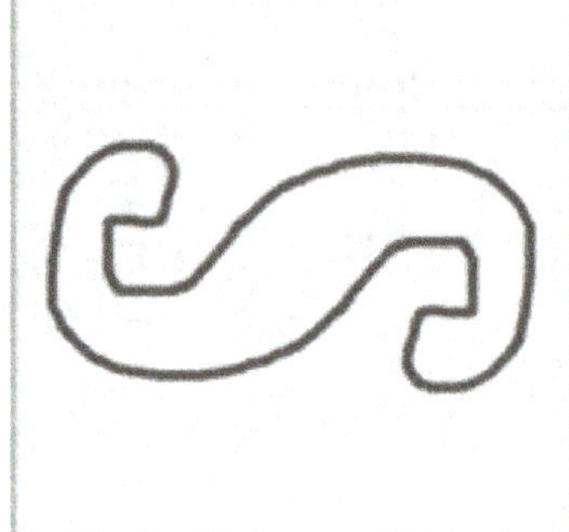	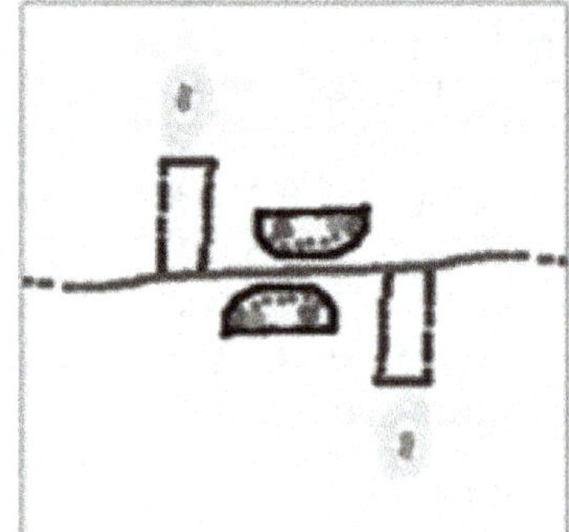
	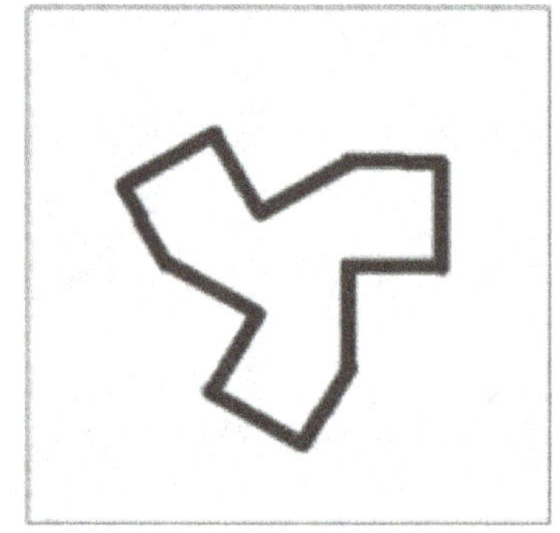	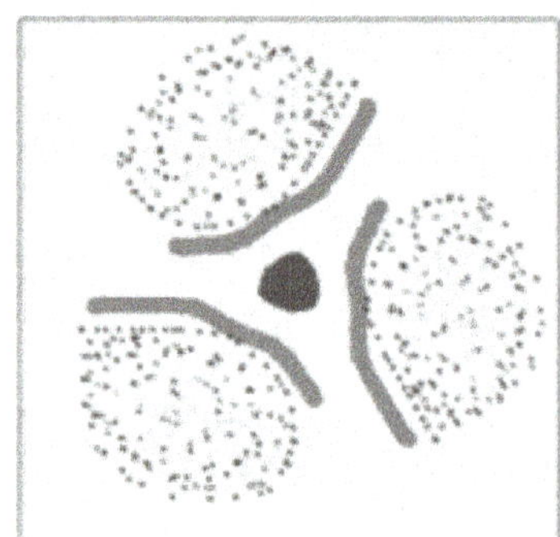

Point Symmetry

Point Symmetry is when every part has a matching part:

- ■ The same distance from the central point
- ■ But in the opposite direction

It is also the same as "Rotational Symmetry of Order 2" above

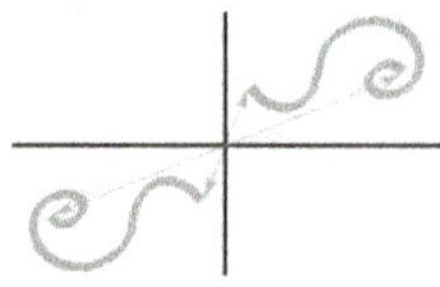

Do you know?

The line of symmetry divides the objects in such a way that it forms two parts that are mirror images of each other.

- ➡ Point is represented by a dot on which length, breadth and height cannot be measured.
- ➡ The distance between two points is called a line.
- ➡ The corner point of an angle is called the vertex and the two straight sides are called arms.
- ➡ Symmetry is when one shape becomes exactly like another if you flip, slide or turn it.
- ➡ With Rotational Symmetry, the image is rotated (around a central point) so that it appears 2 or more times.

1. The angle 89° is:
   - (a) Acute
   - (b) Right
   - (c) Obtuse
   - (d) Reflex

2. The angle 234° is:
   - (a) Acute
   - (b) Obtuse
   - (c) Straight
   - (d) Reflex

3. The angle 98° is:
   - (a) Acute
   - (b) Right
   - (c) Obtuse
   - (d) Reflex

4. Which is closest to the size of angle AOB?

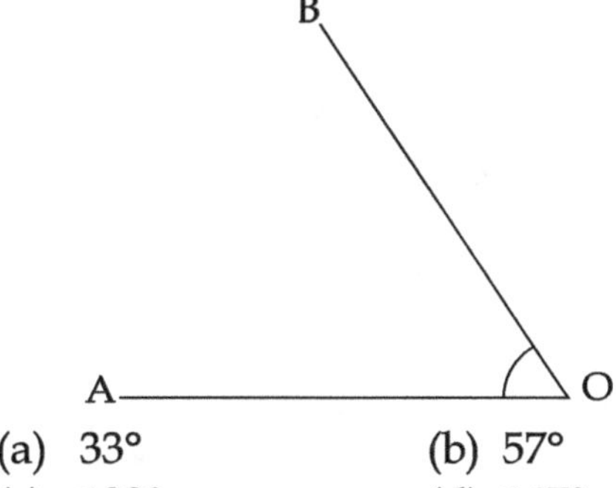

   - (a) 33°
   - (b) 57°
   - (c) 123°
   - (d) 147°

5. Which is closest to the size of angle COD?

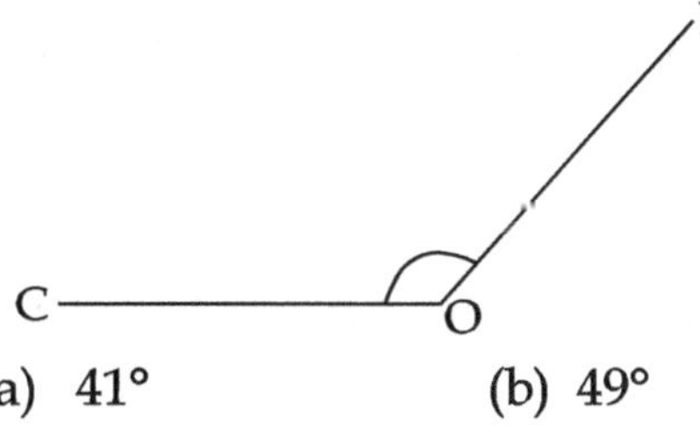

   - (a) 41°
   - (b) 49°
   - (c) 131°
   - (d) 169°

6. Which is closest to the size of reflex angle FOE?

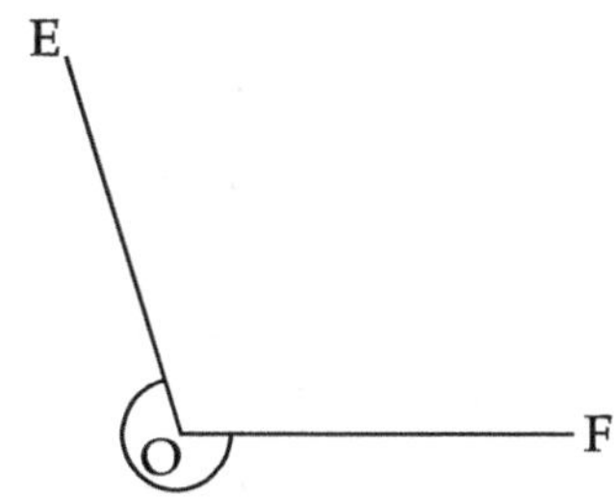

   - (a) 106°
   - (b) 164°
   - (c) 254°
   - (d) 286°

7. For the angle shown in the diagram, the arrow points to its:

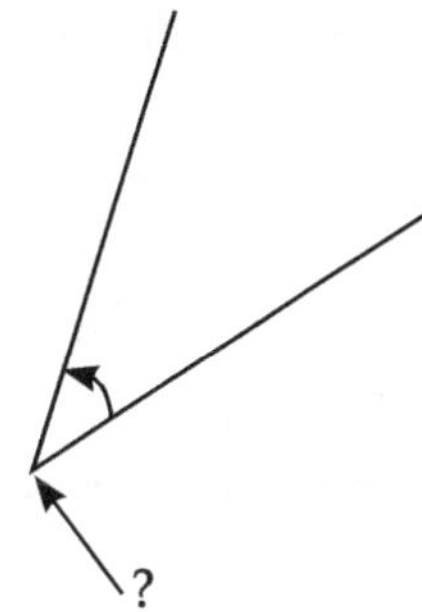

   - (a) arm
   - (b) corner
   - (c) vertex
   - (d) bend

8. By using the three letters on the shape that define the angle, angle α is written as:

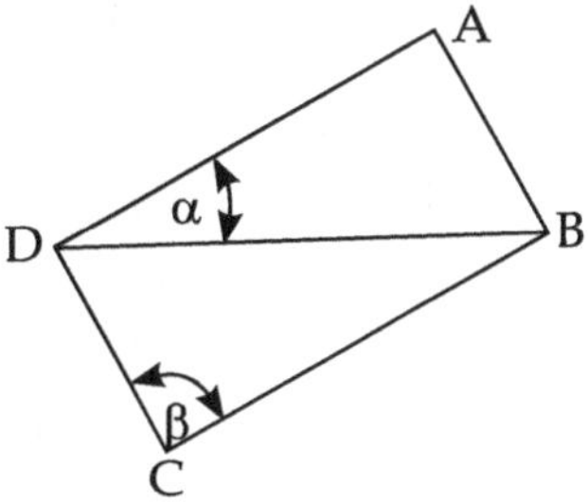

   - (a) ∠ABD
   - (b) ∠ADB
   - (c) ∠BAD
   - (d) ∠BDC

9. By using the three letters on the shape that define the angle, angle β is written as:

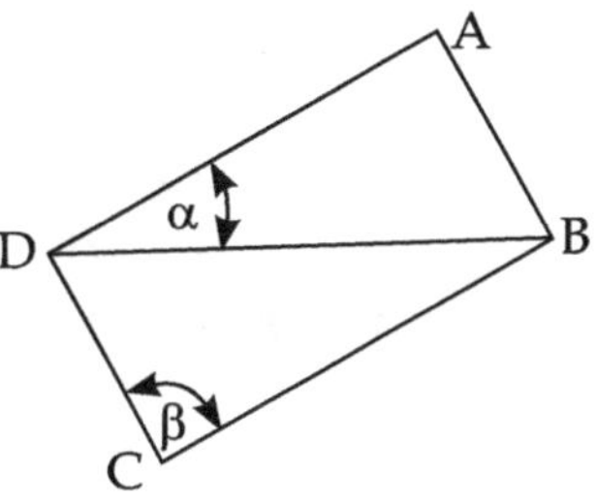

   - (a) ∠DCB
   - (b) ∠BDC
   - (c) ∠CBD
   - (d) ∠ACB

10. If two acute angles are added together, which of the following is NOT possible for their sum:
   - (a) Acute
   - (b) Right
   - (c) Obtuse
   - (d) Straight

11. Which one of the following angles is not acute?

(a) 79°   (b) 89°
(c) 91°   (d) 1°

12. Which one of the following angles is acute?

(a) Half a right angle
(b) A right angle
(c) One and a half right angles
(d) Two right angles

13. How many acute angles are there in the diagram?

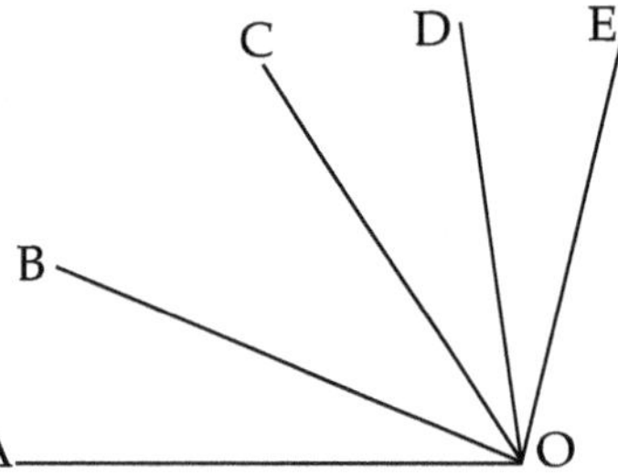

(Think of all possibilities.)

(a) 10   (b) 9
(c) 7   (d) 4

14. How many acute angles are there in this pentagram?

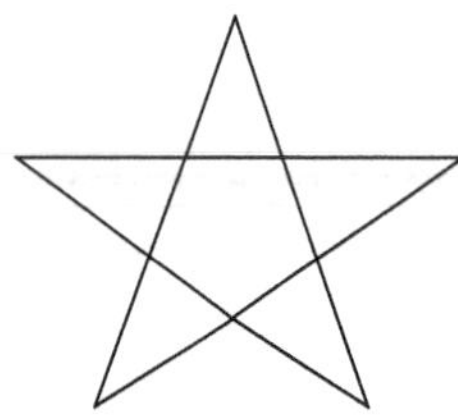

(a) 5   (b) 10
(c) 15   (d) 20

15. How many acute angles are there in the diagram?

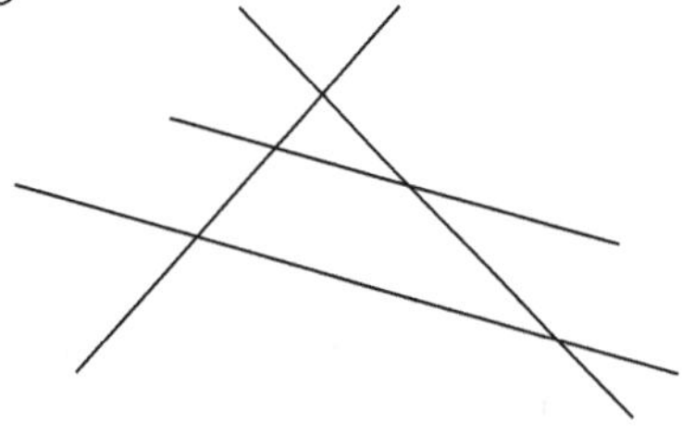

(a) 5   (b) 8
(c) 9   (d) 10

16. How many acute angles are there in the diagram?

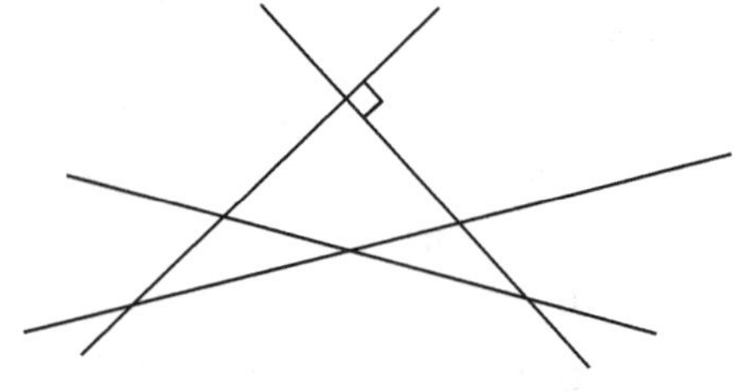

(a) 5   (b) 10
(c) 12   (d) 14

17. How many right angles are there in the diagram?

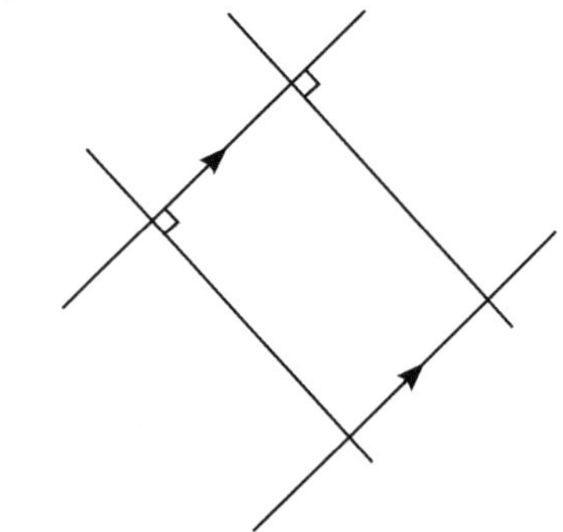

(a) 2   (b) 4
(c) 8   (d) 16

18. How many right angles make two full rotations?

(a) 4   (b) 6
(c) 8   (d) 10

19. Which one of the following angles is not obtuse?

(a) 91°   (b) 149°
(c) 179°   (d) 182°

20. How many obtuse angles are there in the diagram?

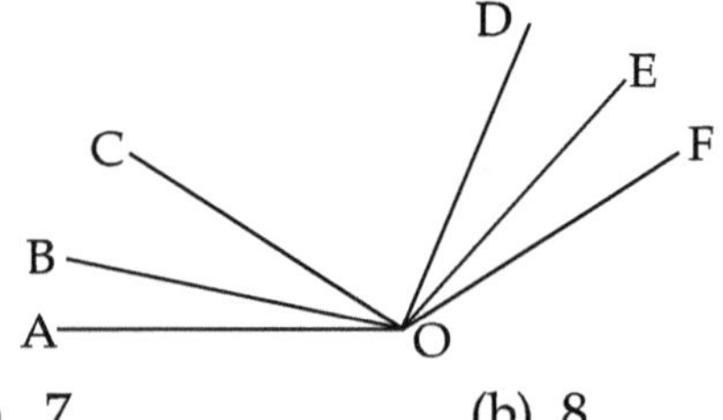

(a) 7   (b) 8
(c) 9   (d) 10

21. How many straight angles are there in three full rotations?

(a) 3   (b) 4
(c) 6   (d) 8

22. Which one of the following angles is not reflex?

(a) 178°   (b) 182°
(c) 270°   (d) 359°

23. Which one of the following angles is reflex?

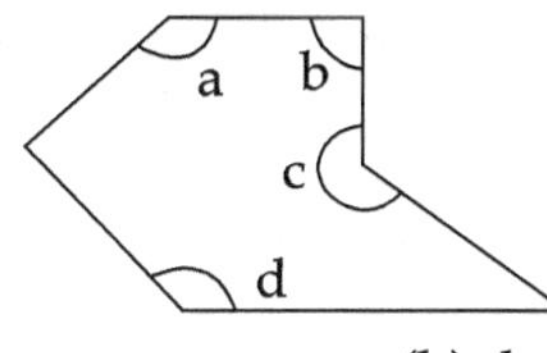

(a) a   (b) b
(c) c   (d) d

24. If angle AOB = 67°, what is the size of reflex angle AOB?

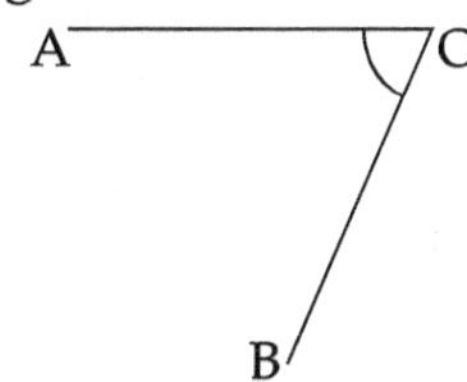

(a) 113°   (b) 247°
(c) 293°   (d) 427°

25. What is the least number of 33° angles you would need to make a reflex angle?

(a) 2   (b) 5
(c) 6   (d) 7

26. Which of the following describes the triangle shown above?

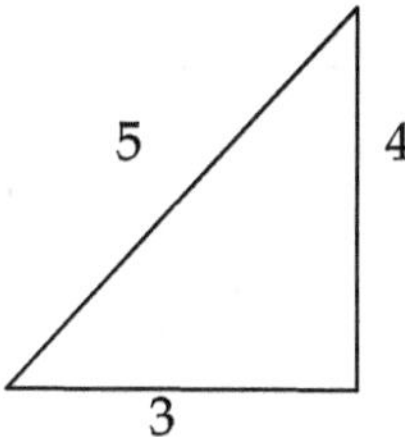

(a) A scalene right angled triangle
(b) A scalene obtuse angled triangle
(c) A scalene acute angled triangle
(d) An isosceles right angled triangle

27. A triangle is isosceles and right angled. Which of the following statements must be false?

(a) The triangle has angles 45°, 45° and 90°
(b) The triangle has two of its sides equal
(c) The triangle has one line of symmetry
(d) The triangle has sides of lengths 3, 4 and 5

28. Shraddha made two copies of the right angled triangle shown and cut them out.

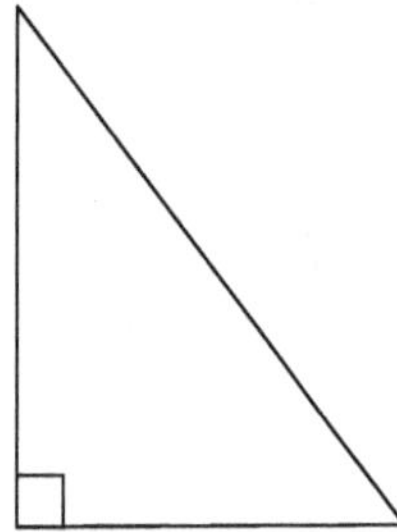

She then joined edges of the triangles together to make shapes. Which of the following shapes was it not possible for Shraddha to make?

(a) A square
(b) A kite
(c) A parallelogram
(d) An isosceles triangle

29. Shraddha made two copies of the following isosceles right angled triangle and cut them out. She then joined edges of the triangles together to make shapes.

Which of the following shapes was it NOT possible for Shraddha to make?

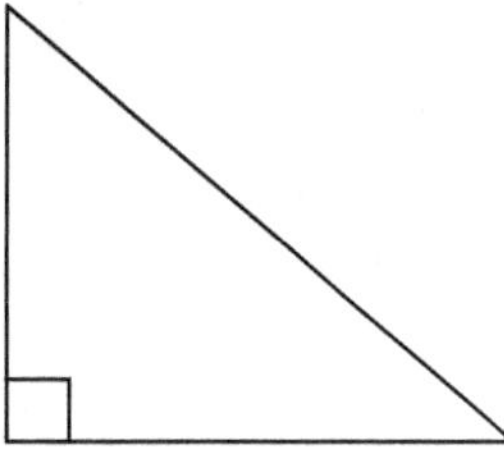

(a) A square
(b) An equilateral triangle
(c) A parallelogram
(d) An isosceles triangle

30. The square is turned one complete about the point O. Which of the following shows the new position of the square?

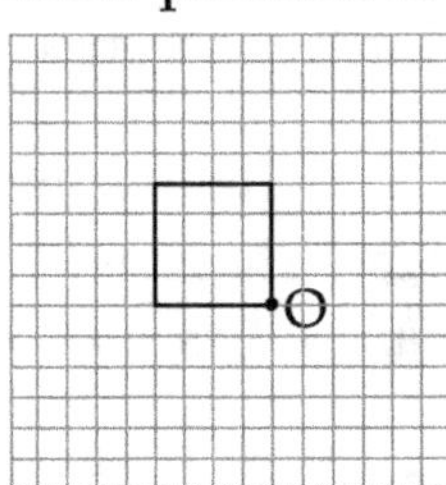

(a)

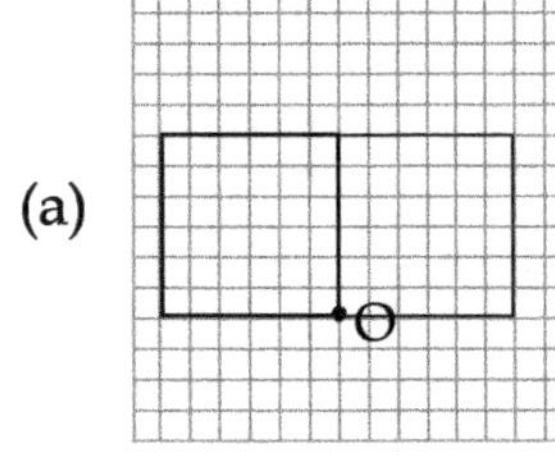

(b)

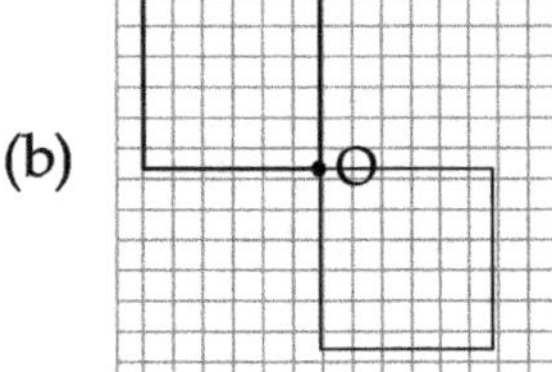

(c)

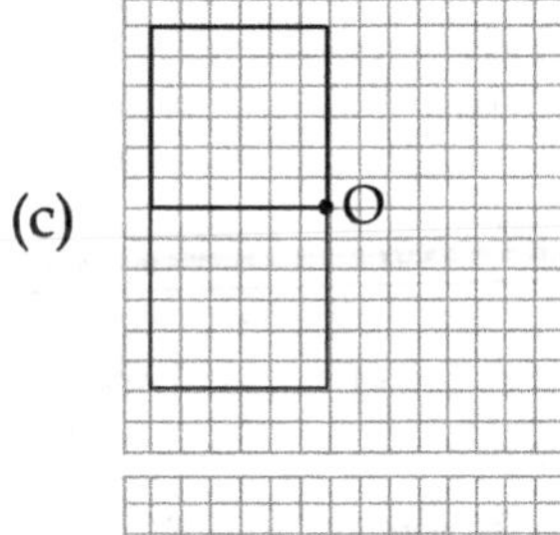

(d)

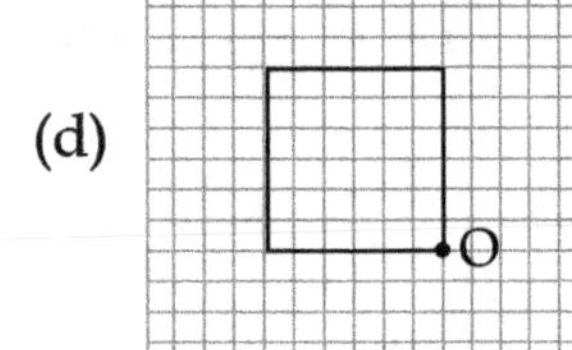

31. How many lines of symmetry does this star have?

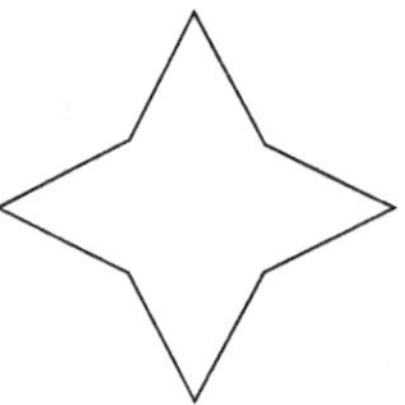

(a) 2   (b) 4
(c) 6   (d) 8

32. What is the order of rotational symmetry of this star?

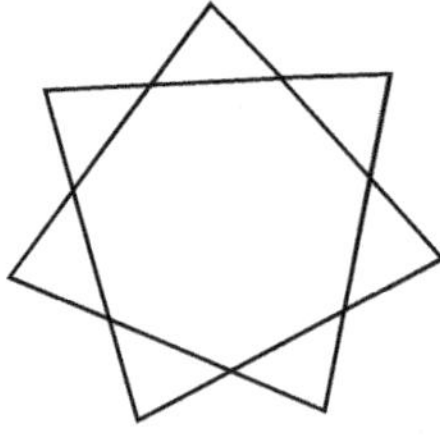

(a) 5   (b) 6
(c) 7   (d) 8

33. What is the order of rotational symmetry of this shape?

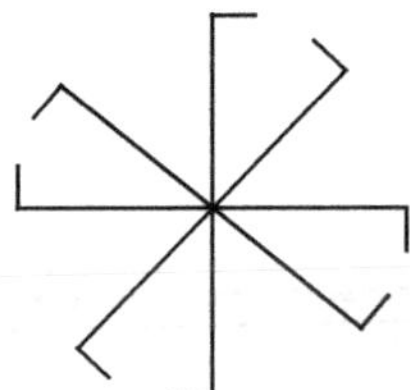

(a) 2   (b) 4
(c) 8   (d) 16

34. At which one of the following times is the angle between the hands of a clock exactly one right angle?
(a) 12:15   (b) 03:00
(c) 03:30   (d) 06:45

SECTION 3
ACHIEVER'S SECTION

Achiever's Section

Important Concepts

Comparison between LAN, MAN & WAN

Inter processor Distance	Processors Located in Same	Example
1 m	Square meter	LAN
10 m	Room	LAN
100 m	Building	LAN
1 km	Campus	LAN
10 km	City	MAN
100 km	Country	WAN
1000 km	Continent	WAN
10,000 km	Planet	Internet

Some basic Internet terminology

WWW	World Wide Web
ISP	Internet Service Provider
URL	Uniform Resource Locator
Server	A computer that provides a service to another computer.
Search engine	Find web pages with specific content.
Cookie	A file left on your computer by a website's browser containing your login, password, user preferences and other personalized information.
Browser	Software used to "browse" the internet. Most common examples are Microsoft Edge and Google Chrome.
Domain name	The unique name that identifies on Internet site.
HTML	Hyper Text Markup Language - computer code used to create documents on the www.
HTTP	Hyper Text transfer Protocol - protocol for moving hypertext files across the Internet.
Downloading	Copying a file from a remote computer to your computer.
Uploading	Copying a file from your computer to a remote computer.
Bookmark	Function used to save a webpage location for future reference.
ASCII	American Standard Code For Information Interchange.
Home page	Page your computer will go to when you initially log onto the Internet.
Hyperlink	Text found on a web page which when clicked, will take you to another web location.
Back	Moves to pervious page on website.

Forward	Moves to next page on website.
Refresh	Starts the process of opening a web page again.
History	Shows a list of pages visited recently.
Mail	Opens a drop-down menu with different options for sending or receiving e-mail.

Some Number Format in Excel

Format style	Display
General	Numbers are shown as integers (e.g. 12S45), decimal fraction (e.g. 1234.5) or in scientific natation (e.g. 1.23E +10).
Number	A number with or without the 1000 separator (e.g. comma) and with Number any number of decimal places. Negative numbers can be displayed with parentheses and/or red.
Currency	A number with the 1,000 separator and an optional dollar sign (which is placed immediately to the left of the number). Negative values are preceded by a minus sign or are displayed with parentheses or in red. Two decimal places display by default
Time	The data in different ways, such as long date (March 18, 2017) or short date (3/18/17 or 18-Mar-17).
Text	The data left aligned by default, is useful for numerical values that have leading zeros and should be treated as text, such as postal codes or phone numbers. Apply text format before typing a leading zero so that the zero displays in the cell.

Common options/button in an Microsoft Edge

Back	Moves to previous page on Website
Forward	Moves to the next page on Website
Stop	Stops opening the Web page
Refresh	Starts the process of opening a Web page again
Home	Takes you to the first page of a Website
Search	Helps to search for any information
Favorites	Lets you "bookmark" your favorite Web sites in a special folder
History	Shows a list of pages visited recently
Mail	Opens a drop-down menu with different options for sending or receiving e-mail
Print	Prints the page you are viewing

5 Ways To Open Task Manager In Windows

Task Manager, in general, has a very huge role to play in disabling the virus from your computer system. There are tons of software available now that can help in carrying out the same process. Task Manager, in short, helps with everything that is going on your computer system. Honestly speaking, you can call it as a backbone of your computer system.

1. CTRL + ALT + DEL Button from the Keyboard

Well, who doesn't know about the famous combination of combination keys, CTRL + ALT + DEL? It is one of the most popular and famous known methods for opening task manager on your Windows system.

While you press Ctrl + Alt + Del button using your keyboard, then a screen appears right in front of you with "Task Manager" option in it. Just click on it and the task manager pane opens for you.

2. Right – Click Taskbar

All that you need to do is, go to your desktop and right click on the screen. From the drop-down menu that appears in front of you, you can easily go for the Task Manager option and Start Task Manager in no time for opening the Task Manager right on your Windows screen.

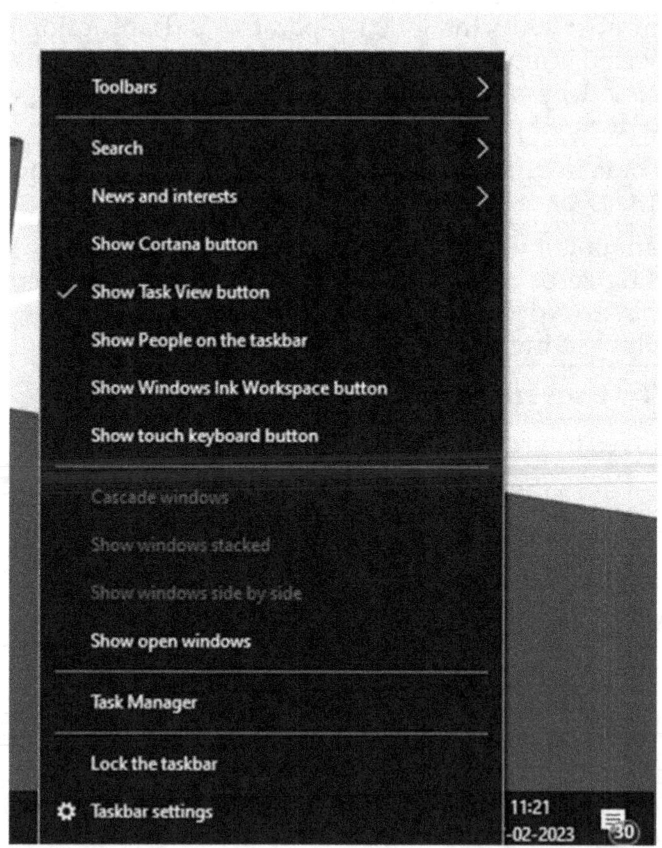

3. Opening Task Manager using Command Prompt

The command prompt is considered to be one of the most convenient ways to open any Windows on any Windows version. Not only that, knowing the right shortcut definitely helps in getting to the window that you have been wanting to visit.

So, for opening Task Manager using the command prompt, all that you need to do is open **cmd** and hit in *taskmgr*. That is all. Hit enter and you are good to go. As soon as you hit on Enter, the task Manager Windows appears right in front of you.

4. Opening Task Manager using Run Command

This method is one of the easiest out of all. Open run Windows as you like it. You can either open it from the start option what can use the window key shortcut, Win + R to appear right in front of you. After the Run Command box pops up on the screen, type in *taskmgr* to view the Task Manager windows.

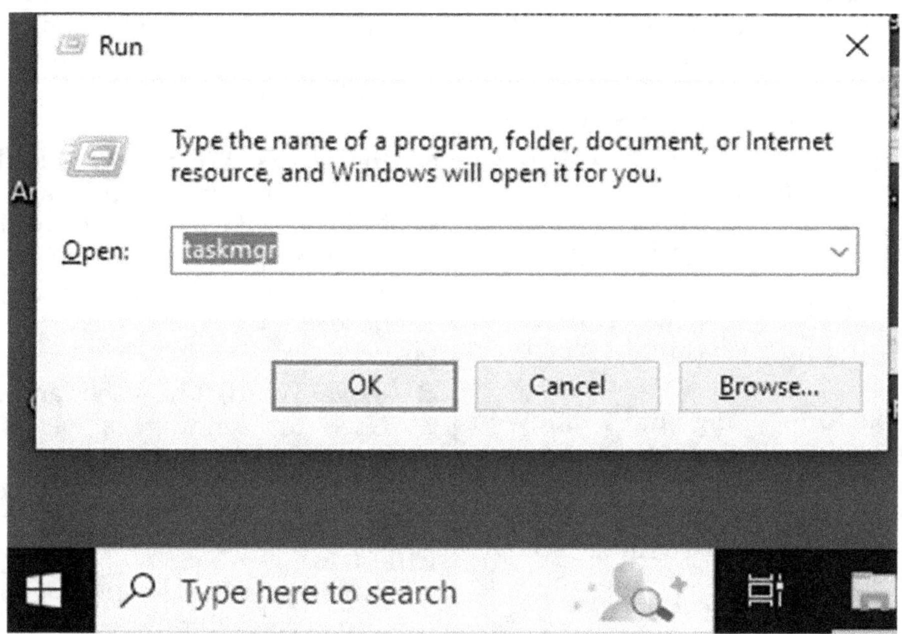

5. Using CTRL + SHIFT + ESC for opening Task Manager

This cool combination of shortcut keys is not known to the most of us. This can also be used in the trick not opening the Task Manager Windows in front of your friends and they will never understand how you do it. Using CTRL + SHIFT + ESC is one of the most convenient and create shortcut keys for opening task manager in Windows.

All you are needed to do is, press all these three buttons together on your computer keyboard. The task manager window will appear right in front of you on your computer screen.

F1 To F12 Shortcut Keys

Function Keys or F-Keys, starting from F1 and ending at F2. All of these have their own use and function. The combination of these keys with Alt and Ctrl buttons is just extraordinary.

Here are the keyboard function Keys and every little detail that you might want to know about it.

F1

- It is most of the times used as a companion and is called the "help key". All the programs open up their help properties when this button is pressed.
- For opening the windows support and help centre, the Windows + F1 key needs to be pressed.

F2

- This key is known for its renaming abilities and renames any icon or file that is highlighted in the different windows version.
- If you use this key in MS Excel, it will edit the current cell you are located at.

- Holding down Alt + Ctrl + F2 will open up a doc window in MS Word.
- Ctrl + F2 will pop up the print preview window in MS Word.

F3

- This key hits off the start function in Windows Explorer.
- Most of the times, for repeating the last command, F3 is commonly used in MS-DOS.
- If you are working on MS Outlook, pressing Windows Key + F3 will open the advanced find window.
- The combo Ctrl + F3 will make sure to lowercase any text that is highlighted in MS Word.
- The keys Shift + F3 will change cases i.e. lower case to upper case in MS Word.

F4

- Responsible for opening Find window in different version of windows.
- It opens the address bar in Internet Explorer as well as Windows Explorer.
- Can also perform the last action.
- The currently active window on MS Windows closes if Alt + F4 is pressed together.
- The currently active tab on MS Windows closes if Ctrl + F4 is held down together.

F5

- This key is mostly known for refreshing or reloading a page or document in any window.
- Starts a slideshow in MS PowerPoint.
- In MS Word, it opens the Find, Replace, and Go To window.
- Also, refreshed any list or items in a folder.
- Using F5 with Ctrl refreshes the whole web page. Along with that, it also clears the cache.

F6

- On some of the laptops, it reduces the volume of the speaker.
- Pressing Ctrl + Shift + F6 together opens another MS word document.

- Takes the cursor to the address bar of Internet Explorer and Mozilla Firefox.

F7

- On some of the laptops, it increases the volume of the speaker.
- For running a thesaurus check on a .docx file, Shift + F7 is used most often.
- Spelling Check and Grammar check in doc file in MS Word can be scrutinized with this key.

F8

- In MacOS, it displays a thumbnail image for the various workplaces.
- This key is also used to recover the recovery system of windows.
- To access the safe mode, F8 is generally used.

F9

- In MS Word, it refreshes any document.
- Used for sending as well as receiving emails in MS Outlook.
- It is also used for reducing the brightness of laptops.

F10

- It activates the menu bar of any opened app in MS Windows.
- Increases the brightness of the laptop.
- Shift + F10 can be used as a correspondence of any other highlighted icon or file.

F11

- It is basically used to enter or to exit the full-screen mode in the present-day Internet Browsers.
- Given access to the hidden recovery files.

F12

- In MS Word, it is known for opening the Save as a window.
- To open a document in word, Ctrl + F12 is used.
- Print a document in MS Word using Ctrl + Shift + F12.
- Shift + F12 really helps you out if you wish to save some file in MS Word.

Mental Ability

1. Find the missing number.

$$
\begin{array}{r}
2\,8,\square 9\,4 \\
+\,2\,8,2\,9\,3 \\
\hline
5\,7,2\,8\,7 \\
\hline
\end{array}
$$

  (a) 9   (b) 0
  (c) 2   (d) 5

2. Which of the following numbers are multiples of 12?
  (a) 96   (b) 108
  (c) 120   (d) All of these

3. Which mixed fraction is shown by the figures given below?

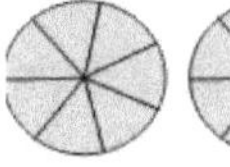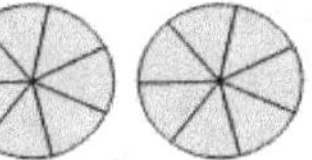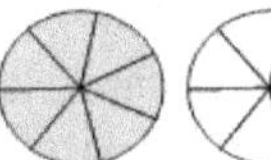

  (a) $4\dfrac{2}{7}$ (b) $4\dfrac{1}{7}$

  (c) $4\dfrac{2}{6}$ (d) $1\dfrac{4}{7}$

4. Tameena left her house on Saturday morning to do some work.
   - First she took 15 minutes to drop off the mail at the post office.
   - Then she took 45 minutes to shop at the toy store.
   - Finally, she took 2 hours and 15 minutes to study at the library.

   If Tameena left the library at 11:30 A.M., at what time did she leave her house to drop off the mail?
  (a) 9:15 A.M.
  (b) 8:45 A.M.
  (c) 9:30 A.M.
  (d) 8:15 A.M.

5. After removing some squares from a big square, the adjoining figure is obtained. The length of one side of a small square is 3 cm. Find the area of the remaining figure.

  (a) 68 cm^2 (b) 603 cm^2
  (c) 612 cm^2 (d) 729 cm^2

6. The calendar given below shows Aditya's schedule for soccer practice and soccer games.

September						
Sun	Mon	Tue	Wed	Thu	Fri	Sat
				1	2 Soccer Practice 4 – 4:30 P.M.	3 Soccer Game 10 A.M.
4	5	Soccer 6 Practice 4 – 5 P.M.	7	Soccer 8 Practice 4 – 5 P.M.	9	Soccer 10 Practice 4 – 5:30 P.M.
11	Soccer 12 Practice 4 – 5 P.M.	13	Soccer 14 Practice 4 – 5 P.M.	15	Soccer 16 Practice 4 – 4:30 P.M.	Soccer 17 Game 10 A.M.
18	19	Soccer 20 Practice 4 – 5 P.M.	21	Soccer 22 Practice 4 – 5 P.M.	23	Soccer 24 Practice 4 – 5:30 P.M.
25	Soccer 26 Practice 4 – 5 P.M.	27	28	Soccer 29 Practice 4 – 5 P.M.	30	

   If Aditya attended every practice in September, what is the total number of minutes he spent at soccer practice during the week of September 11–17?
  (a) 32 mins   (b) 150 mins
  (c) 180 mins   (d) 2½ mins

7. Which statement is true about the adjoining figure?

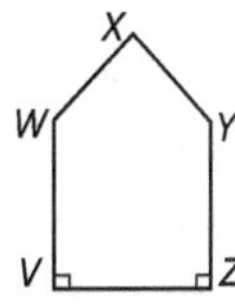

  (a) WX is parallel to YZ.
  (b) WV is perpendicular to YZ.
  (c) WX is parallel to WV.
  (d) WV is perpendicular to VZ.

8. Which set of fractions is ordered from the least to greatest?

  (a) $\dfrac{9}{11}<\dfrac{7}{8}<\dfrac{5}{7}$ (b) $\dfrac{5}{7}<\dfrac{9}{11}<\dfrac{7}{8}$

  (c) $\dfrac{7}{8}<\dfrac{5}{7}<\dfrac{9}{11}$ (d) $\dfrac{9}{11}<\dfrac{5}{7}<\dfrac{7}{8}$

9. Which sign most resembles a ray?

(a)    (b) 

(c)    (d) 

10. Varun saw 3 sticks that were parallel to each other. Which sticks could Varun have seen?

(a) 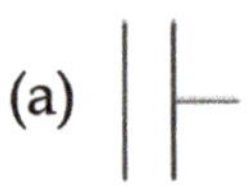   (b) 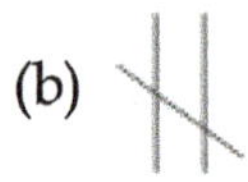

(c) 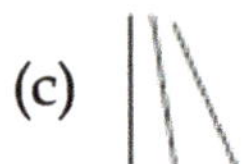   (d) 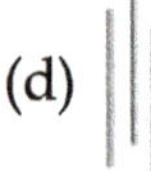

11. Which numbers are both factors of 10?
    (a) 0 and 10   (b) 1 and 20
    (c) 2 and 5   (d) 3 and 7

12. Which clock shows 20 minutes before 12:00?

(a) 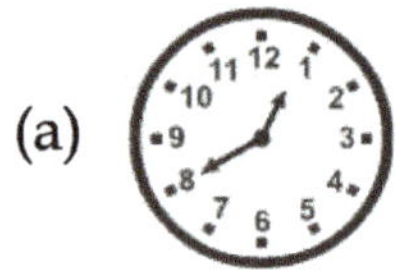   (b) 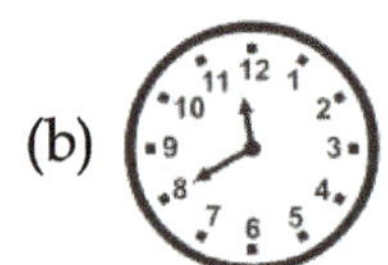

(c)    (d) 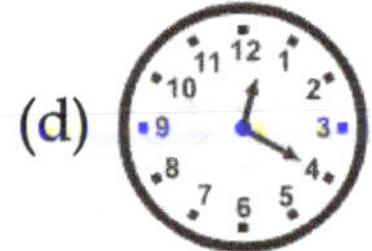

13. A dish has three different flavors of candy in it. The pictograph given below shows the number of candies of each flavor in the dish.

Candy flavours	
Flavour	Number of Candies
Grape	◇ ◇
Lemon	◇ ◇ ◇ ◇
Orange	◇ ◇
Key ◇ = 2 Candies	

How many more lemon candies are in the dish than orange candies?
(a) 2 candies   (b) 4 candies
(c) 6 candies   (d) 8 candies

14. Avinash shaded 1/5 of the shapes in a group. Which of the following could be Avinash's group?

(a) 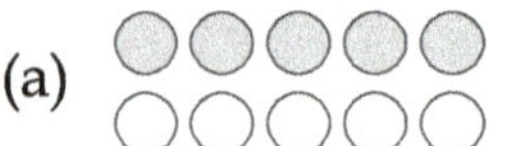   (b) 

(c)    (d)

15. Which of the following is equivalent to the expression given below?

$35{,}720 + 0$

(a) $35{,}720 + 490 \times 490$
(b) $35{,}720 + 490 \div 490$
(c) $35{,}720 + 490 + 490$
(d) $35{,}720 + 490 - 490$

Logical And Analytical Reasoning

16. Tanya is thinking of a number that follows these rules.
    ■ The number is written using each of the digits 1, 4, 6, 7 and 8 exactly once.
    ■ The number is greater than 48,682 and less than 48,722.

    What is Tanya's number?
    (a) 48,617   (b) 48,716
    (c) 48,671   (d) 48,761

17. Which of the following does not have a line of symmetry?

(a) 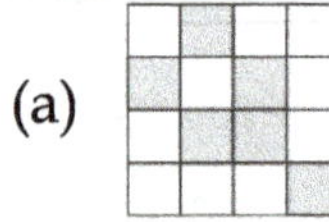   (b) 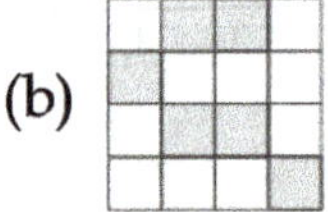

(c) 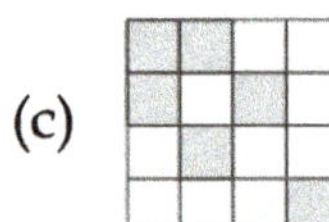   (d) 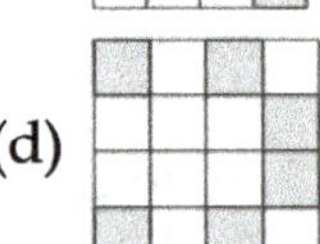

18. In the given input-output table, which rule can be used to find the output number?

Input	Output
12	60
13	65
14	70

(a) Add 5 to the Input number.
(b) Add 48 to the Input number.
(c) Multiply the Input number by 5.
(d) Multiply the Input number by 12.

19. Find the odd one out.

(a) 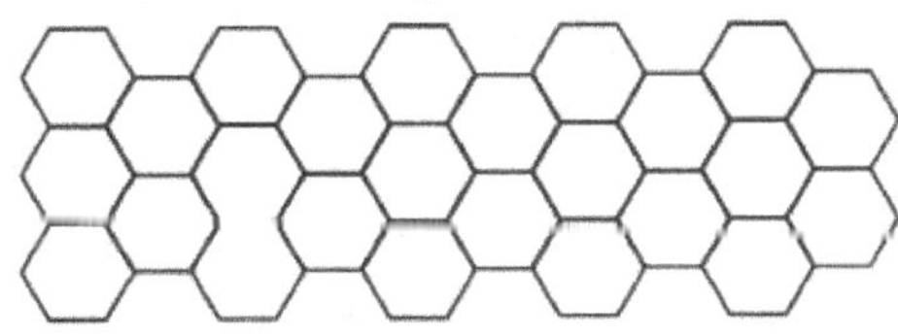   (b)

(c)   (d)

20. The given table shows the costs of mail order items and the shipping amounts.

Mail Order Items	
Cost (Rs.)	Shipping amount (Rs.)
25	10
35	20
45	30
55	40

What is the rule to find the shipping amount?
(a) Multiply cost by 2.5.
(b) Add Rs.15 to cost.
(c) Divide cost by 2.5.
(d) Subtract Rs.15 from cost.

21. How many shapes must be shaded so that 2/5 of the figure is unshaded?

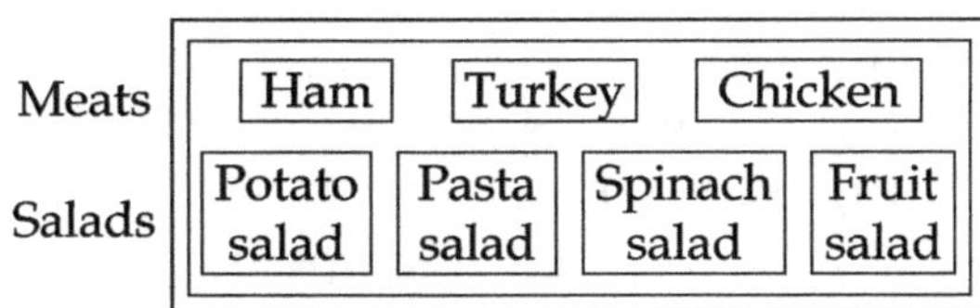

(a) 5   (b) 10
(c) 15   (d) 20

22. The diagram given below shows the types of meats and salads available at a restaurant buffet.

Meats	Ham	Turkey	Chicken	
Salads	Potato salad	Pasta salad	Spinach salad	Fruit salad

How many combinations of 1 meat and 1 salad are possible?
(a) 7   (b) 9
(c) 12   (d) 16

23. The table shows the number of bananas Mr. Gujral needs in order to make different number of bowls of fruit salad.

Fruit Salad	
Number of Bowls	Number of Bananas
6	3
10	5
12	6

Which of the following correctly describes the relationship in the table?
(a) Number of bowls ÷ 2 = number of bananas
(b) Number of bowls × 2 = number of bananas
(c) Number of bowls ÷ 3 = number of bananas
(d) Number of bowls × 3 = number of bananas

24. Which figure from the given options will complete the fig. (X)?

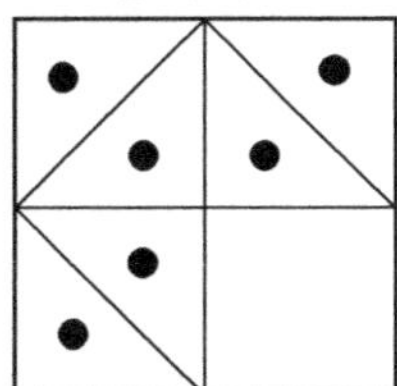

Fig. (X)

(a) 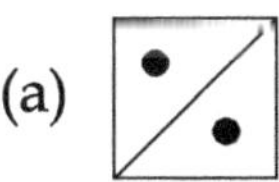   (b) 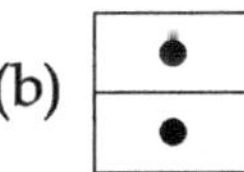

(c) 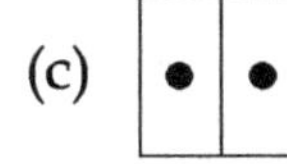   (d) 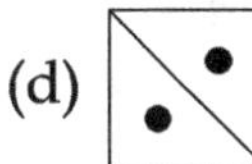

25. The number of triangles in the given figure are ______.

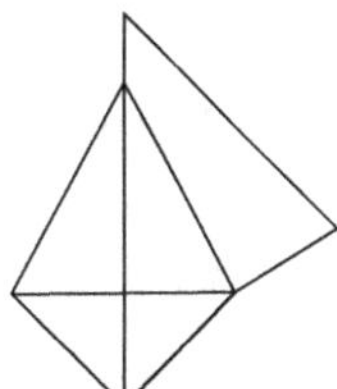

(a) 5   (b) 6
(c) 4   (d) 8

26. A pattern of shapes is shown here.

▢♡♡△▢♡♡△▢♡♡△▢♡ ? ?

The pattern repeats after every 4 shapes. What are the next 2 shapes in the pattern?

(a) ▢♡ (b) △▢
(c) ♡♡ (d) ♡△

27. How many ● do you need to balance the last set-up?

(a) 8 (b) 10
(c) 12 (d) 14

28.)(|)(|)(Which comes next?

(a) (b)
(c) (d)

29. What is the number in the START box?

| START | → | + 32 | → | × 18 | → | 360 |

(a) 202.5 (b) 640
(c) 1120 (d) 207360

30. Find the odd one out.

(a) (b)
(c) (d)

Computers & Information Technology

31. This man is known for starting the company Microsoft back in the year 1975. Since then, he has become one of the richest people in the world. His name is ______.

(a) Steve Jobs
(b) Bill Gates
(c) Konrad Zuse
(d) Charles Babbage

32. What key combination is used when the the computer fails to respond?
(a) Ctrl + Alt + G
(b) Ctrl + Shift + Del
(c) Ctrl + Alt + Del
(d) Ctrl + Space + Del

33. This invention replaced Vacuum Tubes and made computers much smaller and faster. However, it was eventually replaced by another invention.
(a) RAM (b) ENIAC
(c) Transformer (d) Transistor

34. What is a hard disk drive?
(a) Something that plays music
(b) It stores information and data
(c) It is a place to share photos.
(d) A type of RAM

35. If in the find option, I turn on "Match Case", then what would the computer search for if I type "Computer".
(a) Computer (b) computer
(c) COMPUTER (d) All of these

36. What is Internet?
(a) Internet is a network of printers.
(b) Internet is pages linked together.
(c) Internet is millions of computers around the world connected to each other.
(d) Internet is the secret mission of US army.

37. The earliest computer was ______.
(a) Embedded computer
(b) Abacus
(c) Calculators
(d) Supercomputers

38. Which one of the following stores the largest amount of information?
(a) Digital Versatile Disc (DVD)
(b) Compact Disk (CD)
(c) Floppy Disk
(d) Pen Drive

39. A ______ is a specific type of online search tool that finds Web sites, Web pages and Internet files that match one or more keywords you enter.
   (a) System Software (b) Network
   (c) Search engine (d) Website

40. Complete the sequence.
   Hardware → ? → ? → User
   (a) Application software, Operating system software
   (b) Operating system software, Application software
   (c) Application software, User
   (d) Operating system software, Hardware

41. Which button did Kavita use to make the style change to the words "Cars unlimited" in the image?

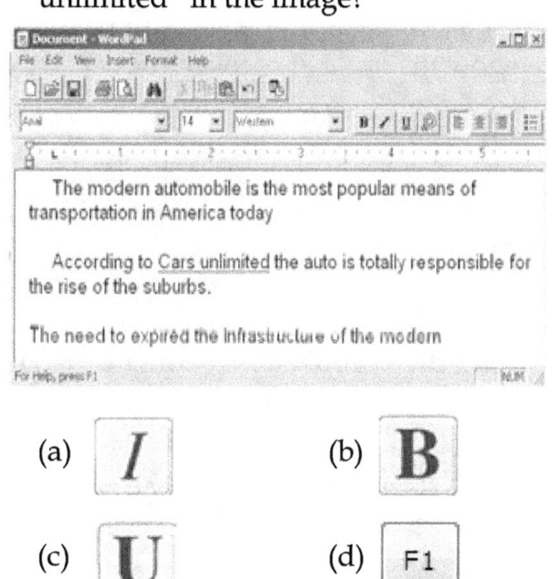

   (a) I
   (b) **B**
   (c) U
   (d) F1

42. Notepad is a ______.
   (a) Spreadsheet editor (b) Website creator
   (c) Text editor (d) None of these

43. The ______ that we use today is the ______ generation computer.
   (a) Fourth   (b) Second
   (c) Third   (d) Fifth

44. Icon clicked for pasting text in a Word document is ______.
   (a)   (b)
   (c)   (d)

45. 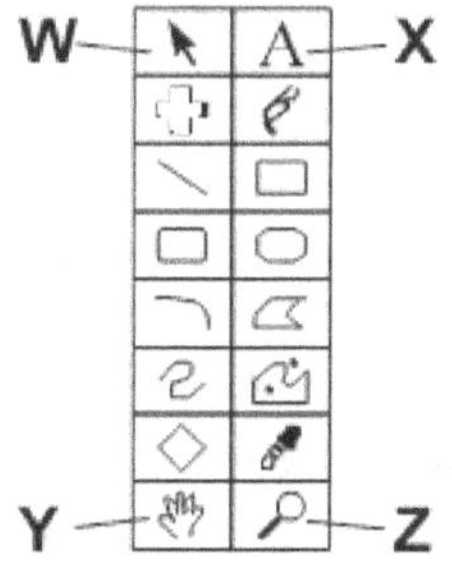 shows ______.
   (a) Curve line tool
   (b) Airbrush tool
   (c) Rectangle tool
   (d) Colour tool

46. Anu is using MS Paint. Which tool will allow her to put text under the graphics?

   (a) W   (b) X
   (c) Y   (d) Z

47. Which of the following is not a logo primitive?
   (a) FD   (b) BD
   (c) BK   (d) CS

48. Command "?Print 12 – 6" ↵ gives result ____.
   (a) 18   (b) –6
   (c) 6   (d) 0

49. Which part of the computer allows it to send and receive data via telephone lines?
   (a) ISP   (b) Modem
   (c) Internet (d) Electronic mail

50. An artificial environment created with the help of computer hardware and software is ______.
   (a) Multimedia (b) Virtual reality
   (c) Images   (d) Games

Mental Ability

1. The given bar graph shows the different kinds of vegetables sold.

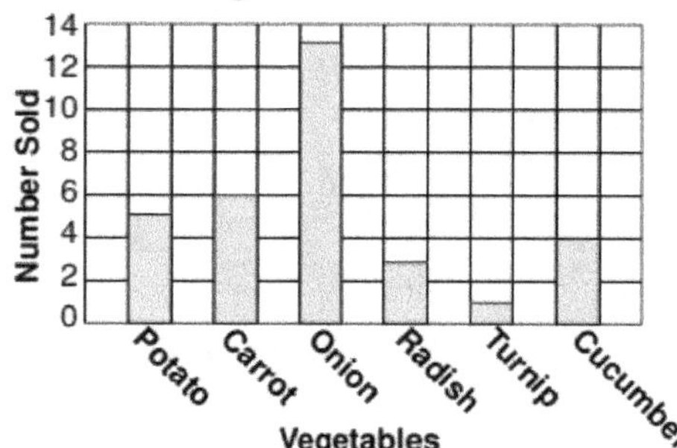

Which of these statements is false from the information in the graph?
 (a) Fewer cucumbers were sold than onions.
 (b) The same number of potatoes and carrots were sold.
 (c) More onions were sold than all other vegetables.
 (d) Turnips were sold the least.

2. In the cafeteria at a school, there are 8 tables for each grade. Which grade can have exactly 9 students sitting at each table?

Students in each grade at school	
Kindergarten	71
First Grade	64
Second Grade	81
Third Grade	63
Fourth Grade	80
Fifth Grade	72

 (a) 1st Grade   (b) 2nd Grade
 (c) 3rd Grade   (d) 5th Grade

3. On Saturday, 2,759 people went to the afternoon concert and 6,387 people went to the night concert. About how many people went to the concert on Saturday?
 (a) 4,000   (b) 6,000
 (c) 8,000   (d) 9,000

4. Which mixed fraction represents the shaded parts of the model?

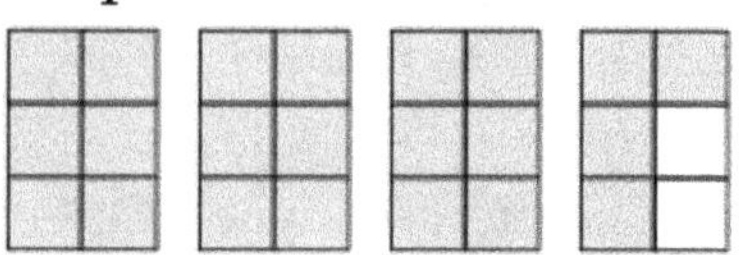

 (a) $3\dfrac{2}{6}$ (b) $3\dfrac{4}{6}$

 (c) $4\dfrac{2}{6}$ (d) $4\dfrac{4}{6}$

5. Mohit has 30 tokens to use on games at the video games parlour. For each game he plays, he uses the same number of tokens. If Mohit plays 5 different games, which number sentence could be used to show the number of tokens he can use on each game?
 (a) $30 + 5$ (b) $30 - 5$
 (c) 30×5 (d) $30 \div 5$

6. Which list contains only one prime number?
 (a) 3, 4, 5, 6   (b) 6, 9, 10, 11
 (c) 4, 10, 12, 21   (d) 7, 11, 13, 17

7. John drew a robot using only rectangles and hexagons. Which could be John's drawing?

 (a) 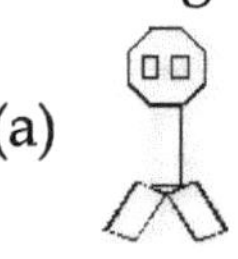   (b) 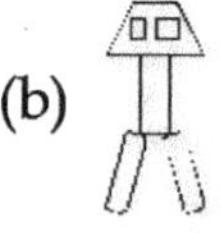

 (c) 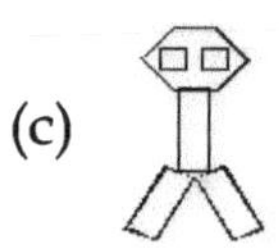   (d) 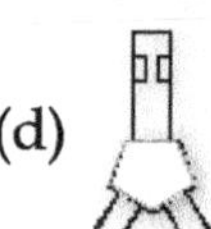

8. A drawing of Misha's garden is shown here.

What is the perimeter of the garden?

(a) 130 m　　　　(b) 150 m
(c) 160 m　　　　(d) 180 m

9. The scale shown here is balanced. The bag of sand weighs 18 kg. Each of the cubes has the same weight. How many kg does one cube weigh?

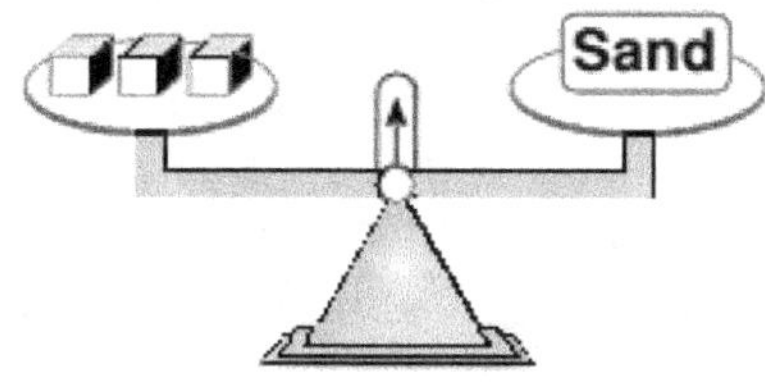

(a) 3 kg　　　　(b) 4 kg
(c) 5 kg　　　　(d) 6 kg

10. The given bar graph shows the average life span of some animals. Which animal has an average life span that is five times longer than the average life span of a polar bear?

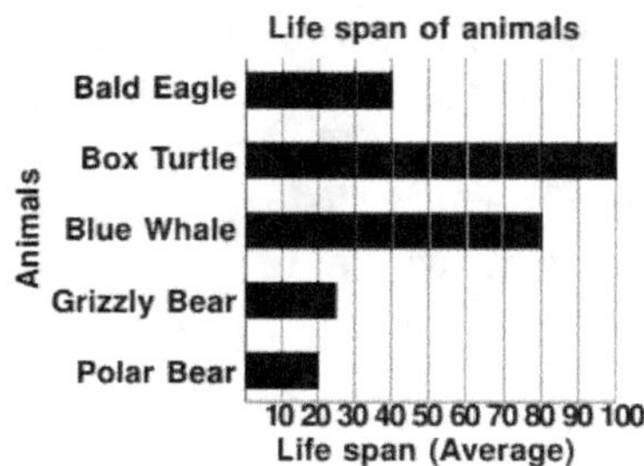

(a) Bald Eagle
(b) Box Turtle
(c) Blue Whale
(d) Grizzly Bear

Logical And Analytical Reasoning

11. The students at Maple Public School are selling flowers. Their goal is to sell 1500 flowers.

On the first day, the students sold 547 flowers.

On the second day, the students sold 655 flowers.

How many flowers must the students sell on the third day to meet their goal?

(a) 298　　　　(b) 308
(c) 1202　　　　(d) 2702

12. What is the value of $48 - 8 \times 4 - 6 \div 2$?

(a) 5　　　　(b) 13
(c) 19　　　　(d) 77

13. There are 20 red and 24 green pencils in a shop. The shopkeeper wants to distribute them equally in boxes. The largest number of pencils that can be put in each box is _____ .

(a) 4　　　　(b) 6
(c) 12　　　　(d) 8

14. Manali was making the house number board for her house using Roman numbers. Which of the following cannot be her house number board?

(a) VX　　　　(b) IXIV
(c) XIIV　　　　(d) None of these

15. Appu's school closed for summer vacations on April 26th and reopened on June 10th. Number of holidays are ___

(a) 46　　　　(b) 45
(c) 44　　　　(d) 47

16. If $\bigcirc + \triangle = 500$, $\bigcirc + \triangle + \triangle = 800$ then $\triangle - \bigcirc$ equals _____ .

(a) 900　　　　(b) 100
(c) 300　　　　(d) 700

17. Which is the heaviest ball?

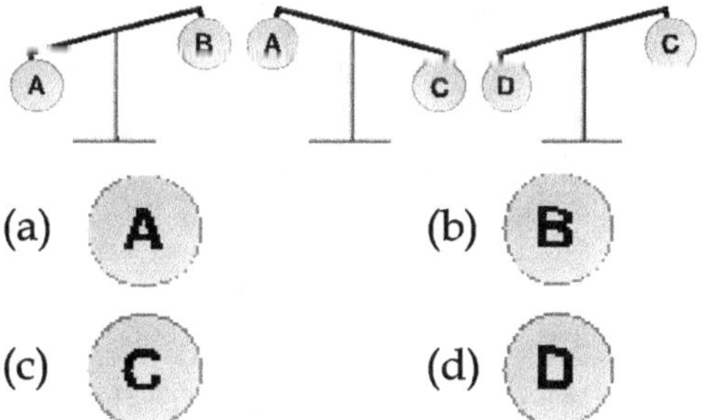

(a) A　　　　(b) B
(c) C　　　　(d) D

18. Find the missing number.

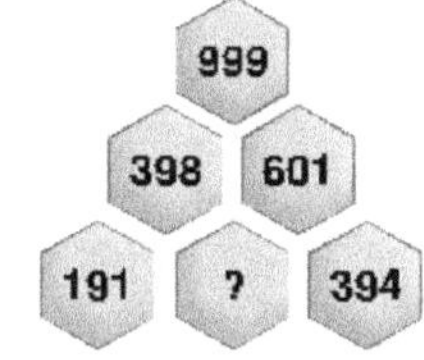

(a) 206　　　　(b) 207
(c) 208　　　　(d) 209

19. Sona folds a piece of paper and cuts as shown in the figure.

Which of the following will she get when she unfolds the paper?

(a) 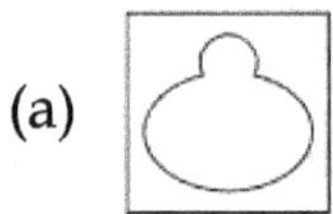 (b) 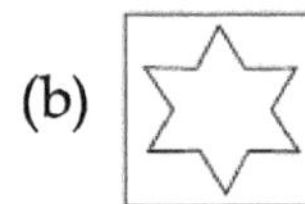

(c) 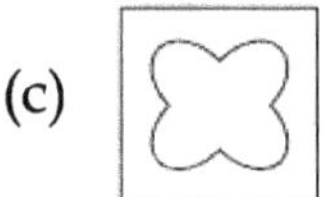 (d) 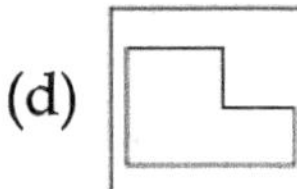

20. What is the mirror image of 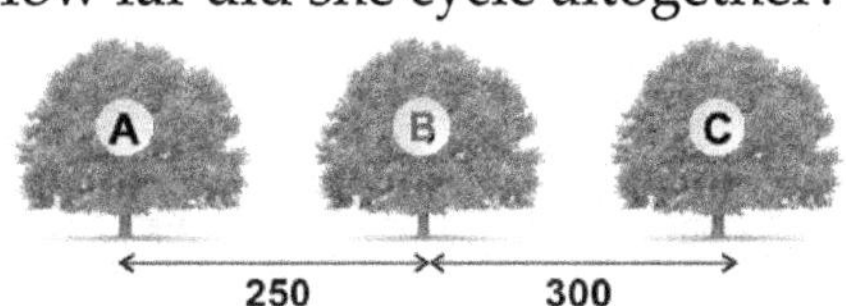 ?

(a) R (b) 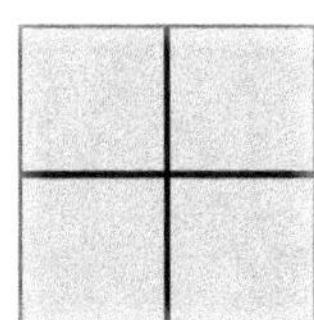

(c)   (d)

Computers & Information Technology

21. If "WHOLE" is coded as "LEHOW" then "MONEY" will be coded as _____ .
    (a) EYNOM (b) YEONM
    (c) MEYON (d) EYONM

22. Anusha cycled from Tree B to Tree C. She then cycled from Tree C to Tree A. How far did she cycle altogether?

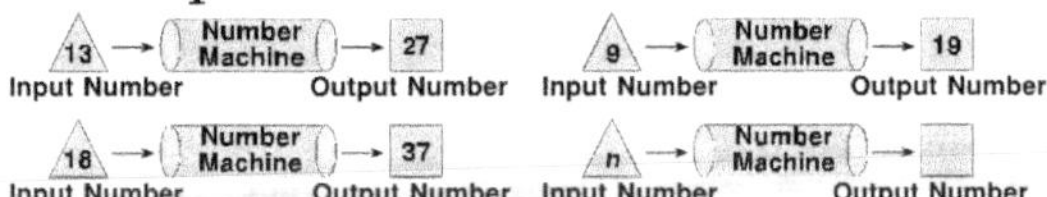

(a) 950 (b) 850
(c) 800 (d) 1050

23. How many squares are there in the given figure?

(a) 5 (b) 6
(c) 8 (d) 4

24. What is the digit in the one's place for the product of 5th Pattern 1?
    Pattern 1 : 2
    Pattern 2 : 2 × 2
    Pattern 3 : 2 × 2 × 2
    (a) 2 (b) 4
    (c) 0 (d) 8

25. Samrat used a pattern for the given table. What rules did he use to go from the first number to the second and from the second number to the third?

First Number	Second Number	Third Number
12	4	7
10	2	5
15	7	10
17	9	12

(a) Add 8, subtract 3
(b) Add 8, add 3
(c) Subtract 8, subtract 3
(d) Subtract 8, add 3

26. Aryan used the number machine shown below to create output numbers from input numbers. The number machine used the same rule each time to create the output number.

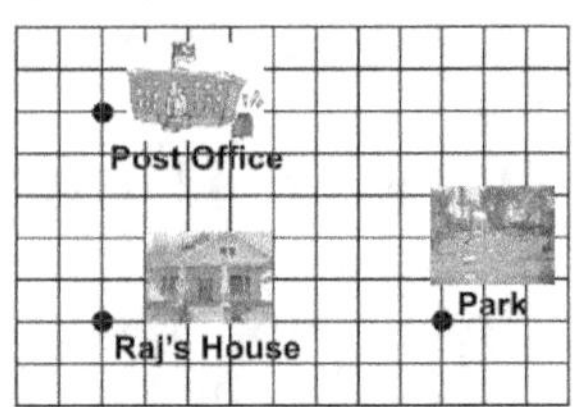

If n is the input number, which expression could be the rule the machine used to create each output number?
(a) 2n – 2 (b) 2n
(c) 2n – 1 (d) 2n + 1

27. On the map, each side of each grid square represents 1 kilometre. How much farther does Raj live from the Park than he lives from the Post Office?

Key

⊢⊣ → 1 km

(a) 3 km (b) 5 km
(c) 8 km (d) 13 km

28. Mr. Abhay drew this pattern of shapes on the chalkboard. He asked his class to find the rule for his pattern. Which answer is correct?

first   second   third   fourth

(a) All the figures have 1 less side each time first second third fourth.

(b) All the figures have 1 less angle each time.

(c) All the figures have 1 more acute angle each time.

(d) Number of sides is increased by 1 in the following figure than the previous figure.

29. Kartik has an apple, an orange and a banana. He is only allowed to have two for his snack. How many different combinations of 2 fruits could Kartik have for his snack?

(a) 2   (b) 3

(c) 6   (d) 9

30. Roy made the given pattern:

If the pattern continues, which shape will be in the last blank?

(a) ◯   (b) ⊗

(c) △   (d) ▢

31. Meeku is setting up his new e-mail account. He needs to ensure privacy and security. Which of the following should he do?

(a) Pick a password used by another person.

(b) Use personal information for the new password.

(c) Pick random letters for the new password.

(d) Use a combination of words and numbers for the new password.

32. A network of computers and other devices that is confined to a related space is known as ______ .

(a) Global Network

(b) Local Area Network

(c) Peer-to-peer Network

(d) Metropolitan Network

33. A ______ is a website in which information is posted on a regular basis.

(a) Forum

(b) Blog

(c) Browsing

(d) Chatt

34. Multimedia is a combination of a few components, which are ______ .

(a) Audio, video and animations

(b) Coreldraw, MS-Access, Pag

(c) Operating system, MS Word, Text effect

(d) None of these

35. By default, your documents print in ______ mode.

(a) Landscape

(b) Portrait

(c) Page setup

(d) Print

36. Why can you not just start typing text on a blank PowerPoint slide?

(a) You should use MS-Word if you want to type text.

(b) The only way to add text is through the Auto content wizard.

(c) You need to select the Autotext button.

(d) You must draw a text box first

37. What is a slide-show in PowerPoint?

(a) A special effect used in slide transitions.

(b) A series of slides displayed in sequence.

(c) The term for an individual slide in PowerPoint.

(d) The button used to preview the slide you are currently working on.

38. Which of these mathematical expressions uses a superscript character?

$$6^3, \frac{1}{4}, 36\%, \sqrt{5}$$

(a) 6^3 (b) 1/4
(c) 36%   (d) 5

39. When viewing a video file, which button takes you to the final frame?

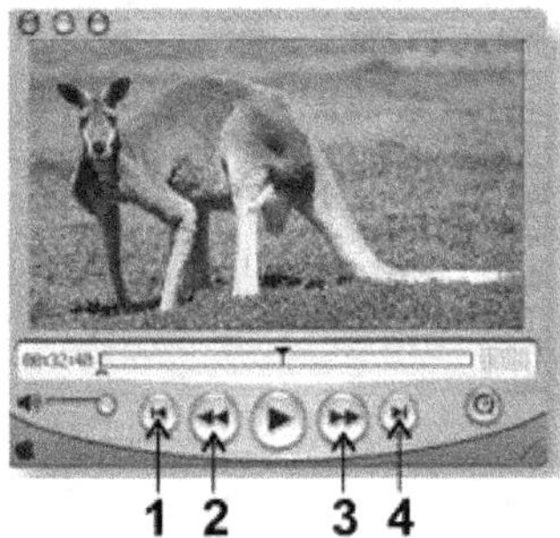

(a) 1   (b) 2
(c) 3   (d) 4

40. Multimedia is used in ______ .
(a) Education
(b) Advertising
(c) Playing Games
(d) All of these

41. Which device is used as the standard pointing device in a Graphical User Environment?
(a) Keyboard
(b) Mouse
(c) Joystick
(d) Track ball

42. Victor Middle School purchased a single-user copy of a word processing program. They may do which of the following?
(a) Copy it onto all the computers in the lab.
(b) Use it on only one computer in the lab.
(c) Use it on all the computers in the classroom.
(d) Duplicate the disk and give it to everyone in the class.

43. You have copied and pasted an image of a Tasmanian bird from the internet into a word processor document. Which handle should you drag to keep the image in the same proportions while re-sizing it?

(a) 1   (b) 2
(c) 3   (d) 4

44. Figure 1 was rotated to form Figure 2. Which handle in Figure 1 was used to rotate the image?

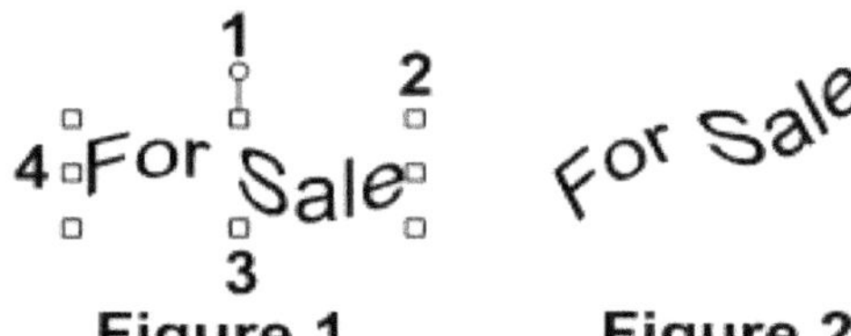

(a) 1   (b) 2
(c) 3   (d) 4

45. Your history assignment is over 30 pages long. You want to include the page number at the bottom of each page. What would be the best method to do this?
(a) Insert a reference line.
(b) Type in each page number.
(c) Insert the page number in the footer.
(d) Insert the page number in the header.

Achievers Section

46. You are sitting at a computer waiting for a web page to load but it seems to be taking much longer than usual. What could you do to load the page faster?
(a) Click the Back icon.
(b) Turn off the computer.
(c) Click the History icon.
(d) Click the Refresh/Reload icon.

47. The following is a file path taken from the footer in a document.

F:\SCIENCE MATERIALS\year 10\reactions.doc

What is the name of the file that has been accessed?

(a) F :
(b) year 10
(c) reactions.doc
(d) SCIENCE MATERIALS

48. You are on page 2 of a word-processing document of 100 pages. You open this dialogue box.

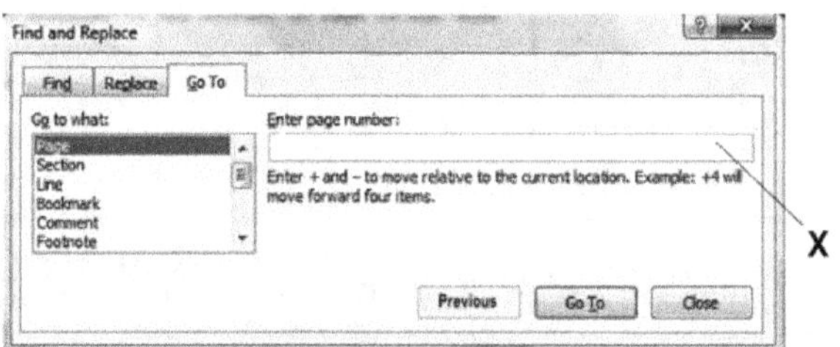

If you type '60' in the box labelled X, what will happen when you click 'OK'?

(a) A new section will be created on page 60.
(b) You will be taken to page 60.
(c) Page 60 will be deleted.
(d) Page 60 will be printed.

49. To open a disk, you position the mouse pointer on the disk icon, and then ___.

(a) Drag mouse while holding button down.
(b) Double click the mouse button.
(c) Roll mouse around.
(d) Roll and then click mouse.

50. You are about to compose an e-mail. Which section must be filled before the message can be sent?

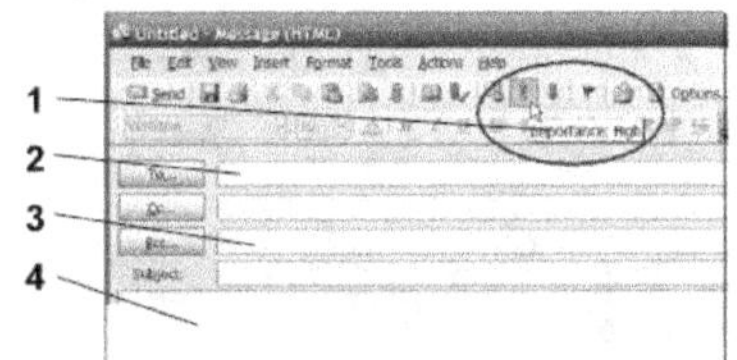

(a) 1   (b) 2
(c) 3   (d) 4

Answer Keys

Scan the QR Code to see the Hints and Solutions

Access Content Online on Dropbox: https://www.dropbox.com/scl/fi/x1il8nzpuzwm1qyz8yycu/NSO-01-Science-Olympiad-Hints-and-Solutions.pdf?rlkey=kzkx1753ie7dfs4rlkt3yo4pa&dl=0

SECTION 1: COMPUTERS AND IT

1. FUNDAMENTALS OF COMPUTER

Answer Key									
1. (b)	2. (a)	3. (d)	4. (a)	5. (d)	6. (c)	7. (d)	8. (d)	9. (b)	10. (c)
11. (a)	12. (b)	13. (d)	14. (a)	15. (a)	16. (c)	17. (b)	18. (b)	19. (c)	20. (c)
21. (b)	22. (d)	23. (b)	24. (b)	25. (d)	26. (c)	27. (c)	28. (d)	29. (b)	30. (c)
31. (a)	32. (b)	33. (d)	34. (b)	35. (d)					

HOTS				
1. (c)	2. (b)	3. (b)	4. (b)	5. (b)

2. MEMORY AND STORAGE DEVICES

Answer Key									
1. (a)	2. (a)	3. (d)	4. (a)	5. (b)	6. (c)	7. (b)	8. (a)	9. (a)	10. (c)
11. (d)	12. (b)	13. (b)	14. (c)	15. (b)	16. (d)	17. (b)	18. (c)	19. (d)	20. (b)
21. (d)	22. (a)	23. (c)	24. (b)	25. (c)					

HOTS				
1. (b)	2. (b)	3. (d)	4. (d)	5. (a)

3. INTRODUCTION TO MULTIMEDIA

Answer Key									
1. (d)	2. (c)	3. (a)	4. (c)	5. (c)	6. (c)	7. (b)	8. (b)	9. (d)	10. (a)
11. (d)	12. (c)	13. (c)	14. (c)	15. (b)	16. (c)	17. (b)	18. (a)	19. (b)	20. (b)

HOTS				
1. (c)	2. (a)	3. (b)	4. (c)	5. (b)

4. MS PAINT

Answer Key

1. (a)	2. (a)	3. (b)	4. (b)	5. (b)	6. (a)	7. (d)	8. (c)	9. (b)	10. (b)
11. (d)	12. (d)	13. (d)	14. (d)	15. (a)	16. (d)	17. (a)	18. (d)	19. (c)	20. (c)

HOTS

1. (b)	2. (b)	3. (c)	4. (d)	5. (c)

5. MS WORD

Answer Key

1. (a)	2. (b)	3. (d)	4. (c)	5. (b)	6. (d)	7. (a)	8. (a)	9. (d)	10. (c)
11. (b)	12. (a)	13. (d)	14. (c)	15. (c)	16. (a)	17. (d)	18. (b)	19. (c)	20. (a)
21. (d)	22. (b)	23. (d)	24. (d)	25. (b)					

HOTS

1. (b)	2. (d)	3. (a)	4. (b)	5. (c)

6. MS POWERPOINT

Answer Key

1. (d)	2. (a)	3. (c)	4. (c)	5. (c)	6. (b)	7. (b)	8. (b)	9. (b)	10. (a)
11. (a)	12. (c)	13. (c)	14. (c)	15. (d)	16. (d)	17. (d)	18. (b)	19. (c)	20. (b)
21. (c)	22. (a)	23. (c)	24. (a)	25. (c)					

HOTS

1. (a)	2. (b)	3. (c)	4. (a)	5. (d)

7. WINDOWS

Answer Key

1. (b)	2. (c)	3. (c)	4. (c)	5. (c)	6. (d)	7. (c)	8. (d)	9. (a)	10. (c)
11. (d)	12. (d)	13. (d)	14. (b)	15. (d)	16. (b)	17. (d)	18. (a)	19. (c)	20. (b)

HOTS

1. (c)	2. (a)	3. (d)	4. (a)	5. (a)

8. NETWORK

		Answer Key							
1. (d)	2. (c)	3. (d)	4. (d)	5. (d)	6. (b)	7. (d)	8. (d)	9. (a)	10. (d)
11. (a)	12. (c)	13. (c)	14. (d)	15. (a)	16. (b)	17. (b)	18. (c)	19. (a)	20. (a)
21. (b)	22. (d)	23. (b)	24. (b)	25. (b)					

	HOTS			
1. (c)	2. (b)	3. (a)	4. (c)	5. (a)

9. INTERNET

		Answer Key							
1. (b)	2. (c)	3. (d)	4. (c)	5. (d)	6. (a)	7. (c)	8. (d)	9. (d)	10. (c)
11. (b)	12. (d)	13. (b)	14. (d)	15. (c)	16. (b)	17. (d)	18. (c)	19. (d)	20. (d)
21. (c)	22. (d)	23. (a)	24. (d)	25. (a)					

	HOTS			
1. (d)	2. (a)	3. (c)	4. (b)	5. (a)

10. LATEST DEVELOPMENT IN IT

		Answer Key							
1. (b)	2. (c)	3. (a)	4. (d)	5. (c)	6. (a)	7. (a)	8. (b)	9. (b)	10. (c)
11. (b)	12. (a)	13. (c)	14. (a)	15. (b)	16. (c)	17. (d)	18. (c)	19. (b)	20. (c)
21. (c)	22. (a)	23. (b)	24. (b)	25. (d)					

	HOTS			
1. (a)	2. (b)	3. (d)	4. (a)	5. (d)

SECTION 2: LOGICAL REASONING

1. PATTERNS

Answer Key									
1. (a)	2. (c)	3. (c)	4. (b)	5. (a)	6. (c)	7. (d)	8. (b)	9. (c)	10. (d)
11. (c)	12. (c)	13. (d)	14. (c)	15. (c)	16. (d)	17. (a)	18. (b)	19. (d)	20. (a)
21. (d)	22. (c)	23. (d)	24. (d)	25. (b)					

2. ANALOGY AND CLASSIFICATION

Answer Key									
1. (d)	2. (c)	3. (b)	4. (d)	5. (a)	6. (a)	7. (d)	8. (d)	9. (c)	10. (c)
11. (d)	12. (b)	13. (a)	14. (b)	15. (c)	16. (d)	17. (a)	18. (d)	19. (d)	20. (b)
21. (c)	22. (d)	23. (b)	24. (c)	25. (b)	26. (b)	27. (a)	28. (c)	29. (a)	30. (c)

3. CODING AND DECODING

Answer Key									
1. (c)	2. (a)	3. (c)	4. (b)	5. (b)	6. (d)	7. (a)	8. (a)	9. (b)	10. (b)
11. (c)	12. (b)	13. (b)	14. (a)	15. (a)	16. (b)	17. (d)	18. (c)	19. (c)	20. (a)
21. (c)	22. (a)	23. (b)	24. (a)	25. (b)	26. (a)	27. (b)			

4. RANKING AND ALPHABET TEST

Answer Key									
1. (b)	2. (c)	3. (d)	4. (d)	5. (d)	6. (d)	7. (c)	8. (c)	9. (d)	10. (d)
11. (c)	12. (d)	13. (a)	14. (d)	15. (c)	16. (d)	17. (c)	18. (c)	19. (b)	20. (d)
21. (c)	22. (c)	23. (c)	24. (a)	25. (c)					

5. DIRECTION SENSE TEST

Answer Key									
1. (d)	2. (a)	3. (c)	4. (c)	5. (a)	6. (a)	7. (b)	8. (c)	9. (a)	10. (d)
11. (b)	12. (c)	13. (a)	14. (c)	15. (b)	16. (d)	17. (b)	18. (d)	19. (d)	20. (d)
21. (a)	22. (c)	23. (d)	24. (a)	25. (d)					

Answer Key									
1. (d)	2. (b)	3. (d)	4. (c)	5. (d)	6. (c)	7. (d)	8. (c)	9. (d)	10. (d)
11. (c)	12. (b)	13. (c)	14. (a)	15. (b)	16. (d)	17. (d)	18. (a)	19. (c)	20. (d)

7. GEOMETRICAL SHAPES AND ANGLES

Answer Key									
1. (a)	2. (d)	3. (c)	4. (b)	5. (c)	6. (c)	7. (c)	8. (b)	9. (a)	10. (d)
11. (c)	12. (a)	13. (b)	14. (c)	15. (d)	16. (b)	17. (d)	18. (c)	19. (d)	20. (b)
21. (c)	22. (a)	23. (c)	24. (c)	25. (c)	26. (a)	27. (d)	28. (a)	29. (b)	30. (d)
31. (b)	32. (c)	33. (b)	34. (b)						

MODEL TEST PAPER - 1

Answer Key									
1. (a)	2. (d)	3. (b)	4. (d)	5. (c)	6. (b)	7. (d)	8. (b)	9. (c)	10. (d)
11. (c)	12. (b)	13. (b)	14. (d)	15. (d)	16. (b)	17. (b)	18. (c)	19. (d)	20. (d)
21. (c)	22. (c)	23. (a)	24. (a)	25. (d)	26. (d)	27. (a)	28. (d)	29. (b)	30. (d)
31. (b)	32. (c)	33. (d)	34. (b)	35. (b)	36. (c)	37. (b)	38. (a)	39. (c)	40. (b)
41. (c)	42. (c)	43. (a)	44. (d)	45. (b)	46. (b)	47. (b)	48. (c)	49. (b)	50. (b)

MODEL TEST PAPER - 2

Answer Key									
1. (b)	2. (d)	3. (d)	4. (b)	5. (d)	6. (b)	7. (c)	8. (d)	9. (d)	10. (b)
11. (a)	12. (b)	13. (a)	14. (d)	15. (b)	16. (b)	17. (d)	18. (b)	19. (b)	20. (c)
21. (d)	22. (b)	23. (a)	24. (a)	25. (d)	26. (d)	27. (a)	28. (d)	29. (b)	30. (b)
31. (d)	32. (b)	33. (b)	34. (a)	35. (b)	36. (d)	37. (b)	38. (a)	39. (d)	40. (d)
41. (b)	42. (b)	43. (c)	44. (a)	45. (c)	46. (d)	47. (c)	48. (b)	49. (b)	50. (b)

Appendix

There are different organizations that conduct these examinations and covering all of them is not needed as the focus should be to understand the main type of exams conducted. They are similar for these organizations with the difference being the change in name of the exam.

Science Olympiad Foundation (SOF)

S. No.	Name of Exam	Grade
1.	National Science Olympiad (NSO)	Class 1-10
2.	National Cyber Olympiad (NCO)	Class 1-10
3.	International Mathematics Olympiad (IMO)	Class 1-10
4.	International English Olympiad (IEO)	Class 1-10
5.	International Commerce Olympiad (ICO)	Class 1-10
6.	International General Knowledge Olympiad (IGKO)	Class 1-10
7.	International Social Studies Olympiad (ISSO)	Class 1-10

Indian Talent Olympiad (ITO)

S. No.	Name of Exam	Grade
1.	International Science Olympiad (ISO)	Class 1-12
2.	International Math Olympiad (IMO)	Class 1-12
3.	English International Olympiad (EIO)	Class 1-12
4.	General Knowledge International Olympiad (GKIO)	Class 1-12
5.	International Computer Olympiad (ICO)	Class 1-12
6.	International Drawing Olympiad (IDO)	Class 1-12
7.	National Essay Olympiad (NESO)	Class 1-12
8.	National Social Studies Olympiad (NSSO)	Class 1-12

EduHeal Foundation

S. No.	Name of Exam	Grade
1.	Eduheal International Cyber Olympiad (ICO)	Class 1-12
2.	Eduheal International English Olympiad (IEO)	Class 1-12
3.	National Interactive Math Olympiad (NIMO)	Class 1-12
4.	National Interactive Science Olympiad (NISO)	Class 1-12
5.	International General Knowledge Olympiad (IGO)	Class 1-12
6.	National Space Science Olympiad (NSSO)	Class 1-12

Humming Bird Education		
S. No.	**Name of Exam**	**Grade**
1.	Humming Bird Commerce Competency Olympiad (HCC)	Class 1-12
2.	Humming Bird Cyber Olympiad (HCO)	Class 1-12
3.	Humming Bird English Olympiad (HEO)	Class 1-12
4.	Humming Bird General Knowledge Olympiad (HGO)	Class 1-12
5.	Humming Bird Hindi Olympiad (HHO)	Class 1-12
6.	Humming Bird Mathematics Olympiad (HMO)	Class 1-12
7.	Humming Bird Science Olympiad (HSO)	Class 1-12
8.	Humming Bird Aptitude and Reasoning Olympiad (ARO)	Class 1-12
9.	Humming Bird Spelling Competition (Spell BEE)	Class 1-12
10.	Humming Bird Language Olympiad	Class 1-12

International Assessments for Indian Schools (IAIS) (MacMillan and EEA Collaboration)		
S. No.	**Name of Exam**	**Grade**
1.	IAIS Maths Olympiad	Class 3-12
2.	IAIS ScienceOlympiad	Class 3-12
3.	IAIS English Olympiad	Class 3-12
4.	IAIS Digital Technologies Olympiad	Class 3-12

SilverZone Foundation		
S. No.	**Name of Exam**	**Grade**
1.	International Informatics Olympiad	Class 1-12
2.	International Olympiad of Mathematics	Class 1-12
3.	International Olympiad of Science	Class 1-12

Unified Council		
S. No.	**Name of Exam**	**Grade**
1.	Unified Council Cyber Exam	Class 1-12
2.	Unified International English Olympiad.	Class 1-12
3.	Unified International Mathematics Olympiad (UIMO)	Class 1-12

Unicus		
S. No.	**Name of Exam**	**Grade**
1.	Unicus Non-Routine Mathematics Olympiad (UNRMO)	Class 1-11
2.	Unicus Mathematics Olympiad (UMO)	Class 1-11

3.	Unicus Science Olympiad (USO)	Class 1-11
4.	Unicus English Olympiad (UEO)	Class 1-11
5.	Unicus Cyber Olympiad (UCO)	Class 1-11
6.	Unicus General knowledge Olympiad (UGKO)	Class 1-11
7.	Unicus Critical Thinking Olympiad (UCTO)	Class 1-11

CREST (Online Mode)		
S. No.	**Name of Exam**	**Grade**
1.	Mathematics (CMO)	Classes KG-10
2.	Science (CSO)	Classes KG-10
3.	English (CEO)	Classes KG-10
4.	Computer (CCO)	Classes 1-10
5.	Reasoning (CRO)	Classes 1-10
6.	Spell Bee Summer (CSB)	Classes 1-8
7.	Spell Bee Winter (CSBW)	Classes 1-8
8.	Mental Maths (MMO)	Classes 1-12
9.	Green Warrior Olympiad (GWO)	Classes 1-12

How To Apply?

Anyone willing to participate in the Olympiad exam can follow these steps to apply for the exam:

- ☞ Log in to the official website of the conducting organization.
- ☞ Find the Registration Option to register
- ☞ Fill up the details such as Student Name, Parent Name, School Name, Class,Postal Address, E-mail Address, Password, etc.
- ☞ Select the subjects you want to apply for. Pay the necessary registration fees and you are done.
- ☞ You will receive necessary details on your email id.

There are no minimum marks required by the Olympiad conducting organizations to apply for the exam.

Awards

Based on the organization rules, students as well as schools participating in these exams are awarded with several recognitions based on the marks they score.